THE

MORAL CATASTROPHE

DAVID HOCKING

HARVEST HOUSE PUBLISHERS
Eugene, Oregon 97402

THE MORAL CATASTROPHE

Copyright © 1990 by Harvest House Publishers
Eugene, Oregon 97402

Library of Congress Cataloging-in-Publication Data

Hocking, David
      The moral catastrophe / David Hocking.
      ISBN 0-89081-746-4 (Cloth)
      ISBN 0-89081-844-4 (Trade Paper)
      1. Christian ethics.   2. United States—Moral conditions.
      I. Title.
      BJ1251.H58   1990
      241'.0973—dc20

                                                                89-35232
                                                                CIP

A NOTE FROM THE AUTHOR

It is not easy to walk with God in this generation as Noah did in his (Genesis 6:8). The similarities are striking when we carefully evaluate the reasons behind God's destruction of that preflood civilization with the moral climate of our present day. Unless a moral and spiritual awakening and revival occur, our culture appears to be headed for disaster.

In the light of the moral catastrophe now confronting us and the need for a moral and spiritual change, it seems fitting to dedicate this treatise to all who will read it and respond to its message. It was initially given as a series of messages to the congregation of believers at Calvary Church of Santa Ana, California. Their encouragement and support provided strong motivation to put these messages into print.

My special thanks to Art Black, director of the nationwide radio broadcast "The Biola Hour," who has continually encouraged me, the radio Bible teacher, to put what I say into print. More than that, he is my friend and a special brother in the Lord. May God bless his heart as he reads the result of his encouragement.

To my grandchildren, I pray that your world might be different because of this book. May the society you encounter be filled with a greater sense of and commitment to moral and spiritual values than the one we have created.

—David Hocking
January, 1990

CONTENTS

MORAL CATASTROPHE

Whatever Happened to Morality?

Something is wrong! Western culture with its history of democratic principles and moral values is struggling desperately. We no longer seem capable of controlling ourselves in our pursuits of pleasure, ease, and material gain. The "good life" has brought corruption, greed, and a self-destructive narcissism.

We talk of human rights but care little for the innocent, handicapped, elderly, and poor. There is plenty of talk but little true compassion and care. The "quality" of life is now more important than the sanctity of life. The rights and privacy of the individual seem more important than our responsibilities to one another and our desire to work for the common good and betterment of society. Whatever happened to words like duty, altruism, responsibility, accountability, and concern for others?

Crime and violent acts flourish in our cities, and our police departments seem helpless in their efforts to control the rampage. We glorify the criminal in our newspapers, television programs, and movies, while the victims are graphically depicted in the process of suffering and dying. Torture, abuse, blood, guns, and knives are used constantly to entertain a culture that willingly watches more violence while it complains of the rise of crime in our society.

Over 1.5 million unborn babies are aborted each year, over 90 percent of which are simply not wanted and are described as "inconveniences." Over 80 percent of all these abortions are performed on unmarried mothers—unwanted pregnancies resulting from sexual activity outside the bonds and responsibilities of marriage. More people have died in our culture from abortion than from all the wars and criminal acts in our history!

Definitions of marriage, family, and even personhood have been radically changed. Nearly half of our marriages end in divorce, forcing millions of our children to be raised in environments of anger, hostility, abuse, and loneliness. The model of parents who stay together for life and consider their main mission in life to support, encourage, love, and train their children is no longer the norm in our culture. The desire to make money, be successful, and have fun dominates the thinking of the majority of Americans. We seem to be running away as fast as we can from the realities of life and the values upon which our society was built.

Our fear of discrimination and our obsession with guaranteeing the rights of our citizens to believe and do whatever they want to has led to a religion of secularism that is bent on eliminating any references to God, the Bible, religious principles, or traditional values. He who believes most gives way to him who believes least, and he who believes least must now give way to him who believes nothing. Believers in moral and traditional values are portrayed as being negative, judgmental, anti-intellectual, and unreasonable. Our shift to a secular culture devoid of any religious commitment or belief is certainly one of the major news stories of this twentieth century!

How Did It Happen?

The question is, "How did all this happen, and what can we do about it?"

The answers will not come easily. Human nature has always relished self-analysis and social research but has never been able to provide adequate solutions. It is one thing to know what is right and wrong but quite another thing to do what is right and avoid what is wrong.

Because of its belief in the ability of each individual to determine the morality of his own actions, our culture questions any institution, document, or person that attempts to impose its moral values upon another person. In a philosophical and social atmosphere devoid of moral absolutes, we now depend totally upon our legal and judicial system to determine what is right and what is wrong for all of us.

Two major factors in American life have contributed to the present moral decline. Though it could take volumes to prove that these two factors are indeed responsible for the present state of things, it should be obvious to most students of American history and culture that they have played a major role:

1) The theory of evolution.

2) Secular humanism.

The theory of evolution finds its roots in modern history from the writings of Charles Darwin. It now permeates our classroom teaching at all levels and is assumed to be fact by millions of Americans, even though its broad conclusions are far from factual and have never been proven by scientific method or research.

It is not our purpose in this book to analyze the tenets of evolution; we simply want to describe the effect upon our society of this theory of the origin, nature, and development of man.

In the September-October issue of *The Humanist* magazine as far back as 1964, the following quote appeared on page 151:

> Darwin's discovery of the principle of evolution sounded the death knell of religious and moral values. It removed the ground from under the feet of traditional religion.

Darwin's theory has no room for God. Man is a highly developed animal and is to be studied in the same way as we would plants or animals. To believe that man is created in the image of God is diametrically opposed to the theories of evolution. Evolution views the universe and all that it contains from the standpoint of time and natural causes. It denies the supernatural.

The result of evolutionary beliefs and applications has been a colossal undermining of Judeo-Christian moral values. The very idea of having moral absolutes to govern our lives is unthinkable in evolutionary circles.

Yet no true scientist in the world, Christian or non-Christian, has much confidence in the guesses of Charles Darwin, since many specifics of Darwin's theory have been proven totally wrong. The incredible thing is that the overall theory he proposed has captured the minds and beliefs of so many people.

THE RELIGION OF HUMANISM

But the most important fact leading to our present moral climate is undoubtedly the religion of secular humanism. Though the roots of humanism go back much further than the proclamation in 1933 of the "Humanist Manifesto," it was this event that brought the beliefs and objectives of secular humanists to the nation's attention. The major points of that manifesto included the following:

1) Religious humanists regard the universe as self-existing and not created.

2) Humanism believes that man is a part of nature and that he has emerged as the result of a continuous process.

3) Holding an organic view of life, humanists find that the traditional dualism of mind and body must be rejected.

4) Humanism recognizes that man's religious culture and civilization clearly depicted by anthropology and history are the product of a gradual development due to his interaction with his natural environment and with his social heritage. The individual born into a particular culture is largely molded to that culture.

5) Humanism asserts that the nature of the universe depicted by modern science makes unacceptable any supernatural or cosmic guarantees of human values.

These first five tenets of the Humanist Manifesto of 1933 are sufficient to show the close connection between evolutionary belief and the beliefs of secular humanism.

One of the signers of this manifesto in 1933 was John Dewey, who is often referred to as "the father of modern education." His influence upon the American educational process was enormous, and it continues to affect us even at this present time.

In 1973 the Humanist Manifesto II was published. In the preface of that document we read the following:

> As in 1933, humanists still believe that traditional theism, especially faith in the prayer-hearing God, assumed to love and care for persons, to hear and understand their prayers and to be able to do something about them, is an unproven and outmoded faith. Salvationism, based on mere affirmation, still appears as harmful, diverting people with false hopes of heaven hereafter. Reasonable minds look to other means of survival.

The preface goes on to say:

> Traditional moral codes and newer irrational cults both fail to meet the pressing needs of today and tomorrow. False "theologies of hope" and messianic ideologies, substituting new dogmas for old, cannot cope with existing world realities. They separate rather than unite peoples.

Especially enlightening are these words from the very first tenet of this new manifesto of 1973:

> But we can discover no divine purpose or providence for the human species. While there is much that we do not know, humans are responsible for what we are or will become. No deity will save us; we must save ourselves.

In the second principle upon which the secular humanist stands as of 1973, the attack against Christianity becomes stronger:

> Promises of immortal salvation or fear of eternal damnation are both illusory and harmful.

The evolutionary commitment of humanists is evident:

> Science affirms that the human species is an emergence from natural evolutionary forces. As far as we know, the total personality is a function of the biological organism transacting in a social and cultural context. There is no credible evidence that life survives the death of the body. We continue to exist in our progeny and in the way that our lives have influenced others in our culture.

Humanism's ethical system (which now controls most of our educational institutions and media conglomerates) is clearly stated in the third tenet of the 1973 manifesto:

> We affirm that moral values derive their source from human experience. Ethics stem from human need and interest. To deny this distorts the whole basis of life. Human life has meaning because we create and develop our futures. Happiness and the creative realization of human needs and desires, individually and in shared enjoyment, are continuous themes of humanism. We strive for the good life, here and now.

That last statement says it all: "We strive for the good life, here and now."

This humanist document is not satisfied with general principles. It makes sure that all who subscribe to it and all who are affected by it understand clearly what its principles mean when applied to all areas of human life and existence. In the arena of human sexuality, the document states the following in tenet six:

> In the area of sexuality, we believe that intolerant attitudes, often cultivated by orthodox

religions and puritanical cultures, unduly re-
press sexual conduct. The right to birth control,
abortion, and divorce should be recognized.
While we do not approve of exploitive, deni-
grating forms of sexual expression, neither do
we wish to prohibit, by law or social sanction,
sexual behavior between consenting adults. The
many varieties of sexual exploration should not
in themselves be considered "evil."

Signers and supporters of this humanist document include such well-known names as author Isaac Asimov; the late
Andrey Sakharov of the Academy of Sciences in the Soviet
Union; Joseph Fletcher, reputed father and founder of "situation ethics"; Betty Friedan of the National Organization of
Women; B.F. Skinner, professor of psychology at Harvard University; and a long list of college and university professors and
presidents.

The American Humanist Association was founded in
1941 in Illinois as a nonprofit, tax-exempt organization, conceived for educational and religious purposes. According to a
multitude of their own writings as well as magazine articles in
the late sixties and early seventies, their agenda contained two
major components: legalized abortion and euthanasia.

SITUATION ETHICS

In his book *Moral Responsibility—Situation Ethics at
Work* (Westminster Press, 1967), Joseph Fletcher writes on
page 34:

It all depends on the situation.... In some
situations unmarried love could be infinitely
more moral than married unlove. Lying could
be more Christian than telling the truth. Stealing could be better than respecting private property. No action is good or right in itself. It
depends on whether it hurts or helps people,
whether or not it serves love's purpose—understanding love to be personal concern—in the situation.

Situation ethics is a philosophy that has no moral absolutes; right and wrong are determined by the situation. Sexual acts such as adultery, homosexuality, promiscuity, etc., can become moral if they demonstrate the purpose of love—a concern for others. (An interesting historical note is that Joseph Fletcher received the "Humanist of the Year" award from the American Humanist Association in 1974.)

The theory of evolution and the teaching of secular humanism have deeply affected the moral climate of this country as well as that of the whole Western world. Traditional moral values have been attacked over and over again by secular humanists, and they have achieved a high degree of success in establishing their views in the fields of politics, education, media, and religion.

Knowing Right from Wrong

What makes something right or wrong? Is it the common good? Is something right if no one is hurt or wrong if other people suffer? Is it right if the majority think it is right? Is it wrong because we voted that it was?

Should our legal system have the authority to determine what is right and wrong? What moral values govern those decisions? Does morality govern the principles and process of law, or does law establish morality?

We claim to have a society that is governed "of the people, by the people, and for the people." Through the process of elected officials (representative government) we control our destiny. Yet we often suffer because the elected leader has few moral values. Three thousand years ago, Israel's King Solomon penned these words in Proverbs 29:2:

> When the righteous are in authority, the
> people rejoice; but when a wicked man rules,
> the people groan.

Our elected leaders are often swayed more by public opinion and the goal of reelection than they are by moral values. But let's face it—our leaders are a reflection of what we the people are and what we believe. We often get what we deserve.

Our failure to understand morality and to apply basic moral principles and values to public life is the root of much of our present distress and moral decline.

Without the existence of God, moral values cannot be fixed or established. Accountability to do what is right and to avoid what is wrong is rooted in the fear of God Himself. The only Person who has the right to determine moral values is the God who made us. But secular society has decided that God did not create humanity or the material universe. The Supreme Being of the humanist is man, not God. Man is the only one who can determine what is right and what is wrong, according to secular humanism. This assumes that humans are capable of doing what is right once they discover what it is. But history proves otherwise.

The foundation of our legal system is a morality rooted in the Judeo-Christian heritage, a belief that standards of morality have been set by God. At the heart of almost all present American law is that set of standards we know to be the Ten Commandments—moral values given by God to Moses over 3000 years ago. The Bible teaches in Romans 3:20 that "by the law is the knowledge of sin." Morality is determined by the law of God and not by the opinions or vote of men and women in our society today. The Bible gives a definition of sin (1 John 3:4) and declares it to be a violation of God's law.

A fascinating passage on the rightful use of the law of God is found in 1 Timothy 1:8-11:

> We know that the law is good if one uses
> it lawfully, knowing this: that the law is not
> made for a righteous person, but for the lawless
> and insubordinate, for the ungodly and for
> sinners, for the unholy and profane, for mur-
> derers of fathers and murderers of mothers, for
> manslayers, for fornicators, for sodomites, for
> kidnappers, for liars, for perjurers, and if there
> is any other thing that is contrary to sound
> doctrine, according to the glorious gospel of the
> blessed God which was committed to my trust.

God's law is not intended for "a righteous person" but for the "lawless, insubordinate, ungodly..." etc. An important passage in the Bible on the validity and use of law in controlling evil is found in Romans 13:1-5:

Let every soul be subject to the governing authorities. For there is no authority except from God, and the authorities that exist are appointed by God. Therefore whoever resists the authority resists the ordinance of God, and those who resist will bring judgment on themselves. For rulers are not a terror to good works, but to evil. Do you want to be unafraid of the authority? Do what is good, and you will have praise from the same. For he is God's minister to you for good. But if you do evil, be afraid; for he does not bear the sword in vain; for he is God's minister, an avenger to execute wrath on him who practices evil. Therefore you must be subject, not only because of wrath but also for conscience sake.

The purpose of law is to control evil. A key issue is the definition of good and evil. Who determines what is right and wrong? This passage teaches that "there is no authority except from God."

Although there are over 600 commandments of God in the Old Testament law (the first five books of the Bible, which Jews call the Torah), the basic summary and essence of them all is the list we call the Ten Commandments. The first four of these commandments deal with our relationship to God Himself, and the final six deal with our relationship with each other.

THE ROOTS OF MORALITY

Consider the impact and significance of God's commandments. We learn four basic things about Him in the first four commandments. Morality is rooted in the authority of God and our personal accountability to Him. When the existence and authority of God is removed from society and its decisions, moral confusion will result.

1) *The uniqueness of God:* "You shall have no other gods before Me."

2) *The worship of God:* "You shall not make for yourself any carved image, or any likeness of anything that is in heaven above, or that is in the earth beneath, or that is in the water under the earth; you shall not bow down to them nor serve them."

3) *The honor of God:* "You shall not take the name of the Lord your God in vain, for the Lord will not hold him guiltless who takes His name in vain."

4) *The blessing of God:* "Remember the Sabbath day, to keep it holy. . . . Therefore the Lord blessed the Sabbath day and hallowed it."

The next six commandments protect basic human rights and urge fundamental human responsibilities in order to insure a just and stable society.

5) *Protection of the family:* "Honor your father and your mother, that your days may be long upon the land which the Lord your God is giving you."

6) *Protection of human life:* "You shall not murder."

7) *Protection of marriage:* "You shall not commit adultery."

8) *Protection of private property:* "You shall not steal."

9) *Protection of truth and integrity:* "You shall not bear false witness against your neighbor."

10) *Protection of individual rights:* "You shall not covet your neighbor's house; you shall not covet your neighbor's wife, nor his manservant, nor his maidservant, nor his ox, nor his donkey, nor anything that is your neighbor's."

The last commandment deals with a serious human problem—the desire to have what someone else has. Covetousness has become a moral cancer that has permeated our material-istic culture. Ephesians 5:5 refers to a "covetous man" as being "an idolater." Much of modern advertising is built on the pres-ence of covetousness within the human heart. Our desire to have what someone else has causes our marketing agencies to appeal to us with less-than-honorable goals and priorities.

The apostle Paul speaks of God's law as being "holy, just, and good" (Romans 7:12). He calls it "spiritual" (Romans 7:14), and reminds us that there is nothing wrong with the law; the problem lies with us: We are "carnal." We want things our own way and we do not like anyone (including God) telling us what to do.

The Bible does not teach that humans are capable of practicing right and avoiding wrong; it presents the opposite. In Romans 3:10-12 we read:

> There is none righteous, no, not one; there
> is none who understands; there is none who
> seeks after God. They have all gone out of the
> way; they have together become unprofitable;
> there is none who does good, no, not one.

What an indictment! Morally, the Bible teaches that we are not capable of making and practicing right decisions. It goes on to explain that we are all sinners, bent toward the wrong (from God's point of view). Romans 3:23 says, "For all have sinned and fall short of the glory of God." The law of God condemns us (James 2:10; Romans 3:19). It reveals God's righ-teous and holy standards and exposes us for our sinful desires and selfishness. The Bible proclaims that we are in need of a Savior, One who can forgive us for our sins and make us what we ought to be. That's the heart of the gospel of Jesus Christ!

FINDING THE ANSWER

The moral catastrophe in our country cries out for abso-lutes. Apart from the existence and authority of God we will remain on the sea of relativity, tossed by the waves of indecision and popular opinion, without direction and without hope. We need a moral reformation, a spiritual and moral revival. We need God's help and deliverance. 2 Chronicles 7:14 gave the nation of Israel an answer to their moral and spiritual decline:

> If My people who are called by My name
> will humble themselves, and pray and seek My
> face, and turn from their wicked ways, then I
> will hear from heaven, and will forgive their sin
> and heal their land.

This important and crucial passage was given to the nation of Israel at a time of moral crisis and pending attack from a foreign power—Babylon. The last chapter of 2 Chronicles records the invasion by Babylon under the leadership of King Nebuchadnezzar, an event that resulted in the destruction of Jerusalem and the temple built by King Solomon. The Jewish people were led into captivity to Babylon for 70 years. It was under Persian leadership that they were allowed to return to the land of Israel.

2 Chronicles 36:14-16 records some of the reasons for this invasion and judgment of God:

> All the leaders of the priests and the people
> transgressed more and more, according to all
> the abominations of the nations, and defiled the
> house of the Lord which He had consecrated in
> Jerusalem. And the Lord God of their fathers
> sent warnings to them by His messengers, rising
> up early and sending them, because He had
> compassion on His people and on His dwelling
> place. But they mocked the messengers of God,
> despised His words, and scoffed at His prophets,
> until the wrath of the Lord arose against His
> people, till there was no remedy.

Proverbs 14:34 states, "Righteousness exalts a nation, but sin is a reproach to any people." The children of Israel had exhausted the patience of God, and He gave them several reasons for the moral catastrophe that had occurred.

1. *Forgetting the Lord.* In 2 Chronicles 36:12,13 we read of Israel's King Zedekiah, who did evil in the sight of the Lord and did not humble himself. It states that he "hardened his heart against turning to the Lord God of Israel."

One giant reason for the moral catastrophe affecting us today is that we have forgotten the Lord God. We are acting like He does not exist nor has any power to do anything for us or against us. How foolish we are, and how wonderful is His patience!

Deuteronomy 8:2 says, "You shall remember that the Lord your God led you all the way...." Verse 11 says, "Beware that you do not forget the Lord your God...." Verse 19 pronounces this judgment:

> Then it shall be, if you by any means forget
> the Lord your God, and follow other gods, and
> serve them and worship them, I testify against
> you this day that you shall surely perish.

2. *Forsaking the commandments of God.* 2 Chronicles 36:16 reveals that the nation of Israel was at such a low ebb spiritually that they "mocked the messengers of God, despised His words, and scoffed at His prophets...." Because of such rejection of God's servants proclaiming His words, the Bible says that "the wrath of the Lord arose against His people till there was no remedy."

Proverbs 29:18 says, "Where there is no revelation, the people cast off restraint; but happy is he who keeps the law." That is our problem! Because we refuse to accept the authority of God and His revelation, there is no restraint upon the moral actions of our society.

God's judgment falls upon His people when they as a group cast aside His laws and decide to run their lives independent of His righteous and holy standards. Even pagan cultures recognize the importance of moral and spiritual values. Though the conception of what is right and what is wrong varies greatly from culture to culture, it is fascinating to observe that throughout the history of the world there has been a general consensus that the moral values of the Ten Commandments are critical to the stability and productivity of any society.

3. *Following false beliefs and sinful practices.* 2 Chronicles 36:14 reveals that "all the leaders of the priests and the people transgressed more and more, according to all the abominations of the nations." After enumerating a number of sexual

practices that should not be allowed among the people of God, Leviticus 18 closes with a warning in verses 29 and 30:

> Whoever commits any of these abominations, the persons who commit them shall be cut off from among their people. Therefore you shall keep My ordinance, so that you do not commit any of these abominable customs which were committed before you, and that you do not defile yourselves by them: I am the Lord your God.

Over 800 years after these words were given to the nation of Israel, the people suffered the consequence of committing "all the abominations of the nations." They were led into captivity to Babylon, and their city and temple were destroyed.

2 Chronicles 7:19 warns the people of God about going after other gods and worshiping them. In verse 22 we read:

> Then they will answer, "Because they forsook the Lord God of their fathers, who brought them out of the land of Egypt, and embraced other gods, and worshiped them and served them; therefore He has brought all this calamity on them."

On our coins in America we find the words "In God We Trust." Yet the growth of occultism, Satanism, secular humanism, and unusual religious beliefs and cults that are foreign to our religious heritage give testimony to the fact that we are bringing inevitable tragedy upon ourselves. We are publicly forgetting the Lord, forsaking His commandments, and following all kinds of false beliefs and sinful practices. May God have mercy upon us!

THE CRISIS IS REAL

The moral catastrophe is real. The loss of moral and traditional values in our country is frightening to those who were raised as children in a much different environment. The survival of the family, the basic unit of our society and culture, is now a serious challenge facing us all.

This book is an attempt to deal with the great moral issues of our time, but it is also a call to every one of us to repent of our complacency and indifference and to do what we can to restore moral values to our society. We need a moral and spiritual revival in this country such as we had in the days of the American Revolution. God's principles of right and wrong must be reestablished in our hearts, our textbooks, our schools, and our government to serve as the foundation of morality and the basis upon which our courts will judge and our politicians will govern!

We need to return to the Bible, and to stop this unnecessary obsession for neutrality. In the realm of moral and traditional values, neutrality leads to disaster, a nation with no moral roots and no will to defend its honor and its values.

We need to remain committed to religious freedom for all, but not at the price of renouncing our moral and spiritual heritage or eliminating our concern for moral values.

The first New England Colony was planted on November 11, 1620, and we read in the Mayflower Compact these words:

> In the name of God, Amen. We whose names are underwritten, the loyal subjects of our dread sovereign Lord, King James, by the grace of God, having undertaken for the glory of God and the advancement of the Christian faith, and honor of our king and country, a voyage to plant the first colony in the northern parts of Virginia, do by these presents solemnly and mutually in the presence of God, and one of another, covenant and combine ourselves together.

Our own Declaration of Independence, signed on July 4, 1776, says this:

> When in the course of human events it becomes necessary for one people to dissolve the political bands which have connected them with another, and to assume among the powers of the

earth the separate and equal station to which
the laws of nature and of nature's God entitle
them, a decent respect to the opinions of mankind require that they should declare the causes
which impel them to the separation....

This special Declaration of Independence goes on to state:

We hold these truths to be self-evident:

That all men are created equal; that they
are endowed by their Creator with certain
inalienable rights; that among these are life,
liberty, and the pursuit of happiness; that to
secure these rights, governments are instituted
among men deriving their just powers from the
consent of the governed.

In the proceedings of the Constitutional Convention
(1787-89), Benjamin Franklin said:

Sir, I have lived a long time; and the longer
I live, the more convincing proofs I see that God
still governs in the affairs of men. If a sparrow
cannot fall to the ground without our Father's
notice, is it possible that we can build an empire
without our Father's aid? I believe the Sacred
Writings which say that "except the Lord build
the house, they labor in vain that build it."

Franklin went on to move that a member of the clergy be
invited to participate in the meetings from day to day, so that
the participants might invoke the wisdom and guidance of the
Father of lights. "Else," he said, "we shall succeed no better
than did the builders of Babel."

James Madison, one of the framers of our Constitution,
said:

We have staked the whole future of American civilization not upon the power of government—far from it. We have staked the future
of all our political institutions upon the capacity
of mankind for self-government; upon the capacity of each and all of us to govern ourselves,

to control ourselves, to sustain ourselves according to the Ten Commandments of God.

George Washington, our first President, said, "The propitious smiles of heaven can never be expected on a nation that disregards the eternal rules of order and right which heaven itself has ordained." He was speaking of the Ten Commandments and the laws of God as found in the Bible.

WHY DENY THE OBVIOUS?

Let's stop running away from the obvious: This nation was built on a moral and spiritual foundation. Though all the founders were not Christians, all of them understood that a just society with freedom for all must be governed by the laws of God, Who alone has the right to determine what is right and what is wrong.

The first amendment in our Constitution reads:

Congress shall make no law respecting an establishment of religion, or prohibiting the free exercise thereof.

The idea of a secular state was foreign to our founding fathers. They desired freedom *of* religion, not freedom *from* religion!

Thirty-five years before July 4, 1776, God sent a man to our colonies by the name of George Whitefield. He called on America to repent. He was followed by John Wesley and Francis Asbury. President Calvin Coolidge accurately observed, "America was born in a revival of religion. Back of that revival were John Wesley, George Whitefield, and Francis Asbury." Any American history textbook or course that leaves out these facts is at best ignorant and at worst deceiving.

General Douglas MacArthur wrote:

History fails to record a single precedent in which nations subject to moral decay have not passed into political and economic decline. There has been either a spiritual awakening to overcome the moral lapse, or a progressive deterioration leading to ultimate national disaster.

It's time for restoration of our moral and traditional values! We've had enough of freedom without moral restraint. We're tired of the attack and constant criticism of those who stand for moral and traditional values. We desperately need to strengthen our understanding and commitments to marriage, the family, integrity in business practices, and ethical standards for all those in authority over us.

The moral catastrophe can be changed to a moral revival! May God help us!

The Right to Life

The young girl confronting me in the hallway of our church seemed desperate as she blurted out, "Pastor, please help me—I'm pregnant, and not married! My parents want me to have an abortion. My friends tell me that it's okay—everybody is doing it these days. The people down at the Planned Parenthood Clinic have urged me to do it. But what I want to know is—Is this baby inside of me a real person? Would I be guilty of murder if I have an abortion?"

No issue of morality is more crucial than the fundamental right to life. If we are weak on this point, we will falter on other moral issues and fail to stand strong for what is right.

Our Constitution guarantees the right to life for all persons regardless of age, handicap, skin color, education, religious belief, etc. But something has gone wrong—human life has been redefined and devaluated by the moral crisis in our country. Issues such as murder, rape, abortion, infanticide, euthanasia, kidnapping, and child abuse have become major problems in our society. These issues dominate our movies and television programs, and instead of deploring the moral depravity of such acts, we find ourselves justifying, defending, and even glorifying these atrocities.

ABORTION: A MORAL CATASTROPHE

No issue is so controversial among Americans as that of abortion. Abortion refers to terminating the life of a baby in the womb of its mother before it ever comes to birth. Prolife advocates argue that life begins at conception and that abortion is murder—the killing of real people in the wombs of their mothers.

29

Prochoice advocates believe in the woman's right to terminate an unwanted pregnancy, arguing that it is her body and that the fetus is not a human being, and that therefore the act of abortion is not murder but rather a fundamental right of a woman to determine whether she wants a baby or not.

As far back as 1967 an American Civil Liberties lawyer, humanist Herman Schwartz, wrote:

> Abortion proponents seek only to permit those who feel it necessary to destroy unborn organisms, often no more than a few inches of protoplasm with no discernible personality at all, in order to reduce human suffering.

But Dr. Paul Adreini, affiliated with the Mayo Clinic, said this:

> Promoting or accepting the right of people to abortion on demand is accepting a utilitarian view of human life—if the fetus is not useful or convenient, like a chair or automobile, then we may dispose of it. Once we accept this utilitarian outlook, once we admit that man has no inviolable right to life—but only a right depending on usefulness—then none of us can be safe from annihilation.

Columnist Mary Kay Williams writes:

> Abortion not only damages another's life, it destroys it. Abortion forfeits the very basic right to life from which all other rights proceed. Without question, it is a moral issue—both deeply personal and highly public. Highly public because there are two parties involved, the mother and the fetus. To deny the fetus this status is to deny all of what modern medical science has been saying about the child's de-velopment in the womb—evidence which should make the fetus more protectable than ever

before. Drawn from the disciplines of biology, genetics, fetology, and perinatology, this evidence affirms that the fetus is different from the parent organism, that fetal life is independent, that the fetus is largely in charge of the pregnancy and the mother is a passive carrier, that the fetus is treated as a separate patient by obstetricians.

Editor James Townsend in *The Educator* says:

> The woman's body is her own, by gift of God, until she engages in activity that invites a guest to share it with her for a period of time, roughly nine months. Having entered into that solemn obligation, she is bound by the law of God and nature not to disturb the tenant. She had a property right in her body and she, for a consideration, voluntarily relinquished a part of that right to another. Her body no longer is completely her own. That is what pregnancy means. Prior to a pregnancy, a woman does have rights—including the right to prevent pregnancy by any means acceptable to her conscience.

THE ROE VERSUS WADE DECISION

On January 22, 1973, the Supreme Court of the United States legalized abortion nationwide. The Court decided in that decision that the unborn were not persons and so had no right to life. Since the Constitution guarantees in its fourteenth amendment that no person shall be deprived of life, liberty, or property without due process of law, it seems apparent that the Court *created social policy* when it made its decision about abortion rather than *accurately interpreting the Constitution*. In the case of Doe Versus Bolton, the Court struck down restrictions on abortion facilities and clearly authorized abortion on demand. Their ruling gave rise to what we now know as abortion clinics. The votes in both cases were seven to two.

Although our Constitution does not use the word "abortion," it seems clear that this document was designed to protect human life. The Supreme Court decided in 1973 that the word "liberty" includes the right to have an abortion, but in the opinion of many legal scholars the Court failed to stand on the fundamental right of the unborn to be protected.

Abortion on demand has created a monster in our society and a giant blemish on our moral and traditional values. A woman may have a legal abortion for just about any reason. Over 90 percent of all abortions are described as "unwanted pregnancies." The sexual revolution that has produced a tremendous amount of pregnant unwed women has only intensified the desire and the demand for abortion. Abortion is America's way of covering up its sexual immorality.

The fact is that the Supreme Court gave women the right to abortion through the nine months of pregnancy. In their view, the baby in the womb, at whatever stage, is not a real human being. Our medical and scientific knowledge has been greatly increased since 1973, and we now realize that all the signs and evidence of human life are possessed by the fetus in the womb.

The argument that the Supreme Court's decision was necessary because of all the women dying from illegal abortions is not an accurate picture of the facts. In 1972 (the year before the Court's decision), the U.S. Centers for Disease Control reported only 39 women who died from such illegal practices.

Over 4000 abortions are performed every day in the United States, and over 23 million babies have been aborted since the Supreme Court's decision—more lives lost than in all of our wars combined!

A baby's heartbeat, brainwave, and response to touch are all present within two months of pregnancy. By 21 days the heart is pumping, and brainwaves have been recorded as early as 40 days.

On July 1, 1976, the Supreme Court ruled in Planned Parenthood Versus Danforth that neither parent of a minor, nor a husband, can veto abortions.

On July 2, 1979, in Bellotti Versus Baird, the Court said that states can require parental consent if they allow minors the option of seeking permission from a judge instead.

On June 15, 1983, in Akron Versus Akron Center for

Reproductive Health, the Court said that states cannot require that second-trimester abortions be performed in hospitals, and struck down a required waiting period before abortion as well as the obligation of the doctor to state that the fetus is human life.

Only 1 percent of all abortions in this country have anything to do with the life or health of the mother. Two million couples are waiting to adopt babies (according to the National Committee for Adoption in Washington D.C.) while over a million-and-a-half babies are aborted each year. What has happened to our sense of moral values when it comes to our unborn babies?

THE HIPPOCRATIC OATH

The Hippocratic Oath of 400 B.C. has been the standard commitment of the medical profession until this present day. It reads:

> I will give no deadly medicine to anyone
> if asked, nor suggest any such counsel; further-
> more, I will not give a woman an instrument
> to produce abortion.

In a shocking book entitled *The Nazi Doctors*, Robert Jay Lifton points out the following facts that led to the tragedy of the Holocaust (and the involvement of medical personnel in that tragedy):

1) All nonbattlefield German killings were medical, that is, carried out by or under the supervision of medical doctors.

2) Medical materialism lent itself directly to purification projects that killed in the name of healing.

3) The claims in favor of euthanasia in Germany were that it was an act of compassion—"mercy-killing." Transportation for patients to killing centers was carried out by the "Charitable Transport Company for the Sick."

4) Anything society could find to decrease the physician's perception of the condemned people as human increased his ability to kill for the state. The main justification for abortion was the claim that the fetus was not a human being.

5) The Nazis based their justification for direct medical killing on the simple concept of "life unworthy of life."

6) The Nazis were successful in translating their most murderous actions into technological problems.

These facts from Nazi Germany are already evident within our culture and its medical community. In a far cry from the ancient Hippocratic Oath to which our medical profession supposedly adheres, our medical personnel make handsome profits from abortions and now advocate stronger legislation for euthanasia—the killing of the elderly, the disabled, or any other member of humanity who may seem undesirable or unwanted. God help us!

Tertullian, church leader in the second century A.D., wrote:

> For us, indeed, as homicide is forbidden,
> it is not lawful to destroy what is conceived in
> the womb.

The Vatican speaks for millions of Roman Catholics and states in no uncertain terms:

> Nothing and no one can in any way permit
> the killing of an innocent human being, whether
> fetus or an embryo, an infant or an adult, an
> old person or one suffering from an incurable
> disease, or a person who is dying. Furthermore,
> no one is permitted to ask for this act of killing,
> either for himself or herself or for another
> person.

ABORTION METHODS

While many Americans continue to listen to pleas of a woman's right to an abortion, few are willing to face the actual methods and practices that kill the unborn babies. The most common methods used in the United States are:

1) *Suction curettage or dilatation and curettage.*

   During the first three months a suction tube and/or loop-shaped steel knife are used to cut the baby's body and placenta into pieces and suck them into a jar!

2) *Dilatation and evacuation.*

   During the fourth or fifth months forceps are inserted through the cervix into the womb, grasping body parts, twisting them off, and removing them in pieces. The spine and skull are crushed and extracted while a curette is used to scrape out the uterus. The baby's body pieces are reassembled to verify completion!

3) *Saline (salt poisoning).*

   During the fourth through seventh months a long needle is inserted through the mother's abdomen into the amniotic fluid surrounding the baby. A strong salt solution is injected, which the baby swallows and "breathes," causing a slow poisoning while the baby's outer layer of skin is burned away. Within 24 hours the mother usually delivers a dead baby, although some babies actually survive this method and are born with severe complications.

4) *Prostaglandin.*

   In the fourth through eighth months hormone-like compounds are injected, causing contractions which force the expulsion of the baby. Side-effects and live births are possible.

5) *Intracardiac injection.*

During the third or fourth months ultrasound imaging is used to guide a long needle into the baby's heart, which injects a fluid causing immediate death. This method is used for "multiple-pregnancy reduction" (elimination of one or more babies in cases of triplets, etc.).

6) *Hysterotomy or cesarean section.*

After the fourth month an incision is made through the mother's abdomen into the womb. The baby is removed and allowed to die by neglect or killed by strangulation or other direct acts while still inside the womb.

These methods are used daily by a society that prides itself on human rights and compassionate responses to human need. Our society does all it can to keep the above facts from women seeking abortions.

WHEN DOES HUMAN LIFE BEGIN?

Some scholars have stated that this question is the most fundamental moral question of our time. It is the one question we avoid most and the only one that can deliver us from our present dilemma and moral confusion. It is the main question that deals with the sanctity of human life. Our current attitudes toward life in our society are arising from a moral relativism that is unbelievably critical of moral absolutes. It seems as though today's culture is profoundly afraid of what it might discover by studying the question of the origin of human life. Have we been wrong? Are we tolerating mass murder and daily contributing to it by our ignorance, silence, and passivity?

Let's start with God. Yes, that's where the problem centers—in the existence of God. The origin of human life is not merely a scientific question; it is a religious issue.

Earlier in this book we mentioned that the two movements that have contributed greatly to our moral catastrophe are evolution and secular humanism (which bases its beliefs upon evolutionary understandings). Evolution has no room for God. It has devaluated human life because it sees the life question as a biological one. In its view, the universe and all it contains—and its subsequent elements that came together in some way to produce animal life and eventually human life— just happened!

The Bible contains a different answer. It begins with these words in Genesis 1:1:

> In the beginning God created the heavens
> and the earth.

In the Genesis account we learn several interesting things about the creation of human life. Consider first the teaching of Genesis 1:26-28:

> Then God said, "Let us make man in Our
> image, according to Our likeness; let them have
> dominion over the fish of the sea, over the birds
> of the air, and over the cattle, over all the earth
> and over every creeping thing that creeps on
> the earth." So God created man in His own
> image; in the image of God He created him;
> male and female He created them. Then God
> blessed them, and God said to them, "Be fruitful
> and multiply; fill the earth and subdue it; have
> dominion over the fish of the sea, over the birds
> of the air, and over every living thing that moves
> on the earth."

According to the biblical account, human life was created, not evolved from animal life. The word "created" (*bara* in Hebrew) means to make something out of nothing; no previously existing materials were used.

Not only was human life created by God, but we are told that it was made in God's image and according to God's likeness. Since man was created in the image of God, and God is spirit (John 4:24), having no physical body, then the "image" must refer to man's personality or soul and spirit, and not his physical body.

In Genesis 2:7 we learn how God designed the human body.

> The Lord God formed man of the dust of the ground, and breathed into his nostrils the breath of life; and man became a living being.

Human life is the result of the creative breath (life) of God. The physical body comes from "the dust of the ground." As most of us know, that statement is chemically true: The exact elements of the soil are found in the human anatomy. That is why at physical death the body decays and becomes dust again. The Bible predicted that this would happen (Genesis 3:19).

James 2:26 tells us that "the body without the spirit is dead." Consider these interesting passages in the Book of Job:

> Job 27:3—"As long as my breath is in me, and the breath of God in my nostrils. . . ."

> Job 33:4—"The Spirit of God has made me, and the breath of the Almighty gives me life."

> Job 34:14,15—"If He should set His heart on it, if He should gather to Himself His Spirit and His breath, all flesh would perish together, and man would return to dust."

The "image of God" refers to the spirit and soul of every human being. The "soul" possess all the marks and responses of our personality. The Greek translation of the Hebrew Bible (called the Septuagint) uses the Greek word for "soul" over 900 times. It is used 101 times in the New Testament and is frequently interchangeable with our English word "person." Our English word "psychology," the study of the soul, comes from the Greek word *psyche*. The "soul" loves, thinks, hates, perceives, decides, etc. When groups of people are counted, they are often referred to as "souls" (Acts 7:14; 27:37; 1 Peter 3:20).

WHEN DOES A PERSON RECEIVE A SOUL?

Those who believe in reincarnation believe that souls are in existence before bodies are created. However, Genesis 2:7

contradicts that theory. God made the human body and then breathed into its nostrils the breath of life, with the result being a living soul.

Some people believe that your parents procreate your body, but that the soul (personality) is created by God at the time of physical birth. This religious view would allow (with some reservation) an abortion to take place. However, in Genesis 5:1-3 we read:

> This is the book of the genealogy of Adam.
> In the day that God created man, He made him
> in the likeness of God. He created them male
> and female, and blessed them and called them
> Mankind in the day they were created. And
> Adam lived one hundred and thirty years, and
> begot a son in his own likeness, after his image,
> and named him Seth.

As we have already seen, the words "image" and "likeness" do not refer to a physical body, because God did not have a physical body when Adam and Eve were created. God's creation of male and female resulted in His evaluation that they were now "mankind" (human life). When parents have a child in their own likeness and after their own image, it speaks of the *soul* of the child and not simply the physical body.

Many people believe that parents procreate all elements of human life and that the result is considered to be the work of God. This viewpoint holds that God no longer repeats millions of times what He did originally. Acts 17:26 seems to confirm this understanding:

> He has made from one blood every nation
> of men to dwell on all the face of the earth, and
> has determined their preappointed times and
> the boundaries of their habitation.

Christian theology does not teach that the human body is sinful. It teaches that sin resides in the arena of our *personality*—what we think, feel, and decide. An interesting passage that reflects on the sanctity of human life and the fact of human life existing in the womb from the moment of conception is found in Psalm 51:5. King David said:

Behold, I was brought forth in iniquity, and
in sin my mother conceived me.

According to these words, sin was present at the moment
of conception. The Bible teaches that every person is a sinner,
and that the presence of sin is a consequence of Adam's disobedience to God. We are held accountable for personal sin before
God, but the fact and presence of sin exist in every person's
"heart" because of the original sin and disobedience of Adam.

The fact of human life being in the womb of a woman is
well-established in the Bible.

Genesis 16:11—"You are with child, and you shall
bear a son."

Matthew 1:18—"She was found with child of the
Holy Spirit."

Matthew 1:20—"That which is conceived in her is
of the Holy Spirit."

Luke 1:31—"You will conceive in your womb."

Luke 1:35—"That Holy One who is to be born will
be called the Son of God."

Luke 1:36—"...conceived a son."

Luke 1:41,44—"The babe leaped in her womb for
joy."

One of the most marvelous passages on the existence of
human life within the womb of a woman is found in Psalm
139:13-18. Carefully read these words as they relate to the issue
of human life:

You have formed my inward parts; You have
covered me in my mother's womb. I will praise
You for I am fearfully and wonderfully made;
marvelous are Your works, and that my soul
knows very well. My frame was not hidden from
You when I was made in secret, and skillfully
wrought in the lowest parts of the earth. Your

eyes saw my substance, being yet unformed. And
in Your book they all were written, the days
fashioned for me, when as yet there were none
of them. How precious also are Your thoughts
to me, O God! How great is the sum of them! If
I should count them, they would be more in
number than the sand; when I awake, I am still
with You.

This passage in Psalm 139 gives proof that a real person is
existing in the mother's womb. Deuteronomy 32:6 asks the
question "Has He not made you and established you?" Job
10:8-12 states:

Your hands have made me and fashioned
me, an intricate unity; yet You would destroy
me. Remember, I pray, that You have made me
like clay. And will You turn me into dust again?
Did You not pour me out like milk, and curdle
me like cheese, clothe me with skin and flesh,
and knit me together with bones and sinews?
You have granted me life and favor, and Your
care has preserved my spirit.

Job 31:15 adds, "Did not He who made me in the womb
make them? Did not the same One fashion us in the womb?"
There can be no doubt in any honest person's mind who
has studied the Bible carefully that it teaches the existence of
human life in the womb. A passage such as Exodus 21:22,23
relates powerfully to the issue of abortion in our day:

If men fight, and hurt a woman with child,
so that she gives birth prematurely, yet no
lasting harm follows, he shall surely be punished
accordingly as the woman's husband imposes
on him; and he shall pay as the judges determine. But if any lasting harm follows, then you
shall give life for life.

Here, in a very clear example, the baby in the womb of
this woman is considered as a human being, and if it is killed in
the process of this fight, then the penalty is "life for life." In

other words, the death penalty is used when a baby's life in the womb is destroyed!

Isaiah 44:24 makes it clear: "Thus says the Lord, your Redeemer, and He who formed you from the womb."

Those who attempt to compare the human fetus to an animal or refer to it as an "unwanted pregnancy," a mere piece of unnecessary flesh, had better consider carefully the concern of God for human life. Consider what Matthew 6:25,26 teaches:

> Therefore I say to you, do not worry about your life, what you will eat or what you will drink; nor about your body, what you will put on. Is not life more than food and the body more than clothing? Look at the birds of the air, for they neither sow nor reap nor gather into barns; yet your heavenly Father feeds them. Are you not of more value than they?

Human life is more valuable than food, clothing, or birds!

WHAT ABOUT EUTHANASIA?

Euthanasia (so-called "mercy-killing") builds its case on the "quality of life" rather than the sanctity of life. Proponents speak of human dignity and the "right to die," but underneath it all is a secular view that does not honor human life as being created by God. It rules God out and seeks to make pragmatic decisions on who deserves to live.

Arguments are often presented that deal with intense physical suffering or serious physical handicap. People speak of how a person would be "better off" if he were allowed to take his own life or to instruct someone else to do it for him.

Abortion and euthanasia were moral issues in Hitler's diabolical scheme to rid the world of "undesirables." The moral catastrophe affecting us has not only allowed the death of millions of babies, but now we are discussing how to eliminate thousands of our elderly citizens who are not active and seemingly demonstrate no useful purpose to society. People see the care of the elderly as a strain upon our economic situation, and the rising costs of medical care are continuing to encourage euthanasia advocates toward stronger action in the legislative process.

In *USA Today* in the spring of 1989, an article appeared by Dan Sperling entitled "Ethics of Helping Terminally Ill to Die." The article points out that a recent panel of top physicians has concluded that it is not immoral for doctors to help terminally ill patients commit suicide. The panel was convened by the Society for the Right to Die.

Its report appeared in the *New England Journal of Medicine*. Dr. Sidney H. Wanzer of the Harvard Law School Health Services, the main author of the report, made this statement: "Our goal is comfort and the relief of pain and suffering, so the patient can have a peaceful death." This view sounds good, and was used by Hitler as well.

Their conclusions were that it is ethical for doctors to help patients commit suicide by prescribing drugs and telling them what dose would be lethal. The conditions under which such practices would be condoned were described as "terminal, their outlook hopeless and their depression untreatable."

Terminal patients would be given painkillers to make them comfortable, regardless of the risk of drug addiction or negative health consequences.

Dr. Jan van Eys, chairman of pediatrics at the University of Texas School of Medicine in Houston, Texas, gave another view of the proceedings: "I don't think that is an appropriate role for a physician—to terminate the life of another person deliberately."

In Exodus 4:11 we read God's answer to Moses when he made excuses as to why he could not be God's spokesman to confront Pharaoh of Egypt:

> Who has made man's mouth? Or who makes the mute, the deaf, the seeing, or the blind? Have not I, the Lord?

Physical handicap does not make a person less than a person. Physical suffering or handicap is never a reason for taking a person's life. Deuteronomy 32:39 says:

> Now see that I, even I, am He, and there is no God besides Me; I kill and I make alive; I wound and I heal.

The issues of life and death are in the hands of God, according to the Bible. In 2 Kings 5:7 the king of Israel responded to a letter from the king of Syria about the leprosy of Naaman, his commander of the army of Syria. He said, "Am I God, to kill and make alive, that this man sends a man to me to heal him of his leprosy?"

Hannah, the mother of Samuel the prophet, said in 1 Samuel 2:6, "The Lord kills and makes alive; He brings down to the grave and brings up."

The law of Moses contains restrictions upon the exercise of the death penalty even when capital crime is involved. Deuteronomy 17:6 says, "Whoever is worthy of death shall be put to death on the testimony of two or three witnesses, but he shall not be put to death on the testimony of one witness."

No one person has the right to take another person's life, including the person who wants to die. Suicide is a selfish act, rooted in our failure to trust God and to leave matters of life and death in His hands. Suicide is always harmful to one's friends and family and demonstrates an extreme form of self-centeredness, a life that cares little about others but is consumed with self-pity, depression, and low self-image.

The arguments of euthanasia advocates are clearly rooted in a belief that physical suffering serves no useful purpose. As long as a person can live without pain and suffering, he or she deserves to live; but if the suffering becomes acute and unbearable, then the person should be allowed or instructed to end his or her own life. But the Bible teaches that suffering serves many useful purposes and develops our character in ways that nothing else can do.

When everything was going wrong for Job and his suffering increased, even his own wife said to him (Job 2:9), "Do you still hold to your integrity? Curse God and die!" That is euthanasia in simple terms: Have nothing to do with a belief in God, and go ahead and die!

Job answered her (Job 2:10):

You speak as one of the foolish women
speaks. Shall we indeed accept good from God,
and shall we not accept adversity?

The Bible comments, "In all this Job did not sin with his lips."

Job gave a marvelous analysis of his suffering and the issue of taking his life in Job 27:2-6:

> As God lives, who has taken away my justice, and the Almighty, who has made my soul bitter, as long as my breath is in me, and the breath of God in my nostrils, my lips will not speak wickedness, nor my tongue utter deceit. Far be it from me that I should say you are right; till I die I will not put away my integrity from me. My righteousness I hold fast, and will not let it go; my heart shall not reproach me as long as I live.

What a testimony! As long as the breath of God was in his nostrils, he would trust the Lord. He left the issue of his death in the Lord's hands and would have none of the counsel of wife and friends that his condition warranted suicide or euthanasia. In Job 42:12 we learn that God used all of Job's suffering in a wonderful way and that He richly rewarded Job for his faithfulness during that period of time in his life: "The Lord blessed the latter days of Job more than his beginning."

Watching my mother endure a painful and long convalescent hospital experience has not been easy. Her confinement to a bed because of paralysis and surgery caused a physical helplessness that, combined with emotional despair and discouragement, created a sense of hopelessness within her and a desire for death. Because she is a Christian, she viewed death as a sweet release from her pain, with the confidence that she would be with the Lord she loved. We talked often about heaven and the biblical promise of a new, resurrected body.

In all of this pain and depression, the sanctity and value of her life has increased in my mind and heart. I have learned much from her. Every person, regardless of age, abilities, handicaps, or disease, is deserving of our profoundest care and respect. The issue is clear: It is the *sanctity* of human life, not merely the *quality* of one's life.

What Should Be Our Response?

The right-to-life issue is affecting all other issues that

trouble our nation during its current moral crisis. If a moral revival is to take place, then the following principles must be reestablished in all facets of American life and understanding:

1) God created human life.

2) Human life begins at the moment of conception.

3) Every person has value regardless of age, appearance, abilities, illness, or physical handicaps.

4) People are more important than animals and plants.

5) Human life is sacred and should never be taken by other human beings except by due process of law for capital crimes.

6) Abortion is the taking of a human life and is an act of murder.

7) God loves people and will forgive us of our sins.

8) Adoption of unwanted babies should become the goal and dedication of a compassionate society.

9) Care of the sick and elderly must be strengthened and supported no matter what the costs or personal inconvenience.

10) Life has meaning and purpose because we were made in the image of God and were designed to worship and glorify Him in all that we think, say, and do.

The Sanctity of Marriage

John and Debbie have been married for less than a year, and their marriage is having serious problems. John is very unhappy with Debbie's attitudes and habits; he feels tremendous pressure from her. Debbie can't stand John's arrogance; she says he doesn't care about her anymore. Both have decided to get a divorce. John's parents are upset, but Debbie's mother is supporting the divorce, since she has never liked John anyway. Besides, she herself has been divorced twice, and she says it's no problem.

After a counseling session with a local psychologist who specializes in marital and divorce problems, John and Debbie were encouraged to get a divorce and to start their lives over again with someone else. That pleased John, because he is already interested in another woman—in fact, the girl that was maid of honor in his wedding with Debbie!

The institution of marriage is under enormous attack, and the pressures seem almost too great for marital bliss to survive. What has gone wrong?

Why do so many marriages end in divorce? Why are so many people unhappy in their marriages? Why do the media, movies, and TV present marriage in such a bad light? Why is "living together" more acceptable than marriage? Why do so many Americans stay single, with no intention of getting married?

The recommending of divorce by professional counselors has been going on for quite some time. Because of our obsession with individual rights and freedoms, many of us do not want to struggle and survive—we simply want out!

We find a professional who will agree with us that we are not getting what we deserve or that we are being mistreated, and the usual advice is: Get a divorce . . . you'll get over it! If the children get hurt in the process . . . that's life! All too many Americans have decided to get a divorce and find someone else with whom they hope to succeed in that illusive pursuit we call happiness.

MORAL CHANGES

My wife gave me an article that appeared in *Glamour* magazine in 1989. It was written by Nicholas Dawidoff and dealt with what men expect from marriage today. The article began with these words:

> Time was when a young man had certain
> expectations of adulthood. By day he would work
> hard at getting ahead in the world. Come
> evening he would return to the girl who wore
> his ring, served his string beans, and raised his
> children. In all this he would do as his father
> had done. Then came the sixties and seventies,
> and with them increasing acceptance of pro-
> fessional women, premarital sex, live-in lovers,
> illegitimate children, abortion, and divorce. Yet
> despite this bewildering succession of social
> changes, a single archaic institution has stead-
> fastly maintained its mystique: Marriage may
> require much more of husbands today than in
> the past, but young men still look forward to
> their wedding day.

The fascinating thing about this article is the admission of the moral and social changes that are deeply affecting the institution of marriage today. The writer lists them: "pre-marital sex, live-in lovers, illegitimate children, abortion, and divorce." It is also interesting to note the adjective "archaic" in reference to marriage. If one interprets this to mean that marriage has been around for a long time, fine. But the word also means "outdated and no longer useful."

In 1960 the average age of men walking the aisle to get married was 22.8 years; in 1988 it was 25.9. The average age of women getting married was 20.3 in 1960; in 1988 it was 23.6. Many people cite economic factors in the present delay to get married, while others believe that the sexual revolution and the desire for sexual freedom and exploration has produced a reluctance to get married.

Much of the blame lies at the doorstep of married couples who have never learned to live in harmony and love. Children have grown up in homes filled with shouting, abuse, swearing, alcoholism, and general neglect of marital and family responsibility. Is it any wonder that we are reaping this current generation's attitudes toward marriage?

In conversations with junior high and high school students, we have discovered a reluctance to think about marriage. Most teenagers do not want to experience what their parents go through every day in their home. Teenagers still desire love and romance, but today they feel that it comes outside of marriage rather than within it.

THE GROWING NEED

In the last few years there has been a growing need for clear and understandable teaching about the importance and value of monogamous marriage. Yet sex-education classes in our schools today seem to focus more on physical anatomy, sexual process, warnings about sexual disease, and recommendations about how to handle sexual desire and involvement.

We could debate the benefits or hindrances which such education provides for our children, but the point here is to understand that marriage is not being promoted or taught in the context of moral and traditional values.

Why is it that so many articles in various magazines present marriage as a difficult place to find love and romance? Why is "falling in love" a matter which people must experience outside of marriage? Some of the answers lie in our understanding of marriage. Too often couples take each other for granted and lose the romantic touches of their courtship days.

King Solomon, the wisest of the ancient monarchs, wrote the most beautiful treatise in the world on sex, love, and romance. The Song of Solomon is the very best thing any person could read on how to fall in love and how to experience continuing love within a marriage.

The whole business of "falling in love" and being romantic is hard to comprehend. Many people experience romantic feelings and heightened desires when simply thinking about or seeing another person. It is most difficult to analyze or explain why this occurs. It can happen several times in a person's lifetime or it can be only an article you read, a movie you see, or a passing fantasy in your thoughts.

Many couples start out with romantic feelings and strong desires drawing them into a desire for lifelong commitment. But after they get married they discover that living in the same house with another person and learning all about his or her attitudes, habits, and lifestyle can be something far removed from the days of romance which they experienced when they were dating each other.

When reality sets in and we are faced with all that another person is, that's when true romance can be developed and enjoyed at a level that touches us deeply, profoundly, and securely. What happiness there is in being loved intensely and continually even though the other person knows exactly what you are like!

Even when a couple has a loving, growing, and happy marriage, romantic feelings for other people can occur throughout their married life. It is always a test of loyalty. Marriage means that you say no to having sex with anyone else.

Professional counselors in the field of marriage and family have consistently pointed out the likelihood of a marital partner falling in love with another person who has befriended him or her. It is at this point that many of us make foolish mistakes. We begin to feel cheated in our marriage, disappointed with what our marriage does for us, and discontented with our marital partner—and before we know it we are thinking about divorce.

We all need friends, and marital couples must develop their social relationships with other people without suspicion, resentment, and jealousy. But the sanctity of marriage draws a line: It never seeks to violate the marriage vow or to substitute the other person for one's spouse. When in your heart you want another person instead of your present spouse, you are in big trouble; the seeds of decay are starting to blossom, and the result will be disastrous for your marriage.

WHAT MAKES A MARRIAGE SACRED?

Weddings are special—beautiful occasions that enhance and establish the beauty and sanctity of marriage in the eyes of all who attend the ceremony. The expense is awesome these days for the father of the bride (speaking from experience!), but when all is said and done, it is worth it. When my children were married, I wrote wedding songs for them that would express the importance of marriage in the eyes of God, and I tried to instill in them in every way possible the truth that marriage is sacred—"till death do us part!" The bottom line? The vow!

Many young people today who contemplate marriage are asking about the significance of a marriage license and a vow in ways that were never asked before. Years ago there was a general consensus in society as to the demands and responsibilities of a marriage. It was a commitment for life, and everyone knew it. But today the scene has changed.

Ministers are often asked to delete such words as "vow" and "till death do us part." The vows that are spoken are often designed to be conditional statements, such as "I will love you if . . ." or "I will love you as long as . . ." The blanks are often filled in by the couple. Words like "submit" and "forsake all others" are missing in many contemporary marriage ceremonies.

In the Bible, marriage is sacred because it is rooted in the command of God Himself. Once again, as with other moral issues, the failure to accept the existence and authority of God and our accountability to Him is causing the erosion and decline of our moral and traditional values and commitments.

Matthew 19:1-12 records a confrontation between Jesus Christ and the religious leaders of His day known as the Pharisees, those claiming to be most loyal to God's laws and the traditions of the Jewish faith. The Pharisees posed a question to Jesus Christ: "Is it lawful for a man to divorce his wife for just any reason?"

As in our day, so it was over 1900 years ago: Divorce was easy to obtain and it occurred frequently. The reasons for divorce were varied. One rabbinical scholar spoke of a woman burning bread and insisted that such incompetence should serve as possible grounds for divorce!

One of the reasons the Pharisees posed the question was not only to test the ability and wisdom of Jesus Christ but also to deal with a serious problem. One school of Jewish scholarship followed Rabbi Hillel, a most respected leader and above reproach in his lifestyle and teachings. Hillel leaned toward the view that the divorce law of Moses (Deuteronomy 24:1-4) was established to regulate divorces in his day that had no justifiable or righteous cause. Another school in the days of Jesus Christ was the one led by Rabbi Shammai, who argued that the only grounds for a divorce was sexual immorality. Which position would Jesus defend? Whichever He chose, the other side would be alienated from Him.

The problem of interpretation centered around the phrase in Deuteronomy 24:1 which speaks of a husband who has found "some uncleanness" in his wife. Was this "uncleanness" sexual misbehavior, or was it anything that irritated the husband? Did the "uncleanness" imply that what she did was regarded as such by the community, or did it refer only to what her husband might think?

The arguments continued for many years among Jewish scholars. The fact was that divorce was easily obtained and was a serious problem in Israel as well as throughout the entire Roman Empire.

Jesus began His answer by referring to God's original plan for marriage (Matthew 19:4-6):

> Have you not read that He who made them
> at the beginning made them male and female,
> and said, "For this reason a man shall leave his
> father and mother and be joined to his wife, and
> the two shall become one flesh"? So then they
> are no longer two but one flesh. Therefore what
> God has joined together, let not man separate.

THE FOUNDATION OF MARRIAGE

The basis of marriage is the command of God. Its sanctity rests upon divine revelation and not human opinion. Within the context of Jesus' answer we also have the clear teaching of a family unit. He mentioned "a man" and "his father and mother." The traditional definition of a family is "a father, a mother, and a child." The family is created by a marriage. A marriage is created when a child leaves his parents and is "joined to his wife." The result is that "the two shall become one flesh."

A father and a son are two; a mother and a daughter are two; a brother and a sister are two; but a husband and a wife are one!

The key phrase in establishing the sanctity of marriage is the wording "be joined to his wife." The whole principle of the vow is based on this one statement.

Deuteronomy 21:21-23 reveals the seriousness of a vow:

> When you make a vow to the Lord your
> God, you shall not delay to pay it; for the Lord
> your God will surely require it of you, and it
> would be sin to you. But if you abstain from
> vowing, it shall not be sin to you. That which
> has gone from your lips you shall keep and
> perform, for you voluntarily vowed to the Lord
> your God what you have promised with your
> mouth.

A person's integrity is developed by keeping his promises and telling the truth at all times. He does not need to swear by anything in order to confirm the validity or truthfulness of his words. In fact, the Bible teaches in James 5:12:

> Above all, my brethren, do not swear, either
> by heaven or by earth or with any other oath.
> But let your "Yes" be "Yes," and your "No," "No,"
> lest you fall into judgment.

We don't need to say "I swear to God I'm telling you the truth" or "I swear on a stack of Bibles that I'm telling you the truth." Does this mean that when you do not "swear" by something or someone we cannot depend on you to tell the truth? A person must speak truthfully at all times! That's what integrity is all about.

Ecclesiastes 5:2-5 warns us about the importance of a vow:

> Do not be rash with your mouth, and let
> not your heart utter anything hastily before
> God. For God is in heaven, and you on earth;
> therefore let your words be few. For a dream
> comes through much activity, and a fool's voice
> is known by his many words. When you make
> a vow to God, do not delay to pay it; for He has
> no pleasure in fools. Pay what you have vowed.
> It is better not to vow than to vow and not pay.

It is easy to make a promise and then break it. Parents are often guilty of promising to do something for their children and then breaking their promise. That is a most serious family issue which can lead to further trouble when the children get older and need someone to depend upon but do not believe that their parents are the ones.

Ecclesiastes warns us about being hasty in making a vow. One of the important reasons for an engagement period of several months is to give the couple time to evaluate and communicate on a level that will make the vow something more than just words they say at weddings. Premarital instruction is extremely important, especially in these days of declining moral values.

MARRIAGE ESSENTIALS

He was only a teenager, but he needed correct information. His remark (which I overheard) to his friends was, "Marriage is for the birds!" He wasn't reflecting upon the beauty of birds having wedding ceremonies, either—he was reflecting his distaste for marriage and his lack of understanding of it! I felt sorry for him, because his parents divorced when he was six years old, and his mother married and divorced twice before he was 15. No wonder his attitudes were not good!

In examining the biblical evidence for marriage and the marriage vow, we discover the following essentials.

1. *Marriage is caused by a man's decision.* Genesis 2:24 speaks of a *man* who leaves his father and his mother. It does not say a *woman*. Jesus quoted the same passage in Matthew 19:5 and agreed. Proverbs 18:22 says, "He who finds a wife finds a good thing, and obtains favor from the Lord." The Bible implies that it is the responsibility of the *man* to initiate the commitment and vow of marriage.

Of course, women should be willing to commit themselves to their prospective husbands with strong words of loyalty and love. But it is fascinating to see how the Bible lays on the *husband* the chief responsibility and accountability in marriage.

The word "leave" implies a role of leadership on the part of the male, and the word "cleave" teaches loyalty. God wants husbands to be faithful and to be leaders. Many sociologists and professionals dealing with marriage and family issues have emphasized that our current crisis could be radically changed if male leadership and loyalty were restored in every marriage and family.

The emphasis in recent years upon the role of women is important and vital to a proper understanding of male/female relationships and responsibilities. Questions of equality need to be addressed, and the male domination of females in our society needs to change.

However, in *marriage* the Bible has clearly designated the husband as the responsible and accountable leader. God holds the husband accountable for the success of the marriage and emphasizes his role as the dominant one in the raising and teaching of children. Most child-rearing today is done by mothers rather than fathers, contrary to the biblical pattern. The ideal is to work as a team, with clear understanding of each partner's respective roles and responsibilities.

2. *Marriage is confessed in the presence of two or three witnesses.* The marriage vow may be said in private between a male and female and be done with great intensity and sincerity, but the Bible teaches the necessity of witnesses. Deuteronomy 17:6 says, "Whoever is worthy of death shall be put to death on

the testimony of two or three witnesses, but he shall not be put to death on the testimony of one witness." In Deuteronomy 19:15 we read, "One witness shall not rise against a man concerning any iniquity or any sin that he commits; by the mouth of two or three witnesses the matter shall be established."

In the New Testament, Jesus spoke of the necessity of two or three witnesses verifying what was said or done when a person had a grievance against another person. In Matthew 18:16 Jesus said, "But if he will not hear you, take with you one or two more, that by the mouth of two or three witnesses every word may be established." In verse 20 He said, "For where two or three are gathered in My name, I am there in the midst of them." His authority is present in multiple witness. A person may deny something that was said or done if only one other person heard it or saw it.

A marriage vow is established in front of witnesses. We are accountable in a public way for what we have said and what we have promised. That makes marriage sacred and solemn.

3. *Marriage is confirmed by sexual unity.* The Bible says that "the two shall become one flesh." Genesis 2:25 adds this note: "They were both naked, the man and his wife, and were not ashamed." Some will read this and say, "I have been naked with a person to whom I was not married and I was not embarrassed at all!" But the word "naked" in Genesis 2:25 deals with transparency and intimacy. Adam and Eve had nothing to hide from each other and no reason to be ashamed in their relationship. In the Book of Hebrews we have this insight about the word "naked" (4:13):

> There is no creature hidden from His sight,
> but all things are naked and open to the eyes
> of Him to whom we must give account.

The words "one flesh" refer to sexual unity. In 1 Corinthians 6:16 there is a warning about sexual immorality:

> Do you not know that he who is joined to
> a harlot is one body with her? For "The two,"
> He says, "shall become one flesh."

Sexual intercourse with a prostitute is described as being "joined" to her and becoming "one body with her." This fact is based on the teaching of marriage that a husband and a wife become "one flesh" when they are "joined" together. Nothing so damages the sanctity of marriage as having sex with someone besides your marital spouse. Sexual immorality (sex outside of marriage) is the enemy of marriage and causes the breakup of marriage. No matter what reasons are given for the many divorces occurring in our country, the number one problem is the failure to be faithful to our marital vows. A person may not have had sexual intercourse with another person outside of marriage, but the thought of having someone else or being discontented with the spouse you have is the seed of decay that separates a husband from a wife emotionally if not literally.

Upon entering a small store next to a service station where I had stopped to get gas, I saw a young boy (about ten years old) at the magazine section reading pornographic material. When I questioned him about this, he told me it was none of my business. If he wanted to look at "sex stuff," he could. He said his dad bought the magazines often and let him read them. He told me that he knew "all about sex" and didn't need anyone telling him about it—especially me.

I immediately told the store manager about this incident, and urged him to get the magazines out of his store, or at least put them out of the reach of children. He was obviously not happy with my confrontation. (More about this in Chapter 5.)

This generation thinks that sex is a game we play—that it can be enjoyed, used, and viewed without limitation or restraint. We attack the Bible for its information about sex without realizing what it really says. Do we really know "all about sex"?

HOW IMPORTANT IS SEX?

Sex is a huge subject in the Bible. Contrary to what many Americans believe, the Bible contains a wealth of information about sex, and it is surprisingly bold, frank, and specific in its details and discussions.

When we use the word "sex" in ordinary discussions with each other, we might refer to three different aspects of it.

1. *Sex refers to physical anatomy* (male and female). We answer the question "What sex are you?" on an application form or in an interview process with either "male" or "female." The Bible emphasizes the distinctiveness of both male and female and urges that the differences be recognized and maintained. Since we were created in the image of God, it is important to realize that the original creation of human life according to Genesis 1:27 included both male and female.

It is important to appreciate your sexuality—the way God made you. If you are female, then thank the Lord for it and do all you can to develop your femininity. If you are male, then rejoice in it and realize that God wants you to be masculine in every way. Both male and female with all their differences were designed by God. You are special and there is no one like you, but in terms of sexuality, about half of the human race knows what you are going through in terms of feelings, needs, and desires.

2. *Sex refers to physical attraction* ("sexy"). There is nothing wrong with being physically attractive. The Bible speaks of people like that (e.g. Joseph in Genesis 39:6), and does not condemn them for having a beautiful body. (Read the Song of Solomon carefully; the physical attributes of a person's body are romantically and wonderfully described.)

However, a part of our moral crisis today is the pressure which we put upon each other to be "sexy." Although we complain over sexual harassment in the business world, all of our advertising and marketing schemes are rooted in the desire to be sexually attractive. If a given item or product is to be attractive to modern Americans, the packaging of its benefits is often associated with sex or physical attractiveness. This affects cosmetics, clothes, cars, investments, careers, foods, and even toys.

One of the great dangers in today's culture is the exploitation of children. Already visible is the attempt to make children appear sexually attractive in advertising.

The Bible warns women to be especially careful in the area of dress. Godly women who are concerned about morality will avoid wearing clothes that allure the opposite sex to possible sexual involvement or seduce a male into a sexual relationship because of the enticement of what one wears.

There is a great difference between a woman's natural beauty and physical attractiveness and her desire to allure and seduce. Godly men need to be careful in making suggestive and sensual remarks to women. They bear great responsibility in encouraging and promoting sensual talk and provocative dress.

We are paying a tremendous price for our obsession with the word "sexy." It has created a monster that is consuming our energies and destroying our moral character.

3. *Sex refers to physical acts* ("Let's have sex!"). Our moral catastrophe in America is very much connected to the sexual activity that is tolerated and even encouraged among our young people. Our only escape is to speak of "safe sex" and to urge young people (and old as well) to use condoms!

But the only truly safe sex is that reserved for marriage between a husband and a wife. A marriage is sacred because a man agrees to have sexual intercourse with his wife alone! A marriage is sacred because a woman agrees to have sexual intercourse with her husband alone! The marriage vows should always include the words "to forsake all others and cleave to her/him alone until death do us part."

SEX IN MARRIAGE

Sex is important, and the Bible urges that it be experienced within the bonds of marriage. Hebrews 13:4 makes this clear:

> Marriage is honorable among all, and the
> bed undefiled; but fornicators and adulterers
> God will judge.

Sex within marriage is honorable. There is no defilement in the sexual activity between a husband and a wife. But outside of marriage sex deserves the judgment of God. It destroys relationships and damages self-image. It hurts people in a multitude of ways that are not clearly understood when the sexual activity takes place.

The Bible teaches two things about sex in marriage and its sacredness:

1. *It is the duty of a spouse* (1 Corinthians 7:1-5).

> Concerning the things of which you wrote
> to me: It is good for a man not to touch a
> woman. Nevertheless, because of sexual im-
> morality, let each man have his own wife, and
> let each woman have her own husband. Let the
> husband render to his wife the affection due her,
> and likewise also the wife to her husband. The
> wife does not have authority over her own body,
> but the husband does. And likewise the husband
> does not have authority over his own body, but
> the wife does. Do not deprive one another except
> with consent for a time, that you may give
> yourselves to fasting and prayer; and come
> together again so that Satan does not tempt you
> because of your lack of self-control.

To avoid the wrong use of our sexual desires, God designed marriage. It is not right to engage in premarital sex or extra-marital sex, according to the Bible. The moral crisis in our country will not change until we restore in our hearts and lifestyles the loyalty of marriage vows and the commitment to have sex only with a marital spouse to whom we have spoken a vow.

It is never right for a person to withhold sex from his or her spouse; that is a clear violation of what the Bible teaches. The Bible warns the married to be careful about sexual absti-nence. It says that we can be easily tempted to have sexual satisfaction with someone else because we are not able to con-trol our sexual desires.

In our culture a person's individual rights have been promoted constantly before our eyes. The cult of the individual has replaced the concern for community and others. In mar-riage, an independent spirit is destructive to marital harmony and unity. 1 Corinthians 11:11 reminds us that "neither is man independent of woman, nor woman independent of man, in the Lord." We are to understand our need for one another.

In relation to sexual fulfillment, the Bible urges couples to understand that each person in a marriage relinquishes the right of control to his physical body and desires when he gets married. 1 Corinthians 7:4 says that neither the wife nor the husband "has authority" over her or his own body. That belongs to your spouse. Your body is to be given to your spouse to enjoy. We are warned about holding back in sexual matters (1 Corinthians 7:5).

2. *It should be the desire of a spouse* (Proverbs 5:18-20). The sexual union of a husband and a wife is sacred and is based on their commitment to each other to forsake all others "till death do us part." It is essential to be loyal to each other. Yet the sexual issue is more involved than just loyalty by avoiding sex with others. It is also something more than just performing a duty, though that should be done.

Sex between a husband and a wife should be based on strong sexual desire, a desire that is filled with romance and that flourishes unrestrained because of the vows that they spoke to each other on their wedding day. There should be complete freedom—no inhibitions, no hesitation.

Proverbs 5:18-20 describes such passion:

> Let your fountain be blessed, and rejoice
> with the wife of your youth. As a loving deer
> and a graceful doe, let her breasts satisfy you
> at all times; and always be enraptured with her
> love. For why should you, my son, be enraptured
> by an immoral woman, and be embraced in the
> arms of a seductress?

One has no need for a prostitute if he follows the advice of this passage! There will be no cause for having sex with someone else if you do what this Scripture says.

1) Rejoice with the wife of your youth!

You are to be excited and happy with your marital spouse. When you are disappointed, discontented, or simply feeling neglected, watch out! The Bible urges you to get excited about the one you married. Are you?

2) Let her breasts satisfy you at all times.

There are no details here about the size or appearance of a woman's breasts. It does not matter to a loving and faithful husband. He finds complete satisfaction with his sexual involvement with his wife. He doesn't need to go elsewhere, for she completely satisfies him.

3) Always be enraptured with her love.

The word "love" can be translated "lovemaking," and fits the context much better. The point is that a marital spouse is to be obsessed, entranced, intoxicated, and enraptured with the lovemaking of his spouse. No wonder many of us are disappointed with our marriages! We are not to be passive in matters of sexual activity; we are to be overwhelmed with the passionate, romantic responses of our spouses.

Speaking of the desire of a spouse, read Song of Solomon 2:4-6:

> He brought me to the banqueting house,
> and his banner over me was love. Sustain me
> with cakes of raisins, refresh me with apples,
> for I am lovesick. His left hand is under my
> head, and his right hand embraces me.

This woman is lovesick! She desires intensely her husband's sexual advances and caresses. For more on the Song of Solomon read *Romantic Lovers*, by David and Carole Hocking (published by Harvest House).

Marriage is sacred, based on vows that were spoken in front of witnesses. These vows make sexual satisfaction and fulfillment what God intended for them to be from the beginning.

THE SEXUAL REVOLUTION

Today's sexual understanding and practices are far from moral values, and we are suffering greatly because of it. The present moral catastrophe cannot be intelligently evaluated without realizing that we have come a long way from biblical morality and responsible sexual behavior.

In the Old Testament law are listed sexual sins that required the death penalty. The laws of God reveal to us the righteous and holy character of God and determine the nature and consequences of sinful behavior. Sin is sin because of God's decision, not because of our feelings or determinations. Consider the list of sexual sins that deserved the death penalty under the law:

Adultery—Exodus 20:14; Leviticus 20:10.

Incest—Leviticus chapters 18 and 20; Deuteronomy 27:20, 22,23.

Bestiality—Leviticus 20:15,16; Deuteronomy 27:21.

Homosexuality—Leviticus 18:22; 20:13.

Premarital infidelity—Deuteronomy 22:13-21, 23-27.

The law also required that when sex occurred with an adult virgin (Deuteronomy 22:28,29), marriage must take place and no divorce was ever allowed.

In the New Testament, Jesus emphasized the danger of even mental adultery, and the apostle Paul warned about believer's becoming involved in immoral talk or jokes.

Such standards seem extreme to our sex-saturated society. Our movies, television, and entertainment opportunities are filled with sexual remarks and seductiveness. Comedians can hardly do a program without sexual jokes that are off-color and inappropriate in any context.

SEX OUTSIDE OF MARRIAGE

If God has said that sex outside of marriage is wrong, shouldn't that be enough for us? Yet because we ignore or resist our accountability to God, we demand more reasons for moral behavior.

That's what John, a 43-year-old businessman, tried to tell me. His sexual escapades were "fun and harmless" and did not affect his "sexual prowess." He resented my confrontation about the dangers of sexual immorality, and asked me, "What possible harm can it bring?"

Here are a few reasons why sex outside of marriage is so wrong and destructive.

1. *Immorality destroys the sanctity of marriage and the family.* We should all be concerned about the terrible breakdown in marital and family life in our country. If we really want to see things change, then we must restore biblical morality to the sexual understanding and practices of our society.

Hebrews 13:4 says that the marriage bed is undefiled, but that all other sex deserves the judgment of God.

2. *Immorality causes emotional turmoil.* 1 Peter 2:11 says:

> Beloved, I beg you as sojourners and pilgrims, abstain from fleshy lusts, which war against the soul.

Carnal sexual appetites will cause emotional turmoil in our lives. Sexual desire is not wrong, but when we seek to fulfill it outside of marriage, it is a "fleshly lust" and will fight against us in the arena of our emotions. We will devastate ourselves emotionally if we get involved sexually outside of marriage.

Sexual immorality causes tremendous emotional pain. It leads to depression and the inability to function effectively.

3. *Immorality reduces sexual vitality.* The reality is just the opposite of what most people think. It is amazing how many people believe that if you are sexually active with a large number of people, you are some kind of "superlover," capable of great sexual prowess. What a joke! At first the sexual pleasure and intense desire that you feel deceive you; you think there is no price to be paid. How wrong you are!

The truth is that people who have multiple sexual encounters are destroying the sexual vitality of their lives. Proverbs 5:7-10 describes the problem:

> Hear me now, my children, and do not depart from the words of my mouth. Remove your way far from her [the immoral woman], and do not go near the door of her house, lest you give your honor to others, and your years to the cruel one; lest aliens be filled with your wealth, and your labors go to the house of a foreigner.

There is no reason why a marital couple cannot experience great sexual desire and vitality even in their elderly years. The speed and frequency at which we experience sexual enjoyment may diminish, but the vitality and intensity of what we feel remains. Age simply deepens your emotional oneness when you follow biblical principles in your marriage and stay away from sexual sin. Sex becomes more satisfying and enjoyable when you have been faithful to your marital partner and have fulfilled your marital responsibilities.

Sex doesn't need to get weak, disappointing, and frustrating. It can be wonderful, warm, loving, romantic, and stimulating all the days of your married life. If you want to ruin that possibility, just get involved sexually with a number of other people.

4. *Immorality leads to sexual disease.* A complete chapter will come later on the colossal problem of sexual disease within our contemporary society. But at this point understand that sex outside of marriage brings its own consequences. Proverbs 5:11 speaks of how a person will "mourn at last, when your flesh and your body are consumed." Romans 1:27 speaks of people "receiving in themselves the penalty of their error which was due."

5. *Immorality hinders your relationships with others.* 1 Corinthians 5:9-13 speaks of how believers must withdraw their social relationships with those who are involved in sex outside of marriage. It strains your ability to interact and communicate openly. Friendships are destroyed; feelings are hurt; mutual trust can no longer exist.

6. *Immorality ruins your reputation in front of others.* Our reputation is what people think we are; our character is what God knows us to be. However, your reputation is also important. Consider how religious and political scandals have destroyed the reputations and leadership of people in high places. Sexual immorality is destructive to your leadership and the respect which people give to you.

7. *Immorality destroys your usefulness to God.* This may not mean much to you if you do not have personal faith in God and in His Son, Jesus Christ, but when a person gets involved in sexual sin, his or her ability to serve the Lord effectively is greatly reduced. 2 Timothy 2:19-22 states:

> The solid foundation of God stands, having
> this seal: "The Lord knows those who are His,"

and, "Let everyone who names the name of
Christ depart from iniquity." But in a great
house there are not only vessels of gold and
silver, but also of wood and clay, some for honor
and some for dishonor. Therefore if anyone
cleanses himself from the latter, he will be a
vessel for honor, sanctified and useful for the
Master, prepared for every good work. Flee also
youthful lusts; but pursue righteousness, faith,
love, peace with those who call on the Lord out
of a pure heart.

The issue of sexual behavior is vitally related to our
usefulness in the service of God. We are told to "flee youthful
lusts." They will ruin our testimony and reduce our effective-
ness in serving the Lord.

WHY SO MANY MARRIAGES FAIL

Nearly one out of every two marriages will end in divorce.
What's wrong? Why are so many marriages failing?

Jesus Christ commented on the reason for all the divorces
in the days of Moses. In Matthew 19:8 He said:

Moses, because of the hardness of your
hearts, permitted you to divorce your wives, but
from the beginning it was not so.

"Hardness of heart"—being stubborn and callous—that's
the reason. Hebrews 3:13 says that such hardness is caused by
the deceitfulness of sin. The major reason why people are ending their marriages is because they are simply indifferent to
the command of God and disloyal to their marital vows. They
have no righteous reason; they just can't get along, and label
this "irreconcilable differences."

Jesus said that the law of Moses was a permission, not a
command. It was an attempt to regulate the problem of many
divorces without any righteous grounds.

Righteous or defensible grounds for a divorce are spelled
out clearly in the Bible. Jesus said in Matthew 5:32:

I say to you that whoever divorces his wife
for any reason except sexual immorality causes
her to commit adultery; and whoever marries a
woman who is divorced commits adultery.

In Matthew 19:9 He said:

I say to you, whoever divorces his wife
except for sexual immorality, and marries another, commits adultery; and whoever marries
her who is divorced commits adultery.

The only righteous reason for divorce is sexual immorality, since immorality breaks the marital covenant and destroys
the sexual unity of the marital couple. No wonder it was accepted as righteous grounds for divorce! However, this doesn't
mean that a person would quickly get a divorce upon hearing
that his or her spouse had an affair. It is always better to learn
to forgive and to restore the relationship.

(The apostle Paul added another reason in 1 Corinthians
7:12-15, and that is the willing departure of an unbeliever who
leaves the believing spouse. Verse 15 says, "A brother or a sister
is not under bondage in such cases.")

Sexual unfaithfulness is a major reason why we are losing the sanctity of marriage and why our moral and traditional
values with regard to marriage have been declining. Until we
stop our sexual promiscuity and our toleration of sexual sin, our
marriages will continue to fail.

Disagreements over finances, the raising of children,
career goals, etc., also cause many marriages to fail. The lack
of communication is another serious problem. But to divorce
because of these "irreconcilable differences" is foolish and com-
plicates our moral tragedy in this country. We desperately need
stable marriages in order to produce stable families and to
restore moral and traditional values to our society.

Our individual happiness is not the highest goal we can
have in life, though we have been led to believe that. Happiness
is not found in the abundance of things we have or in the
circumstances of our daily life; happiness is found when we put
our faith in the living God and His Son, Jesus Christ, who died
on a cross over 1900 years ago to pay for our sins, and then rose
from the dead. Eternal life is a gift of God through faith in His

Son, Jesus Christ our Lord. Have you ever made that personal commitment to Jesus Christ?

A person who is committed to God understands that happiness is found by serving others, by loving and caring, and not by selfish pursuit and achievement.

Jim and Helen found out about true happiness after many years of struggle and heartache. Their marriage of 32 years was filled with violence, hostility, alcoholism, and frequent separations. Their kids fell into drugs and rebellion toward their parents. All three left home in their teenage years and would have nothing to do with their parents.

One day Jim and Helen went for help. A pastor who tried to counsel them about their marital and family problems soon realized that neither one of them had a personal relationship with God. They did not own a Bible, and never prayed. It was obvious that their greatest need (as with all of us) was spiritual, not emotional or psychological.

Jim and Helen got on their knees in that pastor's office and committed their lives and future to Jesus Christ as their Lord and Savior. Then things began to change. They started to attend a church where the Bible is taught. They began to read the Bible together and pray together, asking for God's help and wisdom.

Today Jim and Helen are very happy. Their children have also become Christians, and the love and harmony in this marriage and family is radically different from the past alienation.

WHAT SHOULD BE OUR RESPONSE?

The sanctity of marriage is one of the great moral issues of our time. The moral catastrophe that we are experiencing with the breakup of so many marriages can be changed if we are willing to repent of our sinful attitudes and sexual misconduct and to return to biblical standards of morality.

May the following become our commitment as individuals and as a nation.

> 1) Marriage is sacred because it was commanded
>   and instituted by God.

2) Marriage is based on vows between a man and a woman in front of two or three witnesses that pledge sexual loyalty to each other until death.

3) Sexual unity, satisfaction, and fulfillment are to take place within the bonds of matrimony.

4) Sexual intercourse outside of marriage is wrong and deserves the judgment of God and society.

5) Divorce is a tragic response to marital difficulty, and should be sought only after repeated attempts to reconcile have failed. For believers, the only acceptable grounds for divorce are sexual immorality and the willing departure of an unbeliever.

6) The sanctity and blessing of marriage must be taught to our children but can be best communicated by the loving example of parents.

7) The greatest deterrent to marital failure is a personal commitment to biblical standards of morality and trust in the living God.

✦ 4 ✦

The Value of Children

When our first child was born, I was overwhelmed with the thought of being a father and having a child of my own. When I picked him up at the hospital shortly after my wife delivered, I knew that something very special and valuable had been placed into our hands. It was a sacred trust and a wonderful treasure.

Now that our children are grown, our love for children has continued to grow even stronger. It's wonderful to be grandparents, but it seems that children everywhere have become a special joy to our hearts. We love kids! There is nothing sweeter than to hold a newborn baby in your arms and marvel at the gift of human life. Our secular society with its emphasis on "things" and success has been on a downward course that reduces the value of human life and is especially callous toward our children.

Two million children a year are reported missing, and many of these are runaways. Over 5000 bodies of children are found each year in the United States, and many are unidentifiable. Hundreds of our teenagers are committing suicide each year, and thousands of our children are molested or exposed to perverted and hideous acts of sex and violence.

Over one-and-a-half million babies are aborted each year, and many who are born are declared to be undesirable or unwanted because of physical handicap or parental inconvenience.

Needless to say, we have a serious moral problem confronting our culture when it comes to the value of children!

In *The Desert Sun*, a newspaper serving Palm Springs,

California, an article appeared on June 8, 1989, entitled "America's mentally ill children 'under-served,' study warns."

The article, written by Paul Recer of the Associated Press staff, says:

> As many as 14 million American children suffer from some mental disorder, a problem that is costing society billions of dollars and depriving the nation of productive citizens.
>
> "There is a stigma associated with mental illness and there is a major problem in how children's problems are perceived," said James F. Leckman of Yale University, the chairman of an Institute of Medicine committee that prepared the study.
>
> Mentally ill children have historically been "under-served," he said, noting that "this is a clear and persistent problem in our society."

The report went on to say that 12 percent of America's children are mentally disturbed, and that the total number may be as high as 14 million children. The report identified a variety of problems that have produced mental illness among our children, including developmental impairments that slow education and learning; emotional disturbances that include anxiety, depression, or both; and behavioral problems that include disruptive and antisocial acts.

NEGLECTED AND EXPLOITED

Our children are being ignored and exploited. We seem to be unaware of or indifferent to the growing problem of disturbed children who are being raised in a society devoid of traditional moral values.

Bain de Soleil, which markets lotions and similar items for women, produced an ad for a new suntan lotion in which a mother and her little daughter wore a bikini bathing suit. In spite of efforts used by the firm to justify the ad, critics pointed out that the child was wearing a gold earring and a black bikini, and lounged with her legs outstretched, clearly portrayed along with her mother as a sex object.

In *USA Today* on April 8, 1989, an article appeared on the subject of "infant mortality." Lynda Johnson Robb, a member of the National Commission to Prevent Infant Mortality, was being interviewed. She was quoted as saying:

> There are so many babies that even if we save their lives, they may have mental or physical handicaps. One of the shocking things is that although we are able to save babies now who never would have survived, we still have the same percentage of low-birth-weight babies being born now that we did 20 years ago.

When asked why Japan has the world's lowest infant-mortality rate, she said:

> They put a higher premium on their babies. They have made it a national concern.

In 1988, 40,000 babies died in the United States from birth to age one. Today hundreds of babies are born with alcohol or drug dependency, and even AIDS. Do we really care?

Half of America's children have a mother in the labor force. By the year 2000, seven out of ten preschoolers will have mothers in the labor force. One in five children lives with only one parent, and one in four of our children never completes high school. More than a million children run away or are thrown out of their homes, and 12.4 million children live below the poverty level.

DINKS AND SILKS

In a March 30, 1989, article in *USA Today*, a woman named Susan Riley was quoted. She quit her nursing job in Dallas in order to care for her 13-month-old son. The article states that she elected to stay home because she couldn't imagine anyone taking the same interest in her son's development as she did. The article quotes her:

It's not always the easiest thing to stay
home with children. Some women would rather
be in the work force fulfilling their own needs.
I have sisters and sisters-in-law who have
chosen to work. We make a lot less money than
they do. We are lowering our standard of living
because I'm at home.

The truth is that many mothers would resent this woman's
implications that her role cannot be replaced by another woman.
Many mothers see children as a hindrance to their goals and
objectives in life. Children have become problems to deal with
(usually with governmental help) rather than blessings to
enjoy.

The world of the "DINKS" is now upon us in many metropolitan areas of our country: "Double Income, No Kids." I like
what a friend of mine said after hearing about the "DINKS." He
responded, "I belong to the SILKS!" I asked "What does that
mean?" He replied, "Single Income, Lots of Kids!"

One of the most serious trends in our society revealing the
disdain we have for our children is the vivid portrayal (by
cartoons for the very young and by all kinds of TV and movie
programming for preteens and teens) of sex, violence, and
occultic themes.

The average Saturday-morning program of cartoons is
enough to convince any thinking American that we are out to
destroy the moral and traditional values of our children. I have
spent some time evaluating these cartoon programs and have
been astonished at what I have seen: programs with satanic
symbols and creatures, subject matter that treats violence with
approval, and animated characters (which often look real) presenting sexual innuendo and suggestiveness to our youngest
children!

The average American child will have watched over
17,000 hours of television by the time he or she reaches age 18.
That means that our children watch about 1000 hours of TV per
year, more time than is spent in school. During that time our
children will have seen some 150,000 violent episodes, including an estimated 25,000 deaths. These facts were reported in a

Reader's Digest article in January 1983. The situation is even worse this year.

That same article revealed a study by the National Institute of Mental Health which involved over 2500 studies on television's influence on behavior. The conclusion was that the evidence is overwhelming that violence on television does lead to aggressive behavior.

A study by Stanford University psychologist Albert Bandura found that "action" cartoons for small children are extremely damaging to the child's mental, social, and emotional behavior. His study reveals that cartoon violence is causing an increasing level of violence among children in our society.

Children are most susceptible to the suggestions implanted in their minds through audio and visual stimuli. Their ability to distinguish fantasy from reality is still in the process of development during their first few years of life. It is very difficult for a child to understand that some cartoon characters are not real people.

The devaluation of children in our society is a serious moral problem, and in many respects is a catastrophe for which we are going to pay continuing serious consequences. Children are not considered to be valuable assets, but are often portrayed as burdens and problems. One lady said about her disobedient child in the line of a grocery store in which I was standing, "Children are a pain in the neck!" This is just a small reflection of what is wrong in our culture in terms of attitudes toward children.

The average child receives very little love and affection from parents. A study done at one of our federal prisons revealed that over 90 percent of the inmates incarcerated for violent crime had never experienced the love and affection of a mother and dad. Many children grow up in hostile, violent atmospheres where their own safety and health is threatened.

THE TRUE VALUE OF CHILDREN

The Bible always refers to children within the context of a family. A family is a mother, a father, and at least one child. This is what we call the traditional definition of a family. Today there are massive efforts to redefine the family. In 1980 President Carter promoted regional conferences across America to deal with the family and its many problems. In those conferences there was a concerted effort to redefine the word "family," and much of what took place turned out to be an attack on the traditional definition of a family—father, mother, and child.

There are over 300 references in the Bible to families. They are considered to be the basic structure of society, the foundation of nations (Genesis 10). Families are paternal when described in biblical passages, with fathers as their leaders and heads (Exodus 6).

Property rights were based on family structure (Leviticus 25:10,41; Numbers 27:1-11; 33:54), and when a census was taken, it was done according to families (Numbers 1:2,18). Movements in the wilderness, as well as encampments, were based on family units (Numbers 2:34).

In the Bible, worship and development of spiritual life was based on family structure and encouragement. The feast of Purim was to be remembered by every family (Esther 9:27,28), and the worship of the Lord was to be done by families (Psalm 22:27; 96:7; Zechariah 14:17). God speaks to families and declares His special relationship to them (Jeremiah 2:4; 31:1).

A traditional definition of a family goes something like this:

> A family is two or more people bound together by heterosexual marriage, physical birth, or legal adoption.

This definition allows for a husband and wife to be considered a family, as well as a father and son or mother and daughter. The ideal is "husband/father, wife/mother, and children of that union."

Consider what the Bible says about the value of children:

Psalm 127:3—"heritage from the Lord"; "His reward."

Psalm 127:4—"like arrows in the hand of a warrior."

Psalm 128:3—"like olive plants all around your table."

Proverbs 17:6—"the crown of old men."

Jesus Christ made some profound statements about the value of children in Matthew 18:1-5. His disciples had asked the question "Who is greatest in the kingdom of heaven?" Jesus set a little child in their midst and replied (verses 3-5):

> Assuredly I say to you, Unless you are converted and become as little children, you will by no means enter the kingdom of heaven. Therefore whoever humbles himself as this little child is the greatest in the kingdom of heaven. And whoever receives one little child like this in My name receives Me.

He said in Matthew 18:14:

> Even so it is not the will of your Father who is in heaven that one of these little ones should perish.

In Matthew 19:14 He made this statement when little children were brought to Him to hold and touch:

> Let the little children come to Me, and do not forbid them; for of such is the kingdom of heaven.

He rebuked those who would try to hinder the little children from coming to Him. Words such as "Children should be seen and not heard" were never heard from the lips of Jesus Christ! He loved little children, and He reminded all of us that we must come to Him like little children if we expect to enter the kingdom of heaven.

If we are to restore our moral values as they relate to children, we must give serious attention to the American family. The Bible presents four essential ingredients for a good family.

PARENTS, LOVE YOUR CHILDREN

In a biblical passage where young married women are instructed by older women on how to handle their families, the point is powerfully made that they are to "love their children" (Titus 2:4).

Many of our present problems regarding children would be solved immediately if we only loved our children the way the Bible teaches.

There are at least five things involved in loving your children.

1. *If you love your children, you treat them as blessings, not burdens.* Psalm 127:3-5 is a fundamental passage in the Bible in revealing the value of children:

> Behold, children are a heritage from the
> Lord; the fruit of the womb is His reward. Like
> arrows in the hand of a warrior, so are the
> children of one's youth. Happy is the man who
> has his quiver full of them; they shall not be
> ashamed, but shall speak with their enemies
> in the gate.

Psalm 128:3-6 adds these beautiful thoughts:

> Your wife shall be like a fruitful vine in
> the very heart of your house, your children like
> olive plants all around your table. Behold, thus
> shall the man be blessed who fears the Lord.
> The Lord bless you out of Zion, and may you see
> the good of Jerusalem all the days of your life.
> Yes, may you see your children's children.

In the New Testament, the apostle Paul referred to his attitude toward the believers of a new congregation in the city of Thessalonica when he said in 1 Thessalonians 2:7:

> We were gentle among you, just as a
> nursing mother cherishes her own children.

What a beautiful expression about the value of children: "cherishes her own children"! Do you cherish your children?

The Bible speaks of a man being blessed who has children, and a quiver full of them. An ancient quiver could hold quite a number of arrows! Today couples wait to have children so that they can pursue their careers and make the money they think they need in order to enjoy life in the future. When they decide to have children, they speak of one or two, no more. Parents with lots of children are looked upon as being unwise and lacking in common sense and fiscal responsibility. Yet the Bible teaches otherwise.

2. *If you love your children, you care about them deeply.* Most parents like to believe that they care about their children. But do they really? Does care mean simply providing food, clothing, and a shelter over their heads? 1 Timothy 5:8 says, "If anyone does not provide for his own, and especially for those of his household, he has denied the faith and is worse than an unbeliever." Yes, parents are to provide the material needs of their children, but caring for children is much more than mere material provision. Psalm 103:13,14 gives us the example of our heavenly Father:

> As a father pities his children, so the Lord
> pities those who fear Him. For He knows our
> frame; He remembers that we are dust.

Care and compassion for our children means that we understand their age, weaknesses, faults, desire for self-image, struggles for independence, mistakes, depravity, and lack of adult understanding and experience. In spite of all their failings we love them deeply, taking them one step at a time to the next level of victory, growth, development, understanding, and achievement.

Our children may often disappoint us. They can cause hurt that runs deep into a parent's heart. They can do foolish things that embarrass and sometimes shock us. But parental care endures, caressing our children and reassuring them of our unconditional love.

The children of our present society are desperately in need of parental love and care. Most children go off to school in the morning without proper assurance and confidence of parental love. Many never experience a warm and loving kiss and embrace, and words of commendation from their parents. The hostility and ugliness of many homes is destroying our children. No wonder mental problems are developing at such a rapid pace among our children!

3. *If you love your children, you will warn them about the dangers of life.* This is a parental task that most of us do not

enjoy because we do not want the responsibility. Yet our children need to be warned about many things. Love does that. Our children may not believe that these warnings are necessary, and may think they can handle anything that comes their way, but that is simply not true of any of us. The younger the child the more necessary it is to warn him, but older children also need to be warned.

The apostle Paul revealed such parental concern in his relationship with a group of people in the city of Corinth. They were having many problems in their relationships with one another, and so he wrote in 1 Corinthians 4:14,15:

> I do not write these things to shame you, but as my beloved children I warn you. For though you might have ten thousand instructors in Christ, yet you do not have many fathers; for in Christ Jesus I have begotten you through the gospel.

Paul was their spiritual father and spoke of his love for them. The reason for his warnings was *love*, and not a judgmental attitude or a desire to suppress their individuality or to keep them from having fun.

The Bible contains a book that parents should read often— the Book of Proverbs. It was written by King Solomon, the wisest of ancient monarchs. This book is filled with wisdom and knowledge about life, people, and relationships. It is fascinating to observe Solomon's instruction to his son; much of it is in the form of warning. He warns him about bad company and sexual immorality; he warns him about priorities in life and financial practices; he warns him about laziness and the need of wisdom in all that he says and does.

If you love your children, you must warn them about many things. Your warnings may not be well-received, and the peer pressure of today's youth will add to their reluctance to listen to anything that parents might say to them in terms of warning, but you must do it anyway if you love your children.

4. *If you love your children, you will correct them.* As with the task of warning, this is a responsibility which most parents

dislike. Children today are being programmed toward rebellion and an independent spirit. This attitude is found in movies, television, and most strongly in contemporary music. Parents are treated with disdain and are often portrayed as being incapable of rational thought.

Proverbs 3:11,12 says:

> My son, do not despise the chastening of
> the Lord, nor detest His correction; for whom
> the Lord loves He corrects, just as a father the
> son in whom he delights.

If a parent does not really delight in his child, one can understand his lack of correction. But if you love your children, you will correct them. You want to keep them from ruining their lives, and you will do whatever you can to prevent them taking a wrong turn or making a wrong decision.

Obviously a parent cannot make all the decisions for a child or stop him from making mistakes. We all learn from the bad decisions we have made as surely as the good ones. Some parents try to maintain complete oversight for too long, never allowing their children to be tested and to accept responsibility for the choices they make. There is a time when a parent needs to let go and allow the child the freedom to decide and to bear the consequences of that decision.

The desire to correct can sometimes be motivated by expectations that are too high or unreasonable for the child. Some parents correct their children in order to produce the children they have always wanted rather than accept fully the personality, ability, and dreams of the children they actually have.

Correction in the Bible is rooted in a desire to do right and to avoid wrong. It is always seen in terms of moral direction. Parents who love their children are instructed to guide them in the way of righteousness, and not allow them to continue in the way of evil. Children are easily deceived by the false promises of our secular society—promises about what will make you important, attractive, or successful. Loving parents must correct on the basis of *morality*—not the kind that is governed by their own feelings or desires, but morality which is rooted in the authority and existence of God Himself.

5. *If you love your children, you will discipline them promptly.* Discipline is a lost art in our permissive society, and

we are paying a tremendous price for its absence in the American family. We have been consumed (and rightly so) with injustice, child abuse, and individual rights. We seem to be highly aware of the failure of parents to handle their children, so we have decided that government or education could do a better job. Instead of supporting and helping parents in their responsibility, we continue to undermine their authority and role in the lives of their children.

Proverbs 13:24 states:

He who spares his rod hates his son, but
he who loves him disciplines him promptly.

True discipline deals with a situation as soon as possible; it does not wait. Waiting is harmful for the child as well as the parent. Notice that parental love responds with discipline.

Because of the crucial nature of parental discipline and our society's current response to this parental responsibility, we need to examine the task of disciplining our children in a way that reflects biblical morality and not society's passion for independence and freedom.

Our failure to discipline our children is leading us into the moral catastrophe of our present culture. Our families have become hotels where kids sleep but do little else; very little communication takes place between parents and children in the average American home. Most American children have their own room, unless they are part of a large family where space must be shared. This fact alone is significant and reflects our material abundance. We have houses that provide children with privacy in separate rooms. However, this has led to serious isolation and withdrawal. Many children have their own TV and stereo system in their room, and find few reasons to ever depart from its walls. A child leaves the room to either leave the house or to get something to eat.

The young father in my office was frustrated and tired of all the hassles of bringing up his children in today's world. One of his three children was entering junior high school, one was in the fourth grade, and one was only three years old. And now he just learned that his wife was pregnant again.

His oldest child was very rebellious, and the fourth-grader talked back to his parents in a way that seemed out of control. This young father (only 32 years old) had given up.

The truth was that, like so many of his contemporaries, he had decided to eliminate spanking in his home. He did not like to discipline his children, and he was paying a terrible price for his failure. I asked him, "Do you love your kids?" He replied, "Yes, but sometimes I wish they belonged to someone else or they were never born in the first place!" When I told him that if he loved his children he would discipline them, he seemed surprised and a little resentful. He asked me why he should discipline his kids, adding, "Doesn't that just make them more rebellious?"

After a lengthy discussion in which I listed some reasons for discipline, we prayed that God would help him be the father he should be. That was several years ago. Today he has a different attitude and his family life brings him much happiness. It wasn't easy to discipline his older child (who was now too old to spank), but the immediate effect upon his other children was amazing to both his wife and himself, for a great measure of order and calm was restored to his family.

PARENTS, DISCIPLINE YOUR CHILDREN

A second essential of a family that is rooted in moral and traditional values is that of loving discipline. Discipline is designed to prevent us from having wrong attitudes toward authority and to provide us with the experiences that give us a measure of maturity. We all need discipline. The key to effective leadership in terms of exercising authority and decision-making is *discipline*. Those lead best who have learned how to be submissive. A willingness to obey builds the ability of a person to ask the same of others.

Very little attention has been given in our society to training parents in how to discipline their children. Often the implication is that parental discipline harms children rather than building their sense of worth. Because we are so sensitive to the issues of child abuse (and we should be!), we are floundering in our understanding of what we should do. The majority of Americans are aware that our children are in need of discipline, but many parents are not sure what to do or how to do it. We have a tendency to criticize methods of parental discipline even though we do not have the experience or moral values to understand its importance. Here are six important points to remember in disciplining your children.

1. *Know why you are doing it.* To discipline our children is not easy. Part of our problem is our understanding of why discipine needs to be applied in the first place. The Bible gives at least five reasons.

a) *To remove foolishness*—Proverbs 22:15.
   Foolishness is bound up in the heart of a child, but the rod of correction will drive it far from him.

b) *To rescue from judgment*—Proverbs 23:13,14.
   Do not withhold correction from a child, for if you beat him with a rod, he will not die. You shall beat him with a rod, and deliver his soul from hell.

c) *To receive wisdom*—Proverbs 29:15.
   The rod and reproof give wisdom, but a child left to himself brings shame to his mother.

d) *To relieve your anxiety*—Proverbs 29:17.
   Correct your son, and he will give you rest; yes, he will give delight to your soul.

e) *To reflect God's character*—Hebrews 12:10,11.
   For they [human fathers] indeed for a few days chastened us as seemed best to them, but He [God] for our profit, that we may be partakers of His holiness. Now no chastening seems to be joyful for the present, but grievous; nevertheless, afterward it yields the peaceable fruit of righteousness to those who have been trained by it.

Some of these statements may run counter to your experience or understanding, but understand this fact: We are in a moral crisis in our society; we have lost our sense of moral and traditional values in the present passion for freedom and individual rights. Isn't the Bible worth a second look? Shouldn't we try to understand the wisdom of the Book of Proverbs regarding child discipline? Doesn't the God of the Bible have anything to contribute to these issues?

Children can be spared from ruining their lives by parental and loving discipline. Children are made wiser by discipline, and disciplined children are a blessing and a delight to their parents. Discipline teaches us about the character of God and the attitudes that we desperately need in order to be effective and successful in our lives.

2. *Make sure you follow what the Bible says.* In disciplining your children it is vital to follow carefully what the Bible actually says, and not what you may have heard from some other person. People can prove almost anything by taking a Bible verse out of context and rephrasing it for their own purposes.

When you discipline your children, the Bible is clear that it is to be the *Lord's* discipline, not yours. Ephesians 6:4 instructs fathers:

> Fathers, do not provoke your children to
> wrath, but bring them up in the training and
> admonition of the Lord.

The word "discipline" is based on the Greek word for training. Discipline is designed to *train and prepare our children for life.* But notice carefully that it is the "training *of the Lord.*"

Proverbs 22:6 is a very important verse on child discipline and development, and a little later in this chapter we will analyze it carefully. But at this point please notice the wording of this verse:

> Train up a child in the way he should go,
> and when he is old he will not depart from it.

The training is to be "in the way he should go." Proverbs contrasts the way of the Lord with the way of the world, the way of righteousness with the way of sin. The verse preceding this important command to train our children speaks of "the way of the perverse." Proverbs uses a poetic device that involves contrast. "The way of the perverse" is contrasted with "the way he should go." Obviously, the way a child should go is the way the Lord God wants him to go!

If our discipline is to be all that it should be, it must be guided by what the Bible actually says. To depart from that or add to it leads to many problems in your relationship with your children.

3. *Understand what happens if you don't discipline.* Some parents leave the children to handle things by themselves, all in the name of teaching them life by making them face it alone. Often this is merely an excuse for a parent who does not want to fulfill the responsibility of being a parent and applying discipline to the children.

Proverbs 13:24 reveals that a parent who does not discipline is expressing *hatred* for the child, not love! Don't say that you love your child and that is why you don't discipline him; you're just deceiving yourself! The reality is that you care more about your own feelings and depend more upon your child's acceptance of you than you do about the child. If you love your child, you will discipline him.

Proverbs 29:15 says that a lack of discipline will lead to shame and embarrassment for the parents. Most of us who have gone through the process of parenting and now have children who are grown and gone realize the accuracy of this proverb!

There is a tragic story in the Bible of a family in which discipline was not applied. Interestingly, it was a religious home where the father was a Jewish priest. His name was Eli, and he had two sons named Hophni and Phinehas. The Bible speaks of these children in a way that would shame or embarrass any parent. 1 Samuel 2:12 says, "The sons of Eli were corrupt; they did not know the Lord." They were involved in religious service, along with their father, but there was no personal relationship with God; they felt nothing in their hearts—it was all hypocrisy and sham.

1 Samuel 2:17 says, "Therefore the sin of the young men was very great before the Lord, for men abhorred the offering of the Lord." Worship was being affected by these religious leaders who were immoral and corrupt. Verse 22 says that these two sons were having sex with women who came to the tabernacle for worship.

When Eli finally tried to confront his sons about their wickedness, the Bible says, "Nevertheless they did not heed the voice of their father" (1 Samuel 2:25).

When God brought his rebuke to Eli for the spiritual condition of things under his leadership, He referred to Eli's sons. In verse 29 God said to Eli, "Why do you...honor your sons more than Me?" In 1 Samuel 3:13 we learn the root reason behind this terrible situation. The Lord told Samuel (who worked for Eli) that He would judge Eli's house and remove his leadership role as priest, and for this reason:

> I have told him that I will judge his house
> forever for the iniquity which he knows, because
> his sons made themselves vile, and he did not
> restrain them.

A lack of discipline in this religious home led to terrible consequences. Eli's sons were never restrained by their father. They were allowed to do whatever they wanted to do, so they became corrupt, immoral, insensitive to people, filled with wrong values and priorities, and ungodly in their attitudes and actions.

Parents, wake up! The problems of our society with regard to our children are enormous and are getting even worse. We must restore biblical discipine and go back to moral values that are rooted in the existence and authority of God.

4. *Use the rod.* You can almost feel the hostility arising over this point! Many secular educators have been led to believe that spanking is a form of child abuse. A generation ago, many parents were persuaded by Dr. Benjamin Spock that spanking was not the best way to discipline their children. A generation is now adult which has been devoid of physical discipline. They continue to follow the example of their parents and have even pushed the issue to the ultimate extreme—children's rights to determine their own lives and the need to protect those rights by legislative action.

But we need to ask a crucial question: Is it all right to use the rod to spank our children? The rod (or stick) is mentioned in Proverbs 13:24; 22:15; 23:13,14; and 29:15 in reference to child discipline. The rod is not our last resort; it should be our first response! The Bible speaks of "blows that hurt" in Proverbs 20:30, and at this point some person will shout "child abuse!"

But wait a minute—child abuse is hitting a child in a spot not designed to receive a blow! Proverbs 10:13 says, "A rod is for the *back* of him who is devoid of understanding." Proverbs 19:29 speaks of "beatings for the *backs* of fools." Proverbs 26:3 says, "A rod for the fool's *back*."

The word for "back" in Hebrew is speaking specifically about a section of the back. It is referring to a person's bottom, that part of a person's body that has been designed to take punishment without experiencing serious physical damage. The bottom can be bruised, but it can receive normal spanking without suffering any serious physical damage. That is a medical fact!

Child abuse is when a parent hits a child on the face or any part of the body except the bottom. A parent is not to discipline in anger, or to spank until a bruise or redness appears on the buttocks. (Some children bruise easily, but this does not necessarily mean that child abuse has occurred.)

Why the rod and not your hand? The parent's hand should be the instrument of love in the mind and heart of the child. Using a stick of some sort (or paddle) separates that which punishes from the one who loves. Using the rod emphasizes the parent's hand as that which brings love, affection, and tenderness to a child.

Before and after spanking, a parent should express love and affection for the child. The discipline should occur in private, not in front of others. When you discipline your child in front of others you are destroying his sense of worth, and this brings serious emotional damage. Make the discipline private, and surround it with good communication and expressions of love.

5. *Do not discipline your children in anger.* Because of a child's disobedience, rebellion, or angry outburst a parent can often lose control, and because of his own anger harm the child more than help the child when applying discipline. The Bible is clear in Ephesians 6:4:

> Fathers, do not provoke your children to wrath, but bring them up in the training and admonition of the Lord.

According to the Bible, the improper use of discipline can produce anger in children. This anger often expresses itself toward others, or else it is held within the child and causes many emotional problems.

Colossians 3:21 adds:

> Fathers, do not provoke your children, lest
> they become discouraged.

Many children just give up. The discipline they get is too severe and causes them to become discouraged and lose heart. Schools often see this kind of child who has no spirit and is inwardly defeated.

6. *Always respond with affectionate love and complete acceptance.* Hebrews 12:5-8 speaks of God's love for His children when He chastens or disciplines them:

> You have forgotten the exhortation which
> speaks to you as to sons:
> "My son, do not despise the chastening of
> the Lord, nor be discouraged when you are
> rebuked by Him; for whom the Lord loves He
> chastens, and scourges every son whom He
> receives."
> If you endure chastening, God deals with
> you as with sons; for what son is there whom
> a father does not chasten? But if you are without
> chastening, of which all have become partakers,
> then you are illegitimate and not sons.

Every person who is loved as a son is chastened or disciplined. If we grew up without discipline, we grew up without the proper kind of parental love. The Bible tells us not to be discouraged or to look down on the discipline we receive, since it is an expression of God's love for us.

When a parent really loves his child, discipline will occur promptly. When the child is small (through the elementary years), spanking can be used effectively—not as a means of releasing parental anger or frustration, but rather as a loving correction of a child's misbehavior and a reminder that all of us need to be submissive to authority in our lives. The failure of a child to respond to a teacher's authority in school or a police officer later in life is often the direct result of a lack of parental discipline in the home and the child's failure to be subject to parental authority.

Even with proper discipline, a child is a unique individual who has responsibility for his or her own actions and attitudes. A child has the capacity to rebel even when the discipline has been right and the parents' love has been obvious. God never holds us accountable for another person's sin. Ezekiel 18:20 says, "The son shall not bear the guilt of the father, nor the father bear the guilt of the son." A child is accountable for his own rebellion no matter what the parent has done or not done. A parent is responsible for what he has done or not done in disciplining the child.

When the child approaches the junior high and high school years, the discipline must change from corporal punishment (spanking) to restriction and limitations. Naturally, most teenagers believe that the restrictions or limitations which a parent sets are too harsh or not fair. It is important to discuss this issue with your children, but understand that you must make the final decision and stick to it.

Surveys show that children in college desired *more* discipline from parents, not less! Though not expressed by the child when he is going through it, the discipline of a parent provides a loving shelter for the child; it causes the child to develop with maturity and to experience a loving support for future decisions which a lack of discipline can never provide.

CHILDREN, RESPECT YOUR PARENTS

Gary seemed like a normal teenager at the local high school. He had a few friends, did fairly well in school, played sports, and attended church regularly. His problem? He hated his parents, and let those around him know about it!

Gary's youth pastor did something about it. He confronted Gary with his attitude problem, and heard a long story about how stupid his parents were, how legalistic and restrictive they were, and how they treated him like a kid. The rebellion in Gary's heart was affecting his younger brother and was troubling his parents greatly. The music and movies in Gary's life contributed to his attitude problem, and a few incidents in which he felt his parents made the wrong decision convinced him that they were unrealistic, old-fashioned in their ideas and values, and unable to deal with the "*real* problems" in the *real* world.

Fortunately for Gary, he had a youth pastor who cared enough to confront him. Because of what his youth pastor told him (on several occasions over a period of a year), Gary's attitude changed completely, and his parents have recently become extremely intelligent in Gary's eyes! Gary, like thousands of kids today, needed to learn about a child's responsibility to his parents.

The third essential of a family with moral and traditional values is that the children respect their parents. Not only are children showing disrespect these days, but institutions that are supposedly designed to help the family are also showing disrespect for the role and responsibility of parents.

In Romans 1:30, one of the sins that deserve the judgment of God is described as disobedience to parents. Speaking of the perilous times that will come in the last days of planet Earth, the apostle Paul lists one of the problems of society as being "disobedient to parents."

The Ten Commandments are clear (Exodus 20:12):

> Honor your father and your mother, that
> your days may be long upon the land which the
> Lord your God is giving you.

Ephesians 6:1-3 quotes the commandment of God in its instruction to children:

> Children, obey your parents in the Lord,
> for this is right. "Honor your father and mother,"
> which is the first commandment with promise:
> "that it may be well with you and you may live
> long on the earth."

Traditional and moral values that are applied to the family always produce respect for parents. If children respect their parents, the following things will be true.

1. *They will always speak well of their parents to others.* Proverbs 20:20 says, "Whoever curses his father or his mother, his lamp will be put out in deep darkness." The future influence of a child's life is directly related to the attitudes expressed toward his parents.

Proverbs 30:11 says, "There is a generation that curses its father, and does not bless its mother."

2. *They will never put down their parents or treat lightly what they say.* It is almost a game that young people play to see how they can prove their acceptability to others by speaking critically of their parents. Proverbs 15:20 says that it is "a foolish man" who "despises his mother." Solomon says to his son in Proverbs 1:8,9:

My son, hear the instruction of your father,
and do not forsake the law of your mother; for
they will be graceful ornaments on your head,
and chains about your neck.

"A wise son makes a glad father" (Proverbs 10:1). It is definitely wise on the part of children to honor and respect their parents. If they do not, serious consequences will result in later life.

3. *They will never do anything to harm their parents or drive them away.* Terrible things are happening to parents today—children killing their parents because of satanic influences, and children striking back and doing physical harm. The stories vary from city to city, but as most police departments know, the incidence of children attacking parents is increasing daily.

Proverbs 19:26 states, "He who mistreats his father and chases away his mother is a son who causes shame and brings reproach." Proverbs 28:24 adds, "Whoever robs his father or his mother and says, 'It is no transgression,' the same is companion to a destroyer."

The problems of alcohol and drug addiction have produced a generation of young people who regularly steal from their parents in order to support their habit.

4. *They will do what is right.* Ephesians 6:1 tells children to obey their parents, "for this is right." A child who respects his or her parents does so because it is the right thing to do. Obedience to parents is not an option or a creative alternative; it

is commanded by God, and disobedience brings serious consequences and judgment from God Himself. Deuteronomy 21:18-21
provides an important insight into the danger of a child's rebellion:

> If a man has a stubborn and rebellious son
> who will not obey the voice of his father or the
> voice of his mother, and who, when they have
> chastened him, will not heed them, then his
> father and his mother shall take hold of him
> and bring him out to the elders of his city, to
> the gate of his city. And they shall say to the
> elders of his city, "This son of ours is stubborn
> and rebellious; he will not obey our voice; he
> is a glutton and a drunkard." Then all the men
> of his city shall stone him to death with stones;
> so you shall put away the evil person from
> among you, and all Israel shall hear and fear.

If you want to know what God thinks of rebellious children, here is a clear example—a principle from His law! 1 Samuel 15:23 says, "Rebellion is as the sin of witchcraft, and stub-
bornness is as iniquity and idolatry."

5. *They will desire to please God.* Colossians 3:20 says,
"Children, obey your parents in all things, for this is well
pleasing to the Lord." Children who respect their parents are
doing what pleases God Himself.

A beautiful summary of a family where children respect
their parents continually and are honored for it is found in
Proverbs 23:24,25:

> The father of the righteous will greatly
> rejoice, and he who begets a wise child will
> delight in him. Let your father and your mother
> be glad, and let her who bore you rejoice.

PARENTS, TRAIN YOUR CHILDREN

The fourth ingredient of a family committed to biblical
morality is that the parents train their children faithfully.

Training our children is not easy, and so some of us have left that role to the school and the church. But whether we like it or not, neither of those institutions can substitute for the parents.

Ephesians 6:4 tells parents to "bring them up" and Proverbs 22:6 says to "train up a child." Training is vital. We are teaching our children *something*, either by what we say and do or by what we do *not* say and do. Children sometimes learn what is wrong or what not to do by the failures and mistakes of their parents, but more often they repeat what their parents did in a given situation even when they are bound and determined to do otherwise!

According to the Bible, training a child involves at least three things:

1) Communication of the will of God.

2) Commitment to the way of God.

3) Confidence in the Word of God.

1. *Communication.* What God desires us to be, say, and do must be communicated by parents to children. Our communication is both verbal and nonverbal. Deuteronomy 6:6-9 provides great advice to parents:

> These words which I command you today
> shall be in your heart; you shall teach them
> diligently to your children, and shall talk of
> them when you sit in your house, when you walk
> by the way, when you lie down, and when you
> rise up. You shall bind them as a sign on your
> hand, and they shall be as frontlets between
> your eyes. You shall write them on the doorposts
> of your house and on your gates.

This kind of teaching and training is a lifestyle, not a class of instruction. Parents who do not *live* this kind of lifestyle have difficulty *telling* it. If God's Word and will are not in the heart of the parent first, then the teaching process breaks down. We wind up saying, "Do what I say, not what I do," and our children detect this hypocrisy immediately.

In one sense the teaching of our children is a full-time job. The Bible says to do it "diligently," and describes all the various places and situations in which a parent might teach a child. We never stop learning, and in another sense we as parents never stop teaching.

2. *Commitment.* Proverbs 22:6 is one of the most important verses that a parent can understand in terms of training his children:

> Train up a child in the way he should go,
> and when he is old he will not depart from it.

In trying to determine the meaning of "the way he should go" Bible scholars and commentators have suggested three possibilities:

1) Whatever way the parent wants him to go.

2) The way the child is designed to go.

3) The way God wants him to go.

The parent went to ABC college, so the child is expected to go to the same school. The parent played the violin, so the child learns to play as well. What happens all too often is that the parent relives his or her life in the child. The expectations of the parent are imposed upon the child, and the child is expected to do whatever the parent has suggested. And many children do just that, especially if it seems financially rewarding to do so.

The second view suggests that each child is uniquely created by God (which is true) and has special abilities and talents (also true) that need to be developed and encouraged. This view argues that parental guidance is necessary alongside of the child's innate desires and gifts in order to insure a proper use and development of the child's talents and abilities.

The third view relies more on the context of the Book of Proverbs and sees the word "way" as crucial to the argument. Consider the following examples from Proverbs:

> 14:12—"There is a way which seems right to a man, but its end is the way of death."

14:14—"The backslider in heart will be filled with his own ways, but a good man will be satisfied from above."

15:9 —"The way of the wicked is an abomination to the Lord, but He loves him who follows righteousness."

15:19—"The way of the slothful man is like a hedge of thorns, but the way of the upright is a highway."

16:2 —"All the ways of a man are pure in his own eyes, but the Lord weighs the spirits."

16:7 —"When a man's ways please the Lord, He makes even his enemies to be at peace with him."

16:9 —"A man's heart plans his way, but the Lord directs his steps."

19:3 —"The foolishness of a man twists his way, and his heart frets against the Lord."

19:16—"He who keeps the commandment keeps his soul, but he who is careless of his ways will die."

20:24—"A man's steps are of the Lord; how then can a man understand his own way?"

21:2 —"Every way of a man is right in his own eyes, but the Lord weighs the hearts."

21:16—"A man who wanders from the way of understanding will rest in the congregation of the dead."

22:5 —"Thorns and snares are in the way of the perverse; he who guards his soul will be far from them."

22:6 —"Train up a child in the way he should go, and when he is old he will not depart from it."

From a negative standpoint we have the way which seems right, the way of the backslider, the way of the wicked, the way of the slothful, the way of the foolish and careless, and the way of the perverse.

From a positive standpoint we have the way of the upright and of righteousness, the way that pleases the Lord, the way which the Lord directs, the way of understanding, and the way in which a child should go.

It seems apparent from the context of Proverbs that the way in which a child should go is the way of the Lord, a life committed to righteousness and the wisdom of God.

3. *Confidence.* Proverbs 22:6 makes this amazing promise: "And when he is old he will not depart from it." Can parents rely upon this guarantee, and what exactly is it saying?

The word "old" refers to one who has become aged. The category demands at least the title "senior citizen." When a child who has been trained in the way of the Lord becomes a senior citizen, then "he will not depart from it." What does the "it" mean?

1. The word "it" refers to the way of the Lord.

2. The word "it" refers to being old.

The second view requires that the last phrase of Proverbs 22:6 would read, "He will not depart *because* of it"—that is, because of being old. Old age will not cause him to depart from the way of the Lord in which he has been trained.

What guarantee is this?

Some say it is no guarantee at all. Some argue that the most you can do is to hope that your children turn out right and try to do the best you can as a parent!

Others opt for a limited guarantee. They say that a child may backslide for a while, but in the end (when he is old) he will come back to his original values and training.

Some take the verse quite literally and say that this is an absolute guarantee. This verse teaches that proper training of a child in the way of the Lord guarantees that the child will not depart from the Lord's way even when he becomes a senior citizen!

The last view is the best. It takes what the Bible says and trusts it implicitly.

When your children rebel against your authority, it is easy to lose perspective and confidence in what the Bible is saying. When Bob and Andrea saw their 18-year-old son rebel, it broke their hearts. His problems seemed to begin when he started drinking (which was encouraged by his friends, who pressured him greatly). He moved from alcohol to drugs, and before his parents realized what was wrong, he became addicted to cocaine. His habit led him to steal in order to buy more drugs.

Bob felt devastated; he had always tried to raise his son according to what the Bible said. Where had he gone wrong? Bob was deeply disturbed over the teaching of Proverbs 22:6. "What kind of guarantee is that?" he asked me. We prayed for God to show Bob and Andrea that this was a time to trust God more than ever and to pray diligently and daily for his son.

About three months later I saw them all in church, sitting together with smiles on their faces. Bob's son had a friend who turned out to be a strong Christian, and through this friend's help and encouragement Bob's son made a commitment to Jesus Christ and was now getting help for his drug problem.

It was said of John the Baptist by a special angelic proclamation to his parents (Luke 1:15-17):

> He will be great in the sight of the Lord,
> and shall drink neither wine nor strong drink.
> He will also be filled with the Holy Spirit, even
> from his mother's womb. And he will turn many
> of the children of Israel to the Lord their God.
> He will also go before Him in the spirit and
> power of Elijah, to turn the hearts of the fathers
> to the children, and the disobedient to the
> wisdom of the just, to make ready a people
> prepared for the Lord.

One of the greatest needs we have in the present moral crisis in America is to turn the hearts of the parents back to the children. May God help us!

WHAT SHOULD BE OUR RESPONSE?

Although the survival of the American family as we have

known it appears to be in serious jeopardy, a moral change could take place in our country and culture if the following would become true.

1) Children would be valued as greatly as adults.

2) No child would be considered insignificant or unworthy of life, liberty, and happiness, regardless of age, ability, appearance, or physical or mental disability.

3) Families would consist of father, mother, and children.

4) Divorces would no longer be tolerated as solutions to family stress and disagreement. So-called irreconcilable differences would not be considered grounds for divorce.

5) Children would be considered as blessings rather than burdens and problems.

6) Children would be loved deeply by their parents, with constant expressions of affection and commendation.

7) Children would be disciplined promptly by their parents.

8) Parents would restore spanking on the bottom as a proper and sufficient method of discipline for preteen children.

9) Children would respect and honor their parents and never be allowed to attack or disobey their parents.

10) Parents would teach and train their children in the way of the Lord, communicating constantly what the Bible says and providing the much-needed example of righteous and moral conduct before their children at all times.

11) Schools, churches, and government agencies would support and encourage the role and responsibility of parents in the training, teaching, and disciplining of children, and never substitute themselves for the parents.

12) Children would no longer be encouraged to make decisions and take action on far-reaching matters without parental consent and approval.

13) Sex education would never take place without a strong commitment on the part of the teacher to moral and spiritual values as found in the Bible.

14) Voluntary prayer along with respect and reading of the Bible would be restored to our public school classrooms.

15) Television programming that targets our children would become more responsible and would eliminate its present emphasis on sex, violence, profanity, drugs, and alcohol. Moral and traditional values would be communicated in a positive and approving manner.

It would not be impossible to see such a change occur in our country. We have the means and the freedom to do so, and hopefully we also sense the *responsibility* to do so, not only for our immediate moral crisis but for future generations as well. May God help us to actually do it!

5

A Pornographic Nightmare

The word "pornography" comes from the Greek words for "prostitute" and "writing." Pornography refers to writings about prostitution and all kinds of sexual activity outside the bonds of matrimony.

There are two kinds of pornography:

1. Soft core—pictures sexual acts that are not illegal.

2. Hard core—pictures illegal acts that have no redeeming social value.

Soft-core pornography is difficult to confront. The sexual acts that may exist between a male and a female who are married (as an example) may be legal, but this does not mean that it is appropriate to show such acts to other people. Viewing intimate sexual activity without the knowledge and experience of marriage and without a strong understanding of morality can be both sexually provocative and dangerous to one's emotional health.

Hard-core pornography has no restriction or limitation. Human depravity can be portrayed in any setting, and the world of pornography will use such depravity and abuse the lives of millions who view it. Torture, horrifying killings, and all kinds of perverted sexual activity are promoted and sold in the world of "hard core." Anything goes, and whatever continues to sell will continue to be produced.

EXPLOITING CHILDREN

One of the greatest tragedies of all is the sexual exploitation of children. Child pornography is a terrible problem in our society, and apparently it is still growing. Thousands of children are abducted each year and never heard from again—many of them used and abused within the secret studios of the hard-core pornographers.

My wife wrote a letter to KLOS Radio in Los Angeles to express her complaint about advertisements on that station for *Penthouse* magazine. The Vice-President and General Manager returned this letter:

> I have just been informed of your complaint regarding commercial matter concerning the "Penthouse" advertisement.
>
> I am a parent of two daughters, ages 5 and 9, and am sympathetic when subjecting our audience to anything that might be construed as distasteful. It is for this reason that KLOS employs a Continuity or Operations Director. It is his responsibility to screen all commercial matter for offensive material before it is aired. This particular advertisement was no exception; it passed through our Continuity Department before being aired. Unfortunately, it is difficult to satisfy everyone.
>
> If you have any other questions regarding our commercial matter, please feel free to call me at your earliest convenience.

In spite of the gracious answer, the letter reveals much of what is wrong in our society. No matter what methodology was used to determine the validity of promoting *Penthouse* magazine, the statement which reveals a great deal about the moral commitment of our culture is "Unfortunately, it is difficult to satisfy everyone." That remark implies that some people were being satisfied by the promotion of *Penthouse* magazine.

WHAT IS OBSCENITY?

In 1957 the United States Supreme Court held that "obscenity is not within the area of constitutionally protected freedom of speech and press." They said that obscene material, in the legal sense, is that which is deliberately designed to arouse a desire for illicit sexual activity, and which by this definition threatens harm to society. The Court has continually emphasized the importance of "contemporary community standards" in determining what is obscene or pornographic.

Is pornography deliberately designed to arouse a desire for illicit sexual activity? Of course it is, and every informed person knows it. Yet since 1957 our definitions of "illicit sexual activity" have been radically changed. What was once considered morally wrong is now morally acceptable and even promoted in our society. Where will it all end? Are we ever going to stop the onslaught of pornographic interests that continue to corrupt the minds and destroy the lives of millions of Americans as well as millions of people in other countries of the world?

Clever pornographic interests and promoters have continued to downplay the fight against pornography by labeling those who want to do something to stop it as "right-wing fundamentalists" or "religious fanatics," even though survey after survey shows that the majority of Americans believe that pornography has gone too far.

Part of the strategy opposing the fight against pornography is to accuse the critics of being against nudity. Yet the actual battle is not against the beauty of the physical body; it is *what pornography does to human nudity* that concerns most Americans. We are not talking about mere pictures or displays of ordinary human nudity when dealing with the subject of pornography; we are talking about all kinds of perverted sexual activity.

Nudity between a husband and a wife is never condemned in the Bible (Genesis 2:25), nor is their sexual enjoyment of each other ever discouraged (Hebrews 13:4 and the Song of Solomon).

Common sense teaches that the display of human nudity outside of marriage and family does emotional harm and contributes to sexual interest and involvement. The prevalent idea that pornography has no harmful effect upon our children and teenagers is utter nonsense!

The 1957 Court ruling held that nudity is not obscene. As a result, magazines and periodicals are free to display it.

In 1968 a special Presidential Commission was appointed by President Johnson. This Commission claimed there was no proof that pornography was harmful to morals, and recommended the repeal of all laws prohibiting it.

In 1970 the Commission gave its official results. The President of the United States was no longer Lyndon B. Johnson, but Richard Nixon (elected to office in the fall of 1968). President Nixon refused to accept the report and Congress declined to act on its recommendations.

The Commission said that pornography plays a healthy role in providing an outlet for sexual urges! With such approval from a government agency, the pornography industry grew into an 8-billion-dollar-a-year business, and has continued to push the limits of "adult" material far beyond the Commission's original intent.

In 1973 the Supreme Court, in Miller Versus California, agreed with the ruling of 1957 that obscenity is not protected by the U.S. Constitution. However, for sexually explicit material to be found illegal under the 1973 decision, it must meet the following three tests:

1) The material must appeal to prurient interests.

2) The material must depict sexual conduct in a patently offensive way.

3) The material must lack serious literary, artistic, political, or scientific value.

In the spring of 1986 a report was released from the United States Attorney General's Commission on Pornography. Eleven commission members were told to determine pornography's nature, extent, and impact on society. In examining pornographic materials that would be considered illegal, the commission wanted to know whether some forms of obscenity cause sexual violence.

Violent pornography was stated to be the use of devices of torture, rape in which a woman begs for more, and material that portrays disfigurement or murder along with sexual activity.

The Commission found that research on these materials

gives undeniable evidence that they increase the likelihood of aggressive behavior, especially toward women. They also concluded that violent obscenity contributes to the belief (called the "rape myth") that women enjoy being hurt and being coerced into sexual acts.

The Commission also condemned another category of pornography that results in degradation, subordination, or humiliation. These forms of obscenity often depict men urinating on a kneeling woman, lesbian activity observed by men, and women lying on a bed pleading for sex from many different men.

The Commission could not reach agreement on the effects of pornography that depicts sexual partners as equal and consenting, whether heterosexual or homosexual, and also sex with animals.

The Commission did agree that any pornographic material forced on children or obtained by children is harmful. They condemned child pornography in no uncertain terms and stated that it constitutes child abuse.

The Commission gave 93 specific recommendations. They advocated strengthening existing laws and urging law enforcement personnel to take action against pornography. The number of state and local law enforcement officers assigned to handle obscenity cases is extremely low and must be increased. At the time of the Commission's report, only 8 out of 6700 police officers in Los Angeles were assigned to pornography cases. In Chicago, only 2 out of 12,000 police officers were handling such cases!

The Commission recommended that possession of child pornography be a felony, and that it be a felony to abuse a child sexually in order to produce pornographic materials. They also recommended a felony charge for conspiring to produce and distribute materials dealing with child pornography and to exchange or deliver a child for these purposes.

ACLU VERSUS DECENCY

Dr. James Dobson, the radio host for the most popular Christian radio broadcast in America ("Focus on the Family") and also a member of the Attorney General's Commission, wrote in a mass mailing: "The refusal by federal officials to enforce the criminal laws on the books is a disgrace and an outrage!" He went on to say, "Aggressive action against pornographers will not occur unless our citizens demand the response of government."

The president of the National Coalition Against Pornography, Jerry Kirk, made this statement: "If Americans know what obscenity is, and know that the key to law enforcement is contemporary community standards, and know that those standards are established by citizens, they will rise up en masse."

Former United States Attorney General Edwin Meese was the head of the Pornography Commission that published the report which links with undeniable evidence pornography and sex crimes. He has been attacked repeatedly by the American Civil Liberties Union, which has spent an enormous amount of its resources and energies in attempting to dismiss the findings of the Commission and especially the testimony and confession of Ted Bundy, a recently executed man guilty of dozens of sex-related murders who attributes much of his criminal motivation to his involvement with pornography.

ACLU spokesman Barry Lynn made a statement that was quoted in several newspapers: "I would no more rely on Bundy's psychological self-analysis than I would rely on his stock market advice!" Former U.S. Attorney General Meese replied, "That response may be clever, but it is utterly disingenuous. No one was better able to tell us what motivated Ted Bundy to commit sexually-related murders than Bundy himself!"

Meese has gone on record many times concerning the ACLU's support of the rights of pornographers. He said, "For the ACLU, it's simply a message they don't want to hear. It interferes uncomfortably with their effort to claim Constitutional protection for every sick and perverse film, magazine, or performance that some purveyor of obscenity wants to foist on society in what has become a lucrative market."

SEX IN ADVERTISING

During the past few years (because of the widescale toleration of pornography and the failure to stop its inroads into mainstream American culture) the marketing and advertising firms have been taking bolder steps in the use of sex and nudity to promote their products. Calvin Klein's Obsession perfume is an example. In one ad, two men and a woman are entangled together on a couch in the nude. The photograph is steamy and the implications are rather obvious. In another ad, a woman is embraced by a man who is kissing her just below her breast (which is exposed in the photograph). It appeared in *House and Garden, Vanity Fair*, and *Essence* magazines, among others.

A girl who is casually dressed is slung over a young man's shoulder and struggling as he carries her toward a garage. The next scene reveals that the jeans are off, a breast is partially exposed, and she is tousled and dazed. The product being advertised? Guess jeans. Guess jeans are bought primarily by teenagers, and the company by its ads is saying it's okay for a man to carry you away into a garage and rape you in the backseat of a car. The ads have glamorized what is violent and exploitive to women.

ADULT VIDEO

A few years ago a *Los Angeles Times* article by Jay Arnold of Associated Press spoke of the home-video explosion, which brings the erotic movie out of the adult theater and into the American home. The article said:

> Men and women who wouldn't be caught dead going to a porno show plunk down as much as $100 at neighborhood video stores to take home copies of such improbably titled video-cassettes as "Blazing Zippers," "Lust at First Bite," or "Aerobisex Girls."

The article goes on to say:

> Other than for child pornography, U.S. law enforcement has adopted a hands-off attitude toward X-rated film materials since the Supreme Court's 1973 obscenity ruling that community standards must apply in deciding what is pornographic. The total U.S. prerecorded video

sales hit $1 billion in 1983, of which 14 percent,
or about $150 million, came from adult videos.

Today the situation is far worse. The video porn business
has swelled to over half a billion dollars a year! Virtually every
type of video store, from the neighborhood mom-and-pop store
to the national chains, carry X-rated videocassettes. It is big
business because it brings in much revenue at low production
costs. In other words, the profit margin is huge.

In May of 1989 *Glamour* magazine reported on the new
dimension which pornography is now pursuing: hard-core software. The article describes a new software program called
MacPlaymate. "It makes all the other porn programs look like
cartoons," says the article. It adds, "People who use it go beyond
voyeurism; they become active participants in the violation of a
woman's body."

A former head of Los Angeles County's District Attorney's organized crime division has said, "Basically, unless
you're using child pornography, it's very hard to show under
current law that adult videos are obscene."

Adult bookstores make pornography available to any
adult over 17 years of age. These bookstores (numbering over
20,000 in America) offer every variety of soft-core and hard-
core pornographic material, and often even provide rooms
where sexual acts can take place while pornography is being
viewed or heard.

One man who became thoroughly destroyed by pornography wrote to his pastor (*Moody Monthly*, April 1989):

> I am an emotional invalid. My addiction
> to pornography paralyzes my spiritual life,
> perverts my view of the world, distorts my social
> life, and destroys any possibility of God using
> me, and I just can't stop. Lust eats me up, yet
> it doesn't satisfy. Pornography promises me
> everything; it produces nothing.

Is there any way to stop the pornographic nightmare?
Does anyone really care? Is it a threat to freedom of speech
to restrict the distribution and sale of pornography in our

country? Is there nothing we can do to protect our children, as well as ourselves? Must we allow the video industry with all its money and influence to control the moral and traditional values of our children and families? Are they correct in saying that we don't have to buy their videos, so if we continue to do so, the problem is with the consumer, not the producer? Is that really true? Don't the producers have any responsibility at all? Are they not appealing to our sexual desires and carnal appetites with full knowledge of how human sexuality is enticed and attracted? Shouldn't they be accountable?

These are serious questions that deal with the heart of our moral catastrophe. Legislation has not helped, and law enforcement appears unable to do anything about the continuing cancer of pornography.

Are businesses at least partly responsible when they (because of financial profit) make pornography available to the consumer, or is the consumer totally responsible for viewing what is available or purchasing what is promoted?

Circle K convenience stores are still the largest retailer of pornographic magazines in America. Should Americans boycott these stores until they remove their pornographic literature?

Are Americans who are concerned about moral values correct in their nationwide boycott of Holiday Inns, which make in-room porn movies available to their guests?

DIAL-A-PORN

One of the most alarming aspects of the pornographic nightmare that we face in this country is the ability of our citizens to dial a number on their telephone and be exposed to all kinds of sexual suggestions and activity. Large numbers of children across our country can listen to vivid dramatizations of sodomy, rape, incest, bestiality, bondage, and sex acts between children and between adults and children.

Dr. Victor Cline, professor of psychology at the University of Utah, has done extensive studies on pornography and its victims. He argues that children who have been exposed to pornography cannot handle the strong sexual feelings that it brings forth.

Cases abound where children have become involved in sexual crime immediately after repeated calls to Dial-A-Porn.

Two boys aged 13 and 15, as well as an 11-year-old girl, called Dial-A-Porn 57 times within a few hours! As a result, the boys raped the girl and another girl in the neighborhood. These facts and many others like them, some even more hideous and horrifying, are well-known to law enforcement officials.

Several years ago I encountered the problem of adult video and its potential dangers to our children. I went to the local athletic club where I was a member, only to discover a group of men and young boys (preteens) watching an adult X-rated videocassette on the TV screen in the locker room of that club. It was not soft-core but hard-core pornography on the screen, and I was shocked by the fact that these grown men had no concern for the young boys who were watching the pornography with them. I turned off the video and spoke strong words of rebuke to the adults in that room, telling them that they ought to be ashamed of themselves.

Upon further discussion with these men, I found out that permission had been given by the club management. I continued my investigation and discovered that this family club did not see anything wrong with such videos but agreed that the children should not be allowed to view them. We decided on the basis of their compromising position to remove ourselves from the membership of that club and to explain why in a letter.

THE SEXUAL REVOLUTION

The last 20 years of American history have been described as a sexual revolution—a radical change from past standards of morality that have guided this nation. But this revolution is not producing more freedom, contrary to what its advocates say, but is rather plunging our country into deeper depravity and greater bondage.

The evidence of sexual change in terms of attitudes, values, and accepted practices is everywhere present in our culture. Our movies and television programs are contributors to the moral decline and the change in sexual values and habits. Things that were once taboo are now socially acceptable and even desirable by many Americans. We speak of homosexuals as "coming out of the closet," a phrase that reveals the current toleration of sexual activities that were once considered to be morally unacceptable and illegal in public and private life.

Sexual affairs are treated lightly unless they are newsworthy by being politically damaging to our nation's leaders, enticing on the pages of the nation's gossip columns, or material for sexual jokes by the nation's comedians. Statistics by various studies on sex (Kinsey, Hite, etc.) reveal that a significant portion of the American population has been involved in a sexual affair at one time or another.

To some people, sexual affairs are expected and exciting, regardless of whose marriage or family is destroyed in the process. Little evidence of true love is seen in the practice of people using one another for no goal or objective other than immediate sexual gratification.

Singles discover that sex is an expected part of dating in today's culture. Refusal to go to bed with someone after a nice dinner and casual conversation can mean the inability to have friends of the opposite sex. Your date life can come to a crashing halt if you decide that sex is not part of the evening's agenda. The game seems to revolve around who can seduce the best and quickest. Little concern is shown for moral and traditional values.

A friend of mine in Seattle, Washington, sent a flyer to me which his company distributed. It advertises an "Exotic Bar Tour" in which people can visit totally nude exotic dancers and, according to the flyer, experience "up close and personal" contact with these nude dancers.

Our metropolitan newspapers are filled with advertisements that are sexually explicit and enticing. Some of the small ads are not only blunt and bold, but they are pornographic in implication and suggestiveness.

One of the most serious and disturbing trends of the sexual revolution is the tolerance of sexual films and instruction in our nation's schools that is not based on moral and traditional values. In 1987 the San Ramon Valley School District in Northern California issued a policy that would not allow R- and X-rated videos and films to be shown to the students, so four teachers, supported by the teachers' union, filed a lawsuit against the administration and school board in Contra Costa County Superior Court in December of 1988, accusing the governing board of this school district of censorship and violation of First Amendment rights guaranteeing freedom of speech.

The teachers argue that the governing board is promoting "perceived moral values and teachings of religious organizations, which thereby permit, indirectly, the teaching of a sectarian or denominational doctrine in the high schools." This argument is so absurd that further comment is totally unnecessary.

Jean Patton, a free-lance writer from Bloomington, Indiana, wrote an article on the nature of censorship in the classroom for *The Indianapolis Star* newspaper. She states in the article that parents have a right to expect that the grammar, vocabulary, standards of propriety, and respect for religion are at least equal to those they maintain in their homes. She made this statement about the National Council of Teachers of English:

> The National Council of Teachers of English has long been sabotaging literature instruction in the public schools and degrading the prestige of all teachers (not only English) by furiously maintaining a presumed "First Amendment" right to use any printed material in the classroom, no matter how obscene, blasphemous, disgusting or illiterate, choosing to label us their critics as "censors."

THE REVOLUTION IS EVERYWHERE

Today many of our nation's classrooms, especially in the area of sex education, are tolerating and promoting sexual lifestyles outside of marriage and are condemning any student, parent, church, or organization that seeks to impose the moral and traditional standard of sex within marriage as the only acceptable sexual expression. Premarital sex is accepted and approved, and homosexual behavior is promoted as a valid alternative to the sanctity of marriage between male and female.

One of the most powerful commentaries on the tragedy of the sexual revolution in America is the promotion of condoms. The viewpoint is expressed frequently in our society that "safe sex" is made possible by using a condom. But in the context of moral and traditional values which have governed this nation in its public and private life throughout its history, the only safe sex is within the bonds of holy matrimony!

Telling our teenagers how to use condoms in order to avoid sexual disease and possible pregnancy is not only unwise and totally inappropriate for public school education, but it is opening the door to further sexual involvement and activity on the part of our youth.

The sexual revolution is everywhere, and is most often portrayed and promoted by the world of contemporary music. A few hours of watching music videos on cable television will convince any objective viewer that the sexual revolution is still marketing its diabolical enticements to our nation's young people, who are the primary viewers of these programs. The words and lyrics of thousands of contemporary songs continue to promote sexual promiscuity and departure from moral and traditional values.

The Bible makes a remarkable statement in Galatians 6:7:

Do not be deceived: God is not mocked; for whatever a man sows, that he will also reap.

Hosea 8:7 says:

They sow the wind and reap the whirlwind.

Our nation is reaping the tragic results of sowing seeds of sexual immorality. We are experiencing the whirlwind of sexual disease and disaster because we have sown the enticing arguments of sexual permissiveness and freedom to explore every possible means for sexual gratification.

In 1978 a National Opinion Research Center study found that 57 percent of Americans are convinced that pornography leads to a breakdown of morals and encourages the crime of rape. Yet more than ten years later, in spite of continuing evidence that the American public is still opposed to pornography, the porn dealers have become more successful than ever, filling their pockets with billions of dollars resulting from the sale of pornographic literature, films, and videos.

How Do We Stop It?

Why is it so difficult to stop pornography? That is a question which troubles many of us. The answers are varied. Consider the following possibilities.

1. *Law enforcement is unable to arrest, convict, and stop the production and distribution of pornography.* Organized crime connections and shrewd businessmen and lawyers who represent the pornographic producers and distributors have cleverly avoided police investigation and prosecution.

2. *The Supreme Court's definition of obscenity is too vague for local government to apply effectively.* The point they made about whether a work has "serious literary, artistic, political, or scientific value" results in great disagreement and debate.

3. *The majority of Americans do not understand the nature and pervasiveness of pornography.* Many Americans still think that pornography refers to pictures of nude women in *Playboy, Penthouse,* or similar magazines. While many people committed to moral and traditional values are properly concerned over the promotion of nudity within these magazines, that is not a correct picture of the problem of pornography in this country. It is far worse than that, and much more violent and degrading.

4. *Many Americans are unwilling to get involved.* Many of us simply do not want to take a stand and thereby be criticized for lack of tolerance, bigotry, and censorship. We have been led to believe that every American has a right to do anything whatsoever that he wants to. But that is not freedom; that is moral anarchy! True freedom must be defined by moral values and law. An individual's rights must always be understood in the light of his accountability to God and his responsibility to other people.

5. *There is a great desire to be tolerant.* Americans have always been a tolerant people. Yet tolerance must be limited or else we will destroy ourselves. Murder and theft, if tolerated, would destroy the structure of human society. Murder robs us of life, and stealing robs us of things, but pornography robs us of

character. Murder destroys the sanctity of life, and stealing destroys property rights, but pornography destroys human values.

The First Amendment of our Constitution guarantees the freedom of speech and of the press. Laws against pornography do not inhibit the freedom to legitimately express ideas; instead, what they limit is *profiteering that is aimed at destroying society*. The pornographer does not seek to communicate his ideas and conviction in order to share them with others or convince others of the truth; he is without conscience and moral concern, selling for profit material that destroys character and treats people as things to be manipulated or exploited.

In a tragic story of pornographic interest, mild-mannered engineer Richard Daniel Starrett of Martinez, Georgia (a suburb of Augusta), assualted teenage girls and young women while his wife was away. His attacks were influenced by pornographic literature that fueled his fantasies.

Police said that Starrett had admitted to kidnapping and assaulting three girls (killing one of them) and assaulting four others in Georgia and South Carolina. He was also considered a prime suspect in unsolved abductions and sexual assaults in Alabama, North Carolina, California, Texas, and Tennessee.

When authorities searched his rented warehouse a mile from his home, they found 935 pornographic books and magazines depicting sexual bondage, horror scenes, and nudity! They also found criminology textbooks and books about serial killer Ted Bundy. Police also found 100 videotapes, some of which were films of Starrett's sexual assaults. According to Lexington County Sheriff James Metts, Starrett said that pornography had stimulated his criminal behavior.

In his book entitled *Christians in a Sex-Crazed Culture* (published by SP Publications), Illinois pastor Bill Hybels records the testimony of a man committed to pornography who attended this pastor's church:

> It all started when I was six years old and I would sneak peeks at our neighbor's *Playboy* magazines. I became so enamored with the female anatomy that I used to cut out advertisements from traditional magazines and carry them with me. Adults thought it was cute and funny that I had the desire to look at pictures

of nude women. It was just further evidence that I was all boy.

This seemingly innocent practice continued for several years. But everything changed dramatically when I was 12 and I discovered sexual self-stimulation. It was like going from cigarettes to heroin. Even though I had some clumsy sexual experiences early on, they were, frankly, disappointing compared to my sexual fantasy life.

In my midteens I was no longer just looking at pictures. I began to read *Playboy Advisor* and *Penthouse Letters*. They helped me to develop what I call my fornication philosophy.

After meeting a girl at age 16 who would later become his wife, he continued his letter.

Even though we enjoyed lovemaking with daily frequency at 16, my appetite only grew more and more insatiable. After a couple of years of marriage, I became obsessed with the need to act out the experiences that were so common in my reading. When those desires went unfulfilled, I turned to X-rated movies and films to supplement my magazine habit. My mind was so filled with these images that even when I was making love to my wife, my thoughts were continually flooded with other images.

After a while I found myself occupying private booths in the X-rated movie arcades, vicariously participating in sexual acts that would never be fulfilled at home. I began putting enormous pressure on my wife to grow with me sexually or I would leave her. I also had several hundred magazine mistresses along with regular trips to the video arcades just to keep my interest up. But nothing satisfied me sexually. Nothing.

Fortunately for this man, he received help. After five years of struggle, defeat, victory, and struggle again, he finally had enough strength to destroy all his pornographic literature and videos and to stop visiting X-rated movies and arcades, and to cease his habit of self-stimulation. Today his marriage is a blessing and he has fully recovered.

It was an addiction to pornography that played a key role in the murder of as many as 24 young women and children by mass murderer Ted Bundy. Just prior to his execution, he revealed his involvement with pornography in an interview with Dr. James Dobson of "Focus on the Family" Radio Broadcast. At the age of 13 Bundy's pornographic habit began with the reading of *Playboy* magazine. As he grew older, more explicit pornography was necessary. Bundy claimed that his obsession with pornography drove him to mutilate and murder young women for sexual gratification.

Dr. Jennings Bryant, head of the radio-television school of communication at the University of Houston, did a study that reveals that even so-called "soft-core" pornography has greater effects than most people realize. He said, "We're talking about more than sexually violent material. We're finding proof that this less violent stuff is doing harm, and something has to be done about it."

An interesting part of Dr. Bryant's study is the fact that men and women who are exposed to nonviolent pornography have altered views about the roles of family, marriage, and morals in society.

Dr. Reo M. Christenson, Professor of Political Science at Miami University in Oxford, Ohio (and the author of six books), makes the following statement:

> The pornographers of America should take warning! The winds of change are blowing. Your days of wine and roses are fading. The public has seen what you do with the freedom you have been granted, and they don't like what they see. Nor do America's feminists. Nor do other women who care about their families, their community and their country. Nor do many of America's leading intellectuals.
>
> The Founding Fathers never intended for the First Amendment to be interpreted as the

courts interpret it today. They were sensible
men, resolved to protect the right of heretics and
dissenters to expound their views on social,
economic, political and religious matters without
fear of government reprisals. But they would
have laughed to scorn any notion that things
resembling *Hustler* magazine, vulgar T-shirts,
naked dancers and X-rated movies could hide
behind the First Amendment. Nothing could
have been further from their intentions, or from
the spirit which motivated the Amendment.

The pornographers have also used the
American Civil Liberties Union as their front
line of defense. The strategy has been brilliant,
successful, and disastrous to those who care
about the quality of life in their communities.

Pornography leaves the impression that sex has no relationship to privacy, that it is unrelated to love, commitment, or
marriage, that perverted forms of sexual activity are the most
gratifying, that sex with animals is desirable, and that there
are no adverse consequences—no venereal disease, divorces, or
moral decay.

More than 50 years ago Professor J.D. Unwin of Cam-
bridge did a study on the sexual practices of more than 80
primitive and more advanced societies. He concluded that sexually permissive behavior led to less cultural energy, less
creativity, less individualism, less mental development, and
less cultural progress in general. Primitive societies with the
greatest sexual freedom made the least cultural advances.

Arnold Toynbee, the great historian and student of world
civilizations, stated that a culture which postpones rather than
stimulates sexual experience in the young is a culture most
prone to progress.

What Does the Bible Say About Pornography?

Pornography is a central issue in the moral catastrophe
facing our present American culture. There is no escaping its

diabolical influence and destructive influence apart from total abstinence and legal limitations.

To bring up the subject of what the Bible has to say about these issues seems to some people in our society to be unnecessary at best and discriminatory at worst. To suggest that we should pay attention to the morality standards of the Bible causes many in our country to organize a campaign to get rid of religious bigotry! Why be so afraid of what the Bible teaches? It has successfully guided the moral values of our country for all these years.

Consider carefully the following matters:

1. *Nudity between a husband and a wife is never condemned in the Bible.* Contrary to what the pornographic industry tries to imply about the teachings of those who follow the Bible, we are not against nudity within a marriage. Genesis 2:25 says that "they were both naked, the man and his wife, and were not ashamed."

In the Bible's warnings about the wrong use of sexual desire (outside of marriage), it speaks of sexual intercourse as though it were "uncovering the nakedness" of a person (cf. Leviticus 18). Leviticus 20:11, in dealing with incest, says, "The man who lies with his father's wife has uncovered his father's nakedness; both of them shall surely be put to death." The words "uncover the nakedness" are not simply references to nudity, but are primarily statements dealing with sexual intercourse outside of marriage.

Sexual immorality (sex outside of marriage) is treated like "uncovering" a person's "nakedness." The word "nakedness" refers to the sexual act, and such exposure is reserved in the Bible for a husband and a wife.

2. *Sexual enjoyment and pleasure between a husband and a wife are never condemned in the Bible.* Again, the pornographic industry tries to imply that religious people who are committed to the moral standards of the Bible are against sexual enjoyment and pleasure. They constantly claim that such people see sex only as a duty or obligation, strictly for the bearing of children. But the Bible actually encourages legitimate sexual enjoyment and pleasure. (For further study on what the Bible teaches about sexual pleasure, see the author's book entitled *Romantic Lovers*, published by Harvest House Publishers.)

One entire book in the Bible, the Song of Solomon, is all about marital lovemaking. It is the Bible's manual on sexual love, sexual pleasure, and sexual satisfaction between a husband and a wife. It is the most beautiful and romantic literature one could ever read. It is sensual, erotic, and graphic in its details, and puts the beauty of love and romance back into the sexual activity between a husband and a wife.

3. *The Bible condemns sexual intercourse outside of marriage.* No point of biblical morality so infuriates the pornography peddlers any more than this one. They mock, laugh, and ridicule the standards of the Bible, making people believe that the Bible is against sexual enjoyment and pleasure. Yet the Bible simply tells the truth: Sex is to be enjoyed within the bonds of holy marriage.

Hebrews 13:4 says:

> Marriage is honorable among all, and the
> bed undefiled; but fornicators and adulterers
> God will judge.

Premarital sex was condemned in the Old Testament law and deserved the death penalty when it occurred with a person who was engaged to another person (Deuteronomy 22:23,24). A rape victim, however, was not condemned—only the one who did the raping (Deuteronomy 22:25-27). Premarital sex between people who were not married was also condemned, although it did not demand the death penalty. Instead, it demanded marriage without the possibility of divorce (Deuteronomy 22:28,29).

The law condemned adultery and demanded the death penalty for it (Leviticus 20:10), and the same went for homosexuality, incest, and bestiality (Leviticus 20:10-16).

4. *The Bible condemns the abuse of children in severe terms.* Child pornography is one of the most tragic aspects of the pornographic nightmare in our country. It deserves the strongest laws and penalties. In Matthew 18:6-10 Jesus Christ spoke these words about children:

> Whoever causes one of these little ones who
> believe in Me to sin, it would be better for him

if a millstone were hung around his neck and
he were drowned in the depth of the sea. Woe
to the world because of offenses! For offenses
must come, but woe to that man by whom the
offense comes! And if your hand or foot causes
you to sin, cut it off and cast it from you. It is
better for you to enter into life lame or maimed,
rather than having two hands or two feet to be
cast into the everlasting fire. And if your eye
causes you to sin, pluck it out and cast it from
you. It is better for you to enter into life with
one eye, rather than having two eyes to be cast
into hell fire. Take heed that you do not despise
one of these little ones, for I say to you that in
heaven their angels always see the face of My
Father who is in heaven.

In verse 14 He added:

Even so it is not the will of your Father who
is in heaven that one of these little ones should
perish.

5. *The Bible urges that believers avoid dirty jokes and
talk that encourages and describes sexual sin and immorality.*
In Ephesians 5:3,4 we read:

But fornicaton and all uncleanness or
covetousness, let it not even be named among
you, as is fitting for saints; neither filthiness,
nor foolish talking, nor coarse jesting, which are
not fitting, but rather giving of thanks.

Verse 12 of that same chapter continues:

It is shameful even to speak of those things
which are done by them in secret.

Pornography is filled with stories of sexual sin and vulgar talk. The sad thing about our American culture is what we
are now observing on a regular basis: the use of profanity and

vulgar language on prime-time television and by media personnel and professional comedians. It seems as though four-letter words of sexual violence and perversion are necessary ingredients for the modern person to communicate. What a tragedy!

6. *The Bible warns us about sexual lust and carnal appetites.* The Bible is not against sexual desire; instead, it urges us to control it within marriage. 1 Corinthians 7:2 teaches that "because of sexual immorality, let each man have his own wife, and let each woman have her own husband." In verse 5 couples are urged to have frequent sex with each other and not to deprive each other of this right and responsibility. The reason? Satan can tempt us for our lack of self-control. Marital sex is a key to satisfaction and sexual control.

Jesus made these insightful remarks in His famous Sermon on the Mount (Matthew 5:27,28):

> You have heard that it was said to those of old, "You shall not commit adultery." But I say to you that whoever looks at a woman to lust for her has already committed adultery with her in his heart.

These words of Jesus Christ are a bold and clear denunciation of the primary motive and goal of pornographic literature!

These verses do not condemn sexual desire. They warn us of the danger of adulterous thoughts contributing to adulterous acts. The word "looks" is a present tense in the original Greek language of the New Testament and implies a habit of life rather than a momentary appreciation of a woman's body. The motive behind the looking is not admiring the physical attributes of the woman but the desire to commit adultery with her. It is not women in general that is being discussed, as though a man's sexual interest in women is being condemned (as pornographers wrongly insinuate); it is the concentration of a man upon a particular woman with the motive to commit adultery that is being condemned. The woman is married, and that is what makes the focus of this man's sexual desire so blatantly wrong.

What we continue to think about and fantasize about eventually becomes our priority and objective. Under the right temptation or provocation, the greatest saint among us will fall because of what we have been thinking about and desiring in our minds.

Pornography creates and arouses our sexual desires, not toward the sexual enjoyment and pleasure of marriage, but rather toward the goal of self-gratification.

7. *The Bible indicates that pornography causes emotional turmoil in believers.* A man in his fifties who had been using pornographic magazines for several years got the courage to talk with me one day about his habit. He is a Christian, and felt tremendous guilt for his practice. He would hide the magazines carefully hoping that his wife and children (now married) would not know what he was doing. His guilt feelings were increasing and his spiritual life was taking a nosedive. The emotional conflict within him was unbearable.

2 Peter 2:7,8 says concerning the presence of Lot, Abraham's nephew, in the environment of ancient Sodom:

> [God] delivered righteous Lot, who was
> oppressed with the filthy conduct of the wicked
> (for that righteous man, dwelling among them,
> tormented his righteous soul from day to day by
> seeing and hearing their lawless deeds).

Pornography (seeing, hearing, and reading) torments the inner feelings of a righteous person, a person who believes in God and the righteous standards of His Word, the Bible. The only solution is total abstinence.

8. *The Bible urges believers to abstain from every form of evil.* In 1 Thessalonians 5:22 we read:

> Abstain from every form of evil.

The word "abstain" means to keep your distance from it. Don't get close to it; don't believe that you are strong enough to handle close observation!

The word "form" refers to that which strikes the eye, or is exposed to view. The basic point here is that any depiction of what is actually a sinful deed according to the Bible is wrong for the believer to practice or watch.

Pornography portrays and encourages the wrong use of sexual desire and improper attitudes toward others. It is lust, not God's love, that is promoted by the porn business!

WHAT SHOULD BE OUR RESPONSE?

Pornography must be confronted, attacked, and defeated, not only in our personal lives but also in the public arena of our communities. Although many attempts have failed, we must not lose hope or courage. Here are some practical suggestions that all of us can apply:

1) Do not rent, purchase, or view any X-rated films, videos, or magazines.

2) Do not enter any adult bookstore or establishment that sells, rents, or promotes pornography in any form (whether soft-core or hard-core).

3) Complain publicly about the presence of pornographic literature or videos in any store, institution, or place of business. Courteously confront the management and state that you resent the presence of such materials and will not continue to do business in any establishment that promotes it.

4) As a parent, request strongly that R-rated or X-rated movies not be shown in public school classrooms. If the request is ignored or denied, insist that your child be allowed to leave the class (without penalty of any kind) while such a movie is shown. If the administration or teaching staff is unresponsive, bring it before the local school board and gather around you a group of concerned parents who will not let the issue be ignored.

5) When you or your family are viewing a film in a local movie theater that is continually using obscene or vulgar language, promoting and

displaying the intimate details of sexual practices that are outside of marital love, or encouraging sexual violence, have the courage to leave the theater and complain to the management.

6) When any video that you are watching on your television screen (or any television program) does any of the above, have the courage and conviction to turn it off!

7) Encourage and support legislation that limits and restricts the activities of pornography. Write your own governmental officials and representatives to express your concern about pornography; ask them what they intend to do about this national disgrace.

8) Do not allow your children to gain understanding about their sexuality and sexual desires from sex education classes in public schools, movies, music, or their peer group friends. Accept your responsibility as a parent and teach your children the importance of moral and traditional values in dealing with their sexual desires.

Do not rebuke or condemn your children for their sexual desires and feelings. Help them to understand that sexual desire is a gift from God and that God wants us to enjoy it and be blessed by it, but that in order for that to take place, it must be satisfied within the bonds of marriage.

Express a great deal of physical affection to your spouse as well as to your children. Don't be afraid of intimacy and open discussions within the context of a loving and supportive family.

9) Depend upon the Bible for adequate and correct information about sexual morality.

10) Know where your children are and what they are doing at all times. Know who their friends are and make sure that your children are comfortable about bringing them home to meet you

and that they are not embarrassed or hesitant about their friends staying at your house or talking with you.

11) Speak positively and openly about sex in front of your children and others. Do not listen to dirty jokes or sexually vulgar talk, and do not allow your children to express such communication.

12) When your children begin to have romantic dates, do not be hesitant to discuss their romantic interests or struggles with their physical desires. Don't condemn or be judgmental of their choices in people they want to date, but encourage them to be careful, wise, and cautious about emotional and physical involvement.

13) Always encourage your male children to honor and respect females, and never to take advantage of their vulnerability or romantic interest in your sons. Teach your sons to protect the honor of the girls they date and to treat them as though they might one day be married to them. Remind them when possible that physical affection must be controlled and that sexual intercourse is only for marriage. Let your sons know that you hold them personally accountable for what takes place on their dates.

14) Encourage your female children to be careful about arousing the sexual desires and interest of the boys they date. Emphasize to your girls the importance of their physical bodies, and that allowing them to be sexually fondled or attacked by a boy's aggressive and strong sexual desire is not right, healthy, or wise. Teach them to be women of strong moral character. Encourage them to be careful about wearing clothes that stimulate or attempt to seduce a

boy's sexual desire, without making them feel guilty or condemned for wanting to be beautiful and attractive to boys.

15) Make sure that what you and your spouse do and say in the area of sexual desire and involvement is not only a commitment to biblical morality, but is what you would want your children to experience and enjoy.

6

Homosexuality: A Genetic Result?

In the past 20 years or so there has been a phenomenal rise in the public awareness of the subject of homosexuality. Gay Rights groups have become powerful political lobbies and have influenced national, state, and local legislation to a degree unparalleled in American political history.

What was once considered to be an illegal sexual practice is now not only tolerated but accepted and approved by our society as an alternative sexual preference and lifestyle.

The only hesitancy that our culture seems to currently apply to the subject of homosexuality is the rise of sexual disease, especially AIDS (Acquired Immune Deficiency Syndrome) among homosexuals.

"Gay rights" activists have brought a new understanding to the meaning of civil rights protection. Little did we realize in the fifties (when civil rights legislation was proposed and passed) that it would include one's sexual preference or lifestyle! Civil rights originally was an issue dealing with discrimination because of race or color of one's skin. Martin Luther King said, "I have a dream that my four little children will one day live in a nation where they will not be judged by the color of their skin, but by the content of their character." Race or color of skin tells us nothing about a person's lifestyle, behavior, or character.

Homosexuals have continued to expand the principles of "civil rights" to include their cause of full acceptance and equality within the political, social, and economic life of this country. They have stated forcefully to the American public that they are a part of the minorities in this country who need legal protection.

Homosexuals have been successful in persuading our courts that behavior-based status is grounds for special protection. They demand special treatment because of their chosen behavior and lifestyle.

Traditionally, true minorities were based on race, color, creed, or national origin, and from a legal point of view were referred to as "discrete and insular minorities." Changing such a fundamental description to a "behavior-based status" opens up minority status to all behavior-based groups, including smokers, adulterers, thieves, prostitutes, pedophiles, etc.

To accept the behavior of homosexuals on an equal basis and standing as those born to a certain race or color is utter legal nonsense and results in terrible consequences.

In the Supreme Court case of Bowers Versus Hardwick in 1986, the Court ruled that homosexuality is not a Constitutional right! The decision clearly spelled out the fact that there is no Constitutional right to engage in homosexual sodomy.

HOMOSEXUALITY IN AMERICAN CULTURE

While homosexuality has been present throughout American history in the past, it has only been in recent times that research, analysis, and public debate have brought its beliefs and practices to the general awareness of the majority of Americans. This fact alone is indeed revolutionary in terms of our history.

Many Americans are familiar with the Kinsey Reports on human sexuality that have continued to be quite controversial. In a book written by Alfred C. Kinsey in 1965 (*Sexual Behavior in the Human Female*, published by Pocket Books of New York), Kinsey spoke about the history of homosexuality. On pages 481 and 482 he said the following:

> The general condemnation of homosexuality
> in our particular culture apparently traces to
> a series of historical circumstances which had
> little to do with the protection of the individual
> or the preservation of the social organization
> of the day. In Hittite, Chaldean, and early

Jewish codes there were no over-all condemnations of such activity, although there were penalties for homosexual activities between persons of particular social status or blood relationships, or homosexual relationships under other particular circumstances, especially when force was involved. The more general condemnation of all homosexual relationships (especially male) originated in Jewish history in about the seventh century B.C. upon the return from the Babylonian exile.

Many of the Talmudic condemnations were based on the fact that such activities represented the way of the Canaanite, the way of the Chaldean, the way of the pagan, and they were originally condemned as a form of idolatry rather than a sexual crime.

Throughout the middle ages homosexuality was associated with heresy. The reform in the custom (the mores) soon, however, became a matter of morals, and finally a question for action under criminal law.

Kinsey could use a history lesson himself, for the Bible condemns homosexuality in the law of Moses, written during the fifteenth century B.C.!

In ancient Greece, homosexuality was widely accepted. Plato's *Symposium* praised the virtues of male homosexuality and even suggested that homosexual lovers would make the best soldiers! Many of the Greek mythological gods and heroes, such as Zeus, Hercules, Poseidon, and Achilles, were linked with homosexual behavior. Homosexual activity was not seen as shameful or sinful.

In the early days of the Roman Empire, homosexual behavior was common and was thriving without any legal restriction or limitation. Marriages between two men or between two women were legal and accepted, and many of the emperors of Rome were homosexual and participated in public ceremonies that married them to men.

By 1979, 39 American cities, towns, and counties had enacted ordinances that banned discrimination against homosexuals in housing and jobs.

In a book by Dennis Altman entitled *The Homosexualization of America*, published by Beacon Press in Boston in 1982, the author states the following:

> No longer sinners, criminals, perverts, neurotics, or deviants, homosexuals are being slowly redefined in less value-laden terms as practitioners of an alternative lifestyle, members of a new community. In a self-proclaimed pluralistic society like the United States, this is probably the most effective way to win tolerance, if not acceptance.

In the book *The Hite Report*, published by Dell Publishing Company and released in 1976, 1981, and 1987, author Shere Hite on pages 391 and 392 makes these comments about homosexuality:

> The arguments over whether lesbianism and/or homosexuality are biological or psychological in origin are still raging in some quarters, but the "answer" hardly matters anymore. Homosexuality, or the desire to be physically intimate with someone of one's own sex at some time, or always, during one's life, can be considered a natural and "normal" variety of life experience. It is "abnormal" only when you posit as "normal" and "healthy" only an interest in reproductive sex. Discussions of why one becomes heterosexual would come to the same nonconclusions. To consider all nonreproductive sexual contact "an error of nature" is a very narrow view.

The Kinsey Reports found that 10 percent of white American males were more or less exclusively homosexual for at least three years of their lives between the ages of 16 and 55. The Report found that 4 percent were exclusively homosexual on a lifelong basis. About 37 percent of the white male population that was studied had in adolescence or adulthood at least one homosexual experience which led to orgasm.

Kinsey estimated that 12 to 13 percent of American women had sexual relations with other women at some time during their adult lives. The Report found that by age 40, 19 percent of females had experienced some kind of homosexual contact, but that only 2 to 3 percent of women could be described as exclusively homosexual on a lifelong basis. The Kinsey report research has been challenged, however, due to what seems to be a limited group of people that was studied and how the studies were conducted.

Most sociologists who have studied the growth of homosexuality in the American culture have estimated that a total of 10 to 15 percent of the population has ever been involved in homosexual activities (lower overall figures than Kinsey claims). The accuracy of these percentages is always open to question, since the evaluations and statistical predictions are made on the basis of only a very limited group of people.

Homosexuality is a major attack upon the moral values of the American culture. The moral crisis that is now upon us has been greatly affected by the gay rights movement and the public exposure of the lifestyle, goals, and activities of homosexuals and lesbians within our society.

Their marches, festivals, parades, and demonstrations have continued to keep the issues of homosexuality in front of the American people. Their strategy has centered in legal change, and through the help of the American Civil Liberties Union and its legal staff they have achieved a remarkable degree of success.

They have been able to affect the political platforms and agendas of our political parties and conventions. The Democratic party has endorsed and accepted their presence and goals to an amazing degree. The Republican party has also been pressured by gay activists, but has chosen so far to exclude homosexual positions as part of its official political ideals and agenda.

Charles Socarides, a psychiatrist writing in the *Journal of the American Medical Association* in 1970, called homosexuality "a dread dysfunction, malignant in character, which has risen to epidemic proportions." Yet in 1974 the American Psychiatric Association officially declared that homosexuality was not an illness.

Dr. Socarides, perhaps the most prominent psychiatric expert in homosexuality, wrote in the *Journal of Psychiatry*:

> Homosexuality, the choice of a partner of the same sex for orgastic satisfaction, is not innate. There is no connection between sexual instinct and the choice of sexual object. Such an object choice is learned, acquired behavior; there is no inevitable genetically inborn propensity towards the choice of a partner of either the same or opposite sex.

What Causes Homosexuality?

Studies to this point are far from conclusive as to the source of homosexuality. Is it a lifelong condition over which a person has no control? Is it a genetic result or a hormonal imbalance? Is it an entirely voluntary choice, consciously and deliberately made at a certain time in one's life? Is it the result of role models that a child is exposed to at home or at school?

Those who continue to argue that homosexuality is the result of the genetic makeup of an individual have very little evidence upon which to base their argument. A 1952 study of twins supposedly supported this theory, but subsequent studies over the past 30 years have revealed that there is no scientific proof whatsoever that homosexuality is a genetic result.

Recent research has led some to speculate on the possibility of hormonal factors predisposing a person to homosexuality. But this research has major limitations. For example, treating adult homosexuals with sex hormones does not alter their sexual orientation in any way. No serious scientist today suggests that the cause of homosexuality is related to prenatal hormones.

Psychological theories can be traced back to Sigmund Freud, who believed that all people have latent homosexual tendencies. Freud also suggested that disordered parent-child relations might lead to homosexuality. A study in 1962 by psychoanalyst Irving Bieber and his associates evaluated the family backgrounds of 106 homosexual men and 100 heterosexual men. They found that many of the homosexual men had over-protective, dominant mothers and weak or passive fathers. Bieber suggested that homosexuality results from fears of heterosexual interactions. Recent studies have revealed that homosexual behavior cannot be connected unequivocably with parental background, although certain factors do seem to appear more frequently in homosexuals than in heterosexuals.

A former American Psychiatric Association president, Judd Marmor, stated in his book *Homosexual Behavior* (published by Basic Books of New York in 1980) that there is "a reasonable amount of evidence that boys exposed to this kind of family background [described above] have a greater than average likelihood of becoming homosexual," but he went on to say that "not all people who have this background become homosexual." He made the following observation:

> Homosexuals can also come from families
> with distant or hostile mothers and overly close
> fathers, from families with ambivalent relation-
> ships with older brothers, from homes with
> absent mothers, absent fathers, idealized fathers,
> and from a variety of broken homes.

An interesting footnote to such studies that try to find factors in parental background is that those families which manifest the traditional roles of father and mother, homes where both father and mother live together in a measure of marital harmony and demonstration of romantic love between each other, and who maintain close and loving relationships with their children, rarely experience a child with homosexual tendencies or behavior patterns.

Many scholars today argue that the primary causes of homosexual behavior stem from learned behavior patterns brought on by the relationship of the child to the parent, or pressure from the child's peer group friends, or by specific decisions on the part of the child to experiment with homosexual activity on the basis of what the child has seen, heard, or fantasized about.

Children are very impressionable, and are vulnerable to adult behavior in particular. For example, the influence of a homosexual man upon a child is a strong factor in a child developing his own homosexual behavior patterns and desires.

Children who are described early as "sissy" boys or "tomboyish" girls are thought by some researchers to have a greater likelihood of becoming homosexual.

The behavioral view suggests why some heterosexuals change their sexual orientation to homosexuality in adulthood. Studies have shown that female rape victims show a tendency to shift to lesbianism.

WHAT HOMOSEXUALITY IS NOT!

Homosexuality is not a genetic result; it is a learned behavior pattern. It is also not simply a sickness. Dr. Paul Gebhard, past director of Indiana University's Institute for Sex Research, has given the following definition of homosexuality:

> Physical contact between two individuals
> of the same gender which both recognize as
> being sexual in nature and which ordinarily
> results in sexual arousal.

Homosexuality is not merely "acting feminine" or "acting masculine." There are many studies which show that feminine-acting men are not necessarily homosexual by nature or choice, and neither are women who manifest masculine characteristics. Studies show that only 5 percent of homosexual men fall into the category of "stereotypes" that heterosexuals continue to promote and attack. Male homosexuals can sometimes appear quite masculine, and female lesbians can sometimes demonstrate a great amount of femininity.

Homosexuality is not a third sexual category, either. God created *male* and *female*, Adam and Eve, not Adam and Steve!

WHAT THE BIBLE SAYS ABOUT HOMOSEXUALITY

America's moral values throughout its short history of a little more than 200 years have been built upon the moral and spiritual values of the Bible, the most widely read and widely distributed book in American history.

In the *Hamline Journal of Public Law and Policy*, Volume 9, Number 2, fall edition of 1989, an article appeared by

Roger J. Magnuson, a lawyer and native of Minnesota. He wrote on the subject of "Civil Rights and Sexual Deviance: The Public Policy Implications of the Gay Rights Movement." He made these observations on page 221:

> Many states make sodomy a crime. These statutes had ancient roots. Sodomy was a criminal offense of common law and was forbidden by the laws of all the thirteen original states at the time the Bill of Rights was ratified.

He continued on page 223 with these insightful remarks:

> The real issue underlying the gay rights controversy is whether law should give special protection to sexual preferences for homosexual behavior. Does the inclination to practice anal or oral sodomy (or related sexual practices) with members of the same sex merit special legal safeguards?

In his concluding statement on page 235 he noted:

> Gay rights laws rely on the persuasive power of a single analogy: an analogy of behavior-based status to true status. That analogy equates a deviant sexual act with color, place of birth, or sex; it cannot bear serious analysis. Civil rights laws should not be expanded to give general protections to behavior-based classes absent a careful analysis of the behavior itself, especially when that behavior has serious adverse effects on society as a whole. Nor should society inhibit the ability of its citizens to make good-faith decisions based on bona fide religious and moral views. Finally, society should acknowledge the existence of homosexual behavior as a social problem, both for the good of society itself and for individuals afflicted with it. The rationale of civil rights requires no less eagerness to safeguard a person's right to make decisions on the content of a person's character

than to prohibit decisions based on the color of
a person's skin.

Our present moral catastrophe is in large part the result
of ignoring the teachings of the Bible and removing its moral
codes and principles from public life and institutions.

1. *The Bible teaches that homosexuality was the sin of
Sodom and Gomorrah that brought about its destruction.* The
issue of Sodom and Gomorrah is a serious one as it relates to the
beliefs and practices of homosexuals. They continue to insist
that the sin which the Bible says brought about the destruction
of those two ancient cities was not homosexuality but rather a
lack of hospitality.

In Genesis 18:20 we read what the Lord said about Sodom
and Gomorrah:

> Because the outcry against Sodom and
> Gomorrah is great, and because their sin is very
> grievous. . . .

Genesis 19:4-13 discusses what happened when the two
angels who appeared as men went to visit Lot and urged him to
get out of the city with his family before God destroyed it.

> Now before they lay down, the men of the
> city, the men of Sodom, both old and young, all
> the people from every quarter, surrounded the
> house. And they called to Lot and said to him,
> "Where are the men who came to you tonight?
> Bring them out to us that we may know them
> carnally." So Lot went out to them through the
> doorway, shut the door behind him, and said,
> "Please, my brethren, do not do so wickedly! See
> now, I have two daughters who have not known
> a man; please, let me bring them out to you, and
> you may do to them as you wish; only do nothing
> to these men, since this is the reason they have
> come under the shadow of my roof." And they
> said, "Stand back!" Then they said, "This one

came in to sojourn, and he keeps acting as a
judge; now we will deal worse with you than
with them." So they pressed hard against the
man Lot, and came near to break down the door.
But the men reached out their hands and pulled
Lot into the house with them and shut the door.
And they struck the men who were at the
doorway of the house with blindness, both small
and great, so that they became weary trying
to find the door. Then the men said to Lot,
"Have you anyone else here? Son-in-law, your
sons, your daughters, and whomever you have
in the city—Take them out of this place! For we
will destroy this place, because the outcry
against them has grown great before the face
of the Lord, and the Lord has sent us to destroy
it."

An interesting viewpoint on this passage is given by
Robert Arthur, who left a heterosexual lifestyle and marriage
and became a committed homosexual and a pastor in the Uni-
versal Fellowship of Metropolitan Community Churches. He
claims to be committed to a conservative theological viewpoint
and states that he believes in the plenary-verbal inspiration of
the Bible in their original languages. He believes, he says, in
the authority and infallibility of the Bible and that everything
in it is completely accurate and definitely true. In his little
booklet entitled *Homosexuality and the Conservative Christian*,
published in 1982 by STI Publications in Los Angeles, he says:

Now of course there are those who would
lift the nineteenth chapter out of context and
try to prove that God destroyed Sodom and
Gomorrah because of their rampant homosexuality. But we can see from the context that well
before their destruction, and this attempted
rape, that God had pronounced their judgment
to Abraham.

He goes on to argue that the sin of Sodom involved the
attempt on the part of human beings to rape the angelic visitors. He says, "We are not reading of homosexuality, but of the

mixing of two distinct orders of creation (humans and angels)." He argues that the sin was rape, not homosexuality. However, on the same basis that he accuses those who believe that the sin of Sodom and Gomorrah was homosexuality and says that this could not be so because God pronounced His judgment to Abraham before the angels came to Lot's house, then neither could the attempted rape of these angels be the reason if in fact the judgment was announced before they even came to Lot's house!

The point of Robert Arthur is completely misleading. It is quite obvious that whatever the sin of Sodom and Gomorrah was which was so grievous to God and brought the destruction of those cities, it was obviously not dependent upon the incident of Genesis 19, although that incident demonstrates the attitude and character of the residents of Sodom which prove what the real sin was. The Hebrew word (*yada*) in Genesis 19:5,8 is normally translated "to know," and is the common word used to indicate sexual relationship. Genesis 4:1 says, "Adam *knew* Eve his wife, and she conceived and bore Cain." Genesis 4:17 says "Cain *knew* his wife, and she conceived and bore Enoch." Verse 25 says, "Adam *knew* his wife again, and she bore a son and named him Seth." Genesis 24:16 says of Rebekah (who became the wife of Isaac), "Now the young woman was very beautiful to behold, a virgin; no man had *known* her."

The men of Sodom were not interested in getting acquainted with these men by having casual conversation and discussing backgrounds, education, occupations, etc. The very answer of Lot in Genesis 19:8 in which he offers his two daughters and says that they "have not *known* a man" clearly reveals that the men of Sodom wanted sex with these two male visitors.

Gay proponents say that the sin was a lack of hospitality. In a sense they are correct—what a lack of hospitality it was! But it was something far worse as well. The lack-of-hospitality view comes from the comments of Ezekiel 16:49,50:

> Look, this was the iniquity of your sister
> Sodom: She and her daughter had pride, fullness
> of food, and abundance of idleness; neither did
> she strengthen the hand of the poor and needy.

And they were haughty and committed abomination before Me; therefore I took them away
as I saw fit.

Verses 56 to 58 add this:

For your sister Sodom was not a byword
in your mouth in the days of your pride, before
your wickedness was uncovered. It was like the
time of the reproach of the daughters of Syria
and all who were around her, and of the daughters of the Philistines, who despise you everywhere. You have paid for your lewdness and your
abominations.

Do these passages reveal that the primary sin of Sodom
and Gomorrah was that of inhospitality? It is true that they had
pride in the midst of abundance and did not care about the poor
and needy, but these offenses did not constitute the primary
problem. Ezekiel 16:50 says that they "committed abomination" before the Lord. Verse 58 calls it "lewdness" and "abominations." Those terms are used of rape in Judges 20:4-6, adultery and prostitution in Jeremiah 13:27, and incest in Ezekiel
22:11, but never of inhospitality.

2 Peter 2:7 calls the sins of Sodom and Gomorrah "the
filthy conduct of the wicked." Verse 8 says that they were guilty
of "lawless deeds." Verse 10 says that they "walk according to
the flesh in the lust of uncleanness and despise authority."
Verse 14 says that they have "eyes full of adultery and that
cannot cease from sin." Verse 18 calls people like those who
lived in Sodom and Gomorrah those who "allure through the
lusts of the flesh, through licentiousness." Verse 19 of 2 Peter 2
says they are "slaves of corruption."

The attempt by gay proponents to deny the obvious point
of the Bible's teaching about the sin of Sodom and Gomorrah
shows why so many people in our secular society today are
trying to eliminate the Bible's morality from public life: The
Bible is quite clear on the issue!

2. *The Bible teaches that homosexuality deserves the
death penalty.* Homosexuality is not the only sin to be so condemned in the Bible. The death penalty in the Mosaic law was

142 ♦ David Hocking

also applied to premeditated murder, incest, rape, prostitution, adultery, premarital sex with an engaged virgin, and bestiality.

Though we do not apply the strong penalties of the Mosaic law in our culture today, these penalties do help us to understand the righteous and just character of our God, and to see the seriousness of our sin. Thank God there is a Savior for our sin, who because of His death on the cross can provide redemption and forgiveness for all who put their trust in Him! We all deserve God's punishment for the sins we have committed, but His love and grace make our forgiveness possible.

Leviticus 18:22 says:

> You shall not lie with a male as with a woman. It is an abomination.

Sexual immorality was the sin of Sodom and Gomorrah, and it is called an abomination in Ezekiel 16:50. Homosexuality is called an abomination in Leviticus 18:22.

Leviticus 18:29 says, "For whoever commits any of these abominations [one of which is homosexuality], the persons who commit them shall be cut off from among their people."

Leviticus 20:13 reveals the serious offense which homosexuality is to the Lord and to His people:

> If a man lies with a male as he lies with a woman, both of them have committed an abomination. They shall surely be put to death. Their blood shall be upon them.

3. *The Bible teaches that homosexuality is unnatural, an example of degrading passion, and worthy of death.* One of the most controversial passages that deals with homosexuality is Romans 1:26-32, which was taught by the apostle Paul, who lived in the days of the Roman Empire and was constantly confronted by homosexual lifestyles. Gay preachers and teachers do amazing things with the interpretation of this passage in order to avoid the obvious point.

> For this reason God gave them up to vile passions. For even their women exchanged the

natural use for what is against nature. Likewise
also the men, leaving the natural use of the
woman, burned in their lust for one another,
men with men committing what is shameful
and receiving in themselves the penalty of their
error which was due. And even as they did not
like to retain God in their knowledge, God gave
them over to a debased mind, to do those things
which are not fitting; being filled with all
unrighteousness, sexual immorality, wickedness,
covetousness, maliciousness; full of envy, murder,
strife, deceit, evil-mindedness; they are whis-
perers, backbiters, haters of God, violent, proud,
boasters, inventors of evil things, disobedient
to parents, undiscerning, untrustworthy, un-
loving, unforgiving, unmerciful; who, knowing
the righteous judgment of God, that those who
practice such things are worthy of death, not
only do the same but also approve of those who
practice them.

Verses 26 and 27 refer to the "natural use." The passage
says that when a woman turns to a woman rather than a man to
fulfill her sexual needs, she is going against nature. When a
man decides that it is all right to experience sexual lust and
satisfaction with another man, it is shameful. The word "shameful" is a Greek word referring to that which is without shape or
plan. Homosexuality is against the original plan of God, which
was for a male and female to satisfy each other sexually. Homosexuality is deviant and abnormal behavior.

Romans 1:27 says that homosexuals receive "in themselves the penalty of their error which was due." The tragic fact
of rampant sexual disease is testimony to the accuracy of these
biblical evaluations.

4. *The Bible teaches that homosexuality is one of many
sins for which the law was given.* The apostle Paul wrote these
words to Timothy, his son in the faith (1 Timothy 1:8-10):

We know that the law is good if one uses
it lawfully, knowing this: that the law is not
made for a righteous person, but for the lawless
and insubordinate, for the ungodly and for

sinners, for the unholy and profane, for murderers of fathers and murderers of mothers, for manslayers, for fornicators, for sodomites, for kidnappers, for liars, for perjurers, and if there is any other thing that is contrary to sound doctrine.

The law gives us the knowledge of sin and shows that the whole world is guilty before God (Romans 3:19,20). Even one offense makes us guilty of all and deserving of the law's penalty, which was death (James 2:10).

The Bible teaches that the law was designed for sinners, and lists a number of categories, one of which is called "sodomites" (New King James Version). Although many attempts are made by gay teachers to prove that the Greek word *arsenokoites* does not refer to homosexuals, the evidence in Greek history is to the contrary. It refers to a male prostitute who took an active role in sexual encounters. The Greek word is composed of the word for "male" and the word for "bed," specifically referring to sexual activity in bed. The primary usage of the word refers to the sexual activities of men with men, and evidence of its application to other kinds of sexual involvement is lacking.

5. *The Bible teaches that the practice of homosexuality will result in eternal condemnation.* Such a statement will not win a popularity contest in downtown San Francisco, but listen to these words of the apostle Paul in writing to the Corinthians (1 Corinthians 6:9,10):

> Do you not know that the unrighteous will not inherit the kingdom of God? Do not be deceived. Neither fornicators, nor idolaters, nor adulterers, nor homosexuals, nor sodomites, nor thieves, nor covetous, nor drunkards, nor revilers, nor extortioners will inherit the kingdom of God.

Those who continue to practice these things without a sense of remorse, confession, and repentance before God are headed for hell, not heaven! That's the clear message of the Bible.

The word for "sodomites" is the same one as the word mentioned above in 1 Timothy 1:10; it refers to male prostitution. The word translated "homosexuals" in 1 Corinthians 6:9, *malakoi* is sometimes translated "effeminate." It appears twice in Matthew 11:8 and once in Luke 7:25 and refers to that which is "soft," such as clothing. Metaphorically, it can refer to a person who lacks masculine characteristics. It is used to describe a man who acts like a woman. In homosexual encounters, one male plays the dominant role of a macho man, while the other plays the role of the female, responding as a female would and manifesting female desires and characteristics. That is the kind of person who likes "soft clothing." The term was used to refer to homosexuals who displayed feminine characteristics.

The important thing to notice about the biblical passage is that those who persist in such a lifestyle (along with other sexual sins) will suffer eternal condemnation!

6. *The Bible teaches that homosexuality is a behavior pattern that can be stopped.* 1 Corinthians 6:11, the verse that immediately follows the above list of sins that lead to eternal condemnation, provides clear evidence that homosexual behavior as well as heterosexual immorality (such as adultery) can be stopped.

> Such were some of you. But you were
> washed, but you were sanctified, but you were
> justified in the name of the Lord Jesus and by
> the Spirit of our God.

What a wonderful encouragement—"such *were* some of you"! Homosexual behavior can be stopped as well as forgiven. Through the wonderful work of Jesus Christ we can be forgiven of our sins! 2 Corinthians 5:17 gives us this encouraging message:

> Therefore, if anyone is in Christ, he is a
> new creation; old things have passed away;
> behold, all things have become new.

God can produce a moral change within the human heart so that previous sinful lifestyles can be forgiven, cleansed, and changed.

John has been an active homosexual since he was 14 years old. To his knowledge there was no evidence of homosexual tendencies or influence in himself until the day he saw such activity pictured in a pornographic magazine given to him by one of his friends. On a day which found him vulnerable and unprepared, he engaged in homosexual acts with his friend. They were alone in his friend's house after school one day. After a swim in his friend's family pool, they removed their bathing suits in his friend's bedroom and decided to play some cards on the bed while remaining nude. It seemed harmless at first, causing both of them to laugh as they fondled each other.

These occasions became more frequent, and at the same time their interest in pornographic magazines and X-rated videos increased. By the age of 18 John was engaging in homosexual activity at least once a week. His sexual desire and interest kept growing. In college John became involved with many different homosexuals. His parents became totally frustrated with his lifestyle, and felt it was hopeless that he would ever change. They began to accept the opinion of many that homosexuality was the result of genetics, even though they had no evidence of it in John's life before age 14.

In college John met a young man who was not a homosexual but took a special interest in him. This friend was a committed Christian who began to witness to John and tell him that his life could be changed by the power of Jesus Christ.

One day in the college gymnasium, John made a personal commitment of his life and future to Jesus Christ. In the months following, he struggled with homosexual desires and thoughts from his past. Through the help of Christian friends, John was completely delivered from his homosexual behavior, and is now married to a wonderful Christian lady with two children. Yes, there is hope, forgiveness, and deliverance!

The homosexual lifestyle is not a happy one at all but leads to great unhappiness along with serious physical, emotional, and social problems. But the greatest tragedy of all is the failure of the homosexual to know of God's forgiveness and power to change. Homosexuality is not normal human behavior; it is abnormal and against nature.

WHAT SHOULD BE OUR RESPONSE?

Hardly any issue has received such prominent attention and widespread publicity in our country as that of homosexuality. Gay rights advocates have kept their concerns and beliefs on the front page of American life. They have been quite successful in convincing many Americans of the fallacy that homosexual rights are civil rights.

What can we do about the growth of homosexuality? What should our attitude be toward homosexuals? What means should we use to protect ourselves and our children from the solicitations and enticements of homosexual people?

1) Always refer to homosexuality as a sin, not a sickness.

2) Understand that homosexuality is a learned behavior pattern, not a genetic result.

3) Do not consider gay rights as civil rights.

4) Do not hate homosexuals; hate *homosexuality* and what it does to people and communities.

5) Do not tolerate the approval and promotion of homosexual acts or lifestyles, especially in the sex-education classes of our public schools.

6) Use your voting rights to defeat gay rights initiatives and agendas that seek community, state, and national approval and acceptance of the homosexual lifestyle.

7) Never believe that "sexual preference" should be added to our understanding and application of human rights or civil rights.

8) Do not discriminate against homosexuals in terms of the rights to which all Americans are entitled, but never be intimidated or pressured to approve or accept their sexual lifestyle and activity.

9) Teach your children what the Bible says about sexual matters, and warn them of sexual sins, including the sin of homosexuality.

10) Do not treat homosexuality as a more terrible sin than adultery among heterosexuals, but never view it as harmless or tolerable.

11) Encourage homosexuals to accept God's love and forgiveness in the work and Person of Jesus Christ. Show them that God's power can give them the inner strength, courage, and conviction to overcome their desire to be involved in homosexual activities.

12) Make sure your own personal beliefs, principles, lifestyle, and example are in line with biblical morality. Make sure your own life demonstrates the commitment that the only safe and right sex is that between a husband and a wife within the bonds of holy matrimony.

7

Sexual Disease and Human Survival

In July 1989 the Center for Disease Control in Atlanta, Georgia, reported that the number of known AIDS cases in the United States had passed the 100,000 figure. In January 1990, the figure has grown to 200,000. They estimate that 1.5 million Americans are infested with the virus, but as yet show no serious symptoms. Over 60,000 Americans have died from the AIDS virus.

Microbiologist and Nobel laureate David Baltimore has given this warning:

> It will probably be the most important public-health problem of the next decade and going into the next century. It threatens to undermine countries.

This quote and many additional frightening statistics were reported in an extensive article in *U.S. News and World Report* in January 1987. The article was entitled "AIDS: At the Dawn of Fear." The situation is now even worse.

The figures which the Centers for Disease Control have reported as to the number of Americans carrying the AIDS virus have been challenged by many people in the medical profession, with some believing that instead of 1.5 million Americans infected, the number is more like 4 million!

Estimates place the number of AIDS cases in 1991 at 270,000 Americans, with 179,000 dead. Heterosexuals will comprise about 10 percent of the total cases, and at least 4000 babies will have contracted the disease by being exposed to the virus while in their mothers' wombs.

At the present rate of reported AIDS cases, in 20 years over 11 million Americans will have AIDS, with 52 million cases of AIDS-related diseases and 8 *billion* people carrying or exposed to the virus worldwide. Let's pray that these statistics never become reality!

More than half of all AIDS cases in the United States are currently found in New York, San Francisco, and Los Angeles.

THE TRUTH ABOUT AIDS

Frankly, after reading the most up-to-date medical information and observing several video presentations, I seriously doubt that any of us knows the full truth about AIDS.

The misconceptions about AIDS seem to multiply weekly. In spite of enormous efforts to keep the public from panicking, the full information is still lacking. For example, we do not know how the first human contracted the sickness. A few years ago experts told us that only 10 percent of those exposed would develop the disease; now they tell us that 25 to 50 percent of those exposed will get AIDS!

The current facts indicate that if you get the disease, you die, though not right away. The process of death is slow, painful, and lonely. The impact on society is different from other killers (such as cancer and heart disease), not only because AIDS is always lethal but also because it can be transmitted in life's most basic human actions of sex, procreation, and expressions of love. As a result, more emotionalism is attached to AIDS than to any other disease.

AIDS is the most serious plague in all of human history. The Black Plague of the Middle Ages resulted in the death of one million people. During the Holocaust under Hitler, 6 million Jews lost their lives. The famine in Africa has taken the lives of 10 million people. But at the present rate, *100 million* people will have the AIDS virus by the year 2000!

Most victims of AIDS become demented, suffering irreversible brain damage. About 80 percent die within three years after confirmation of having AIDS. The HIV virus mutates fives times faster than any known virus in medical and scientific history. It is present in all body fluids (blood, serum, tears, plasma, saliva, milk, and semen).

Ted Koppel of the "Nightline" TV program summed up our current moral catastrophe regarding AIDS when he said:

> We have actually convinced ourselves that slogans will save us. Shoot up if you must, but use a clean needle. Enjoy sex whenever and with whomever you wish, but wear a condom. No! The answer is no! Not because it isn't cool or smart, or because you might end up in jail or dying in an AIDS ward. But no because it's wrong!

Presently, 73 percent of AIDS patients are known to be homosexuals. Only 2 percent of known AIDS patients are heterosexual, and these are primarily involved with prostitution. About 17 percent of AIDS cases reveal drug usage, and 2 percent of AIDS victims became infested through blood transfusion. Another 1 percent are described as hemophiliacs.

THE SURGEON GENERAL'S REPORT

The former Surgeon General of the United States, Dr. C. Everett Koop, brought the AIDS problem to the forefront of American medical concerns. In his national report, still available upon request, he gave the following information:

> AIDS (Acquired Immune Deficiency Syndrome) is a disease which impairs the body's immune system, leaving a person unable to fight infections and diseases. AIDS is caused by a virus called HIV (Human Immunodeficiency Virus). When this virus enters the bloodstream, it attacks the body's immune system, weakening or destroying cells which are crucial to the system's normal functioning.
> Not all persons infected with HIV develop AIDS. Some show no obvious signs of sickness, although they are able to infect others with the virus. Some persons with HIV develop a condition called AIDS Related Complex or ARC. ARC patients exhibit symptoms less severe than those associated with AIDS itself. A certain

percentage of infected persons (25–50%) will develop AIDS within five years of being infected.

Since not everyone with HIV shows readily discernible signs of illness, the AIDS antibody test is essential for correct diagnosis of HIV infection. This test detects antibodies to the HIV virus which the body produces in a vain effort to attack the virus itself. The test, by identifying the AIDS antibody in the bloodstream, tells if someone has been infected with HIV. Those who test positive do not necessarily have AIDS. They may remain well, or develop ARC, or AIDS.

Concerning the future, the Surgeon General of the United States wrote these words in that nationwide report:

AIDS is a life-threatening disease and a major public health issue. Its impact on our society is and will continue to be devastating. By the end of 1991, an estimated 270,000 cases of AIDS will have occurred, with 179,000 deaths within the decade since the disease was first recognized. In the year 1991, an estimated 145,000 patients with AIDS will need health and supportive services at a total cost of between $8 and $16 billion. However, AIDS is preventable. It can be controlled by changes in personal behavior.

ARE CONDOMS THE ANSWER?

Most Americans are aware of the extensive campaign to promote the use of condoms as a way to achieve "safe sex." The World Health Organization began a Global Program on AIDS (GPA) in February 1987. It was endorsed by the World Health Assembly, the United Nations General Assembly, and the London Summit of Ministers of Health. By 1991 its budget is expected to increase from its original 66 million dollars to over 650 million.

According to the GPA's Guidelines for the Development of a National AIDS Prevention and Control Programme, the World Health Organization gave us this advice:

Education leading to widespread change
in behaviour is the key to preventing further
spread of HIV infection.

As to what that "education" involves, the following was stated and has become the major answer which the media and most organizations dealing with the problem have proposed:

An essential aspect of change to be promoted is the use of condoms.

In answering the question "How can I avoid catching AIDS?" a *U.S. News and World Report* article on January 12, 1987, said this:

If you test positive for the AIDS antibody,
shoot drugs or engage in other activities that
increase the chances of catching AIDS, inform
your sex partner, and use a condom if you have
sex. If your partner tests positive, or if you think
he or she has been exposed to AIDS because of
past sexual practices or through the use of
intravenous drugs, a condom should be used.
If you or your partner is in a high-risk group,
avoid oral contact with the genitals or rectum,
as well as sexual activities that might cut or tear
the skin or the tissues of the penis, vagina or
rectum. Avoid sex with prostitutes. Many are
addicted to drugs and often get AIDS by sharing
contaminated needles with other addicts.

Once again, the use of condoms is promoted as the only "safe sex" we can experience.

A physician who attends the church where I teach the Bible (and who is currently dealing with many AIDS patients) made the following statement to me in a written letter:

The figure that 80 percent of AIDS victims
will die within three years is very optimistic.

I believe that 90 percent will die within a year.
The patients I have treated died in a few months
after confirmation of having AIDS.

In his letter to me he described the diseases which AIDS
patients usually acquire. It was not a pleasant experience reading it. He also made the statement:

The use of condoms as a means to safe sex
is a fallacy. There is absolutely no guarantee
that a person using a condom will be prevented
from getting AIDS from an infected person. It
will help, but is not "safe"!

In the Newport Mesa School District of Southern California, parents became concerned about the promotion of "good
and safe sex" in social science courses. The following occurred in
school classrooms:

1) Intimate discussion of male and female eroge-
   nous zones, genital stimulation, faking of orgasm,
   and "how-to" sexually explicit subject matter.

2) Promotion and "helpful hints" on the use of condoms and other contraceptives.

3) Description of deviant and abnormal sexual
   behavior, including sex with the dead and with
   animals.

4) Lectures by homosexual guest speakers advo-
   cating their practices as an acceptable alternate
   lifestyle.

5) Teaching, despite convincing evidence to the
   contrary, that homosexual orientation is a condition that cannot be helped, with adamant
   refusal to present the other side of the issue.

In an effort to stop the so-called "safe sex" teaching in our
public schools that advocates the use of condoms, a new abstinence law (SB 2394) was added to the policy statement of the

California State Board of Education. Under the name of the Family Life and Health Education Program, the following guidelines were established:

> ... Whereas, preadolescent and adolescent sexual intercourse is unlawful in many cases and often results in a loss of self-esteem, school dropout, and an increased risk of contracting sexually transmitted disease as well as, among women, unintended pregnancy and/or sterility; now therefore be it RESOLVED, that a Family Life and Health Education Program that encourages kindergarten through grade twelve students to be abstinent and establishes sexual behavior in the ethical and moral context of marriage be included as a necessary part of our overall educational system....

Congratulations to the State of California! Sexual abstinence outside of marriage is the only true safe sex! The only sexual practices that a person should engage in are those which occur between a husband and a wife in holy matrimony!

In his book *Safe Sex in a Dangerous World* (Vintage Books, 1987), Dr. Art Ulene says this:

> We are told that we can have "safe sex" by using condoms, avoiding anal intercourse, giving up other forms of sexual contact that permit the exchange of body fluids, and limiting the number of our sex partners. These seem like minor inconveniences to endure for being able to continue an active sex life.
>
> But no one talks about condom failures. And few people realize that there is a risk of infection if the one partner you limit yourself to is carrying the AIDS virus. The term "safe sex" means different things to different people, but this is a time when we cannot afford flexible definitions.
>
> The concept of "safe sex" was initiated within the homosexual community. It was, in part, an attempt by this group to protect the

health—but also the lifestyles—of its members. It was also partly an attempt by bathhouse operators to protect their businesses. In retrospect, it is clear that both groups underestimated the danger of AIDS and the need for more dramatic changes in sexual behavior if the spread of this disease was to be stopped, both within the homosexual community and beyond it.

Homosexual men were not the only ones who got the "safe sex" message from posters that were put up in bathhouses. The posters were given prominent coverage by television news programs, and millions of Americans who saw them on their screens at home were left with the impression that "safe sex" was actually possible with an infected partner.

The idea of "safe sex" picked up more steam as medical journals published studies showing that AIDS-like viruses could not penetrate the walls of condoms—at least not in the laboratory. Condom manufacturers worked hard to convince the public that the laboratory results would hold for actual use by humans, although the facts suggest that condoms are—in real life—less than 100 percent effective.

On pages 31 and 32 of this excellent little book Dr. Ulene says:

I think it's time to stop talking about "safe sex." I believe we should be talking about safe partners instead. A safe partner is one who has never been infected with the AIDS virus. With a safe partner, you don't have to worry about getting AIDS yourself—no matter what you do sexually, and no matter how much protection you use while you do it.

Truly "safe sex" is an all-or-nothing thing. Sex is either 100 percent safe or it's not, even when it's "almost safe." If you can't find a safe partner, don't kid yourself into believing that there is a perfectly safe alternative—other than abstinence.

But no one talks about abstinence today. Judging by my mail, it was a somewhat surprised—but approving—"Today" show audience who heard me suggest that abstinence is a reasonable alternative in these dangerous times. And I'll say it again. If you can't be sure that you've got a safe partner, abstinence is the only sexual practice you can consider safe.

SEXUALLY TRANSMITTED DISEASE

In Masters and Johnson's book *Sex and Human Loving* (published by Little, Brown, and Company of Boston in 1988), there is an entire section on the subject of sexually transmitted diseases. Concerning gonorrhea, we read on pages 530 and 531:

> Although the discovery of penicillin as an effective treatment for this disease slowed its spread in the 1940s and 1950s, the incidence of gonorrhea has grown tremendously in the last twenty years and has reached epidemic proportions today. More than a million cases of gonorrhea are reported annually, and these probably represent only a quarter of the actual cases that occur each year.
>
> Gonorrhea is transmitted by any form of sexual contact, ranging from sexual intercourse to fellatio, anal intercourse, and infrequently, cunnilingus or even kissing. A woman who has intercourse once with an infected man has a 50 percent change of getting gonorrhea, while a man who has intercourse once with an infected woman has a lower risk, probably around 20 to 25 percent, of becoming infected. The old excuse, "I caught it from a toilet seat," which was previously laughed at by scientists, has now

been shown to be at least theoretically possible, since the infective bacteria can survive for up to two hours on a toilet seat or on wet toilet paper. However, it is unlikely that this form of transmission is more than a rare occurrence.

Masters and Johnson describe this sexual disease as having "epidemic proportions."

On pages 533 and 534 syphilis is described. The Masters and Johnson report says:

> Syphilis is far less common than gonorrhea today. In 1983 there were about 25,000 new cases reported in America, with a male-female ratio of two to one. Half of the men with syphilis are homosexual or bisexual.
>
> Syphilis is usually transmitted by sexual contacts, but it can also be acquired from a blood transfusion or can be transmitted from a pregnant mother to the fetus.

In describing the disease of genital herpes, the report says on pages 535 and following:

> Genital Herpes currently affects some 40 million Americans, with an additional 500,000 cases occurring annually. Viewed by some as a relatively minor skin infection with annoying but brief symptoms and by others as a life-threatening disease or even a heaven-sent directive against loose morals, the genital herpes epidemic of the 1980s had received almost as much media coverage as a presidential campaign by 1983, when it began to be outshadowed in the press by coverage of the AIDS epidemic.
>
> Genital herpes is generally transmitted by sexual contact. Direct contact with infected genitals can cause transmission via sexual intercourse, rubbing the genitals together, oral-genital contact, anal intercourse, or oral-anal

contact. In addition, normally protected areas
of skin can become infected if there is a cut,
rash, or sore, so that infections of the fingers,
thighs, or other areas of the body are also
possible.

The risk of developing genital herpes in a
woman exposed to an infected man is estimated
to be 80 to 90 percent. A man's risk of developing genital herpes from a single sexual
encounter with an infected woman is estimated
to be about 50 percent.

An amazing statement is given on page 543 concluding a
very informative discussion of genital herpes and its consequences:

While the use of a condom can help prevent
transmission of genital herpes, it is not a
foolproof method (both because it doesn't cover
all lesions and because it isn't always worn from
the start of genital contact) and it may actually
irritate the condition.

AIDS is not the only problem we have; in all the furor and
panic over the presence of AIDS in our society, we have forgotten that other sexually transmitted diseases are continuing to
affect and infect our society. Venereal diseases of all kinds are
continuing to spread ominously.

In a *USA Today* article on April 6, 1989, entitled "Sex-
transmitted virus targets teen-age girls," journalist Gaynelle
Evans wrote:

A sexually transmitted disease linked to
cervical cancer in a growing number of teen
girls is causing concern among doctors. It's
called Human Papilloma Virus (HPV).

HPV now ranks as one of the most common
sexually transmitted diseases. The Centers for
Disease Control estimates that a half-million
people contract it each year; studies show most
victims are teen women, and it is almost always
sexually transmitted.

The infection can cause changes in the cervix that signify cancer. Researchers say HPV is the reason for a growing incidence of cervical cancer in younger women. And studies show that 30 percent to 35 percent of all sexually active teenagers have evidence of an HPV infection. There are a lot of sexually active teenage girls who won't find out they have HPV until it's too late because they are less likely to receive regular medical care than adults.

In 95 percent of all cases where there is cervical cancer, there is evidence of HPV. While the virus is not the cause of cervical cancer, it is definitely a contributor.

Abstinence from sex is the only foolproof way. Using condoms and spermicidal cream are also very helpful.

AIDS PROJECT LOS ANGELES

AIDS Project Los Angeles is a nonprofit public health organization dedicated to providing vital support to people with AIDS and AIDS-related illnesses as well as education to the general community.

According to their purpose statement, this organization seeks to:

1) Support and maintain the best possible quality of life for persons in Los Angeles County with AIDS and AIDS-related illnesses, and their loved ones, by providing and promoting publicly and privately funded vital human services for them.

2) Reduce the overall incidence of human immunodeficiency virus (HIV) infection by providing risk-reduction education and information for persons primarily affected by and at risk for AIDS, and for the general public.

3) Reduce the levels of fear and discrimination directed toward persons affected by AIDS, and to enhance and preserve the dignity and self-respect of those persons, by providing and promoting critically needed education to the public, health-care providers, educators, business and religious leaders, the media, public officials, and other opinion leaders.

4) Ensure the ongoing support for all of these services by involving, educating, and cooperating with a wide range of organizations and individuals in AIDS-related service provision, and by supporting efforts at all levels of the public and private sectors to secure adequate development and finance of AIDS research, education, and human service programs.

Peter Scott, a homosexual rights activist, was the former chairman of AIDS Project Los Angeles, He died of complications from AIDS. A former lawyer who gave up his practice to champion gay rights, Mr. Scott worked to defeat measures to fire gay teachers and an initiative requiring people with AIDS to register with the state. He founded the Municipal Election Committee of Los Angeles, the city's most powerful gay-rights political group.

The AIDS Project Los Angeles produced "A Self-Care Manual" in 1987. In Section Eight of this manual, entitled "A Spiritual Perspective," we gain some insight into the difficulties which the AIDS epidemic has presented to those of us concerned with moral and traditional values. On pages 220 and 221 in this manual we find the following statement which summarizes the moral catastrophe that we face in relation to sexually transmitted diseases:

Is AIDS a punishment or scourge from God? Some would say yes. Indeed, some members of the "religious right" would probably praise God for this tragic epidemic, which is claiming the lives of thousands of gay men and others. The idea that AIDS is a punishment from God is based on three false assumptions: that homosexual acts are sinful; that God causes suffering; and that God punishes sin with disease.

These false assumptions result from a particular way of looking at society, sexuality, and how God works in the world. These assumptions, and the worldview they reflect, are based on the fear called homophobia, and on a tragic misunderstanding of the meaning of God. It is the responsibility of persons of faith to overcome this fear and misunderstanding, to witness to God's love and grace, and to know God's compassion and faithfulness.

The people who wrote this section of this AIDS manual have never studied the Bible carefully or else have chosen to ignore the evidence which the Bible itself teaches. The fact is, the Bible teaches that homosexual acts are sinful, that God does indeed cause suffering, and that God punishes sin with disease.

WHAT THE BIBLE SAYS ABOUT SEXUAL SIN AND DISEASE

The moral catastrophe that our American culture faces is in large part the result of rejecting biblical values and morality. Our hesitancy to understand that our country was built upon these values is contributing to the moral chaos that we are experiencing today. We must take a serious look at biblical instruction on the crucial questions of survival that sexual disease is bringing to our attention.

1. *The Bible teaches that sexual behavior outside of heterosexual marriage is a sin.* Hebrews 13:4 makes it quite clear:

Marriage is honorable among all, and the bed undefiled; but fornicators and adulterers God will judge.

Sex outside of marriage is considered moral defilement. This verse teaches clearly that God will judge sexual practices outside of marriage.

In the Old Testament, the Jewish people were given explicit details about sexual behavior. They were told in Leviticus chapters 18 and 20 that fornication, adultery, incest, homosexuality, sex with animals, prostitution, etc. were sins and abominations to God. People who became involved in such practices were worthy of death.

2. *The Bible teaches that God punishes sinful behavior with disease and death.* Contrary to constant attempts by gay rights activists to prove otherwise, the Bible teaches clearly that God does punish sinful behavior with disease and death. The evidence is overwhelming.

Leviticus 26:14-16 states:

> If you do not obey Me, and do not observe
> all these commandments, and if you despise My
> statutes, or if your soul abhors My judgments,
> so that you do not perform all My command-
> ments, but break My covenant, I also will do
> this to you: I will even appoint terror over you,
> wasting disease and fever which shall consume
> the eyes and cause sorrow of heart.

The Bible teaches that God will bring disease upon those who are disobedient to His laws and commands.

Deuteronomy 28:58-61 continues this obvious point of God causing disease because of disobedience:

> If you do not carefully observe all the words
> of this law that are written in this book, that
> you may fear this glorious and awesome name,
> THE LORD YOUR GOD, then the Lord will
> bring upon you and your descendants extraordi-
> nary plagues—great and prolonged plagues—
> and serious and prolonged sicknesses. Moreover
> He will bring back on you all the diseases of
> Egypt, of which you were afraid, and they shall
> cling to you. Also every sickness and every
> plague which is not written in the book of this
> law will the Lord bring upon you until you are
> destroyed.

The Bible is crystal clear: God will bring disease and plague upon those who do not obey His laws and commandments. No area of disobedience so clearly defies the character and holiness of God as sexual sin. No sins listed in God's law receive more condemnation or comment than those dealing with sexual behavior.

In Micah 6:13 God says:

Therefore I will also make you sick by striking you, by making you desolate because of your sins.

In the New Testament, we also find clear evidence for God's punishment of sinful behavior by bringing disease and death. 1 Corinthians 11:30-32 is an example:

For this reason many are weak and sick among you, and many sleep. For if we would judge ourselves, we would not be judged. But when we are judged, we are chastened by the Lord, that we may not be condemned with the world.

God brings sickness even to the believer—not punishment but chastening (discipline), whose purpose is to correct and restore.

1 John 5:16 speaks of sin that leads to death. Revelation 16 records God's judgment upon the world during a terrible period of time known as the Great Tribulation, a time when God will judge the world for its rebellion and sin. There is a list of seven plagues, the last ones to be brought upon planet Earth by God. In Revelation 16:2 we read of "a foul and loathsome sore" which is to come upon people. Verse 11 says that people "blasphemed the God of heaven because of their pains and their sores, and did not repent of their deeds."

Evidently people will one day be fully aware that their physical plagues are coming directly from the hand of God. But in spite of this knowledge, the plagues will apparently have little effect upon the people's sinful actions and rebellious hearts.

3. *The Bible teaches that sexual sin can result in physical disease.* To say that sexual immorality (sex outside of marriage) can result in physical disease is to provoke immediate hostility in many people. They seem to believe that such teaching eliminates compassion for those who suffer physically from such disease or that it ignores those who suffer innocently (babies in the womb, blood transfusion recipients, spouses, etc.). Yet some of the most compassionate and caring people in our society are those who believe that sexual sin can result in sexual disease. God hates sin but loves sinners.

Proverbs 5 speaks of a young man's involvement with an immoral woman (prostitute). Proverbs 5:11 speaks of the physical consequences:

> You mourn at last, when your flesh and
> your body are consumed.

1 Corinthians 6:18 says:

> Flee sexual immorality. Every sin that a
> man does is outside the body, but he who
> commits sexual immorality sins against his own
> body.

What other meaning can this verse have but that sexual sin leads to sexual disease? Most sin, according to the Bible, affects the soul (personality) but does not directly and immediately damage the physical body. This passage argues that *sexual* sin can cause immediate physical consequences to a person's body. What else but sexually transmitted disease?

Sex within marriage does not cause physical damage, but multiple sexual partners and encounters outside of marriage often lead to physical problems.

Romans 1:26,27 speaks of such physical consequences when it states:

> For this reason God gave them up to vile
> passions. For even their women exchanged the
> natural use for what is against nature. Likewise
> also the men, leaving the natural use of the
> woman, burned in their lust for one another,
> men with men committing what is shameful,

and receiving in themselves the penalty of their error which was due.

The discussion centers on homosexual behavior, with the text saying that such activity is "against nature." The text also states that continuing in these sinful practices results in a penalty which is deserved and which is received "in themselves." The strong implication is that there is a personal and physical consequence of such sinful behavior. It is difficult to escape the probability that this is a reference to sexual disease.

4. *The Bible teaches that physical disease is not always the result of personal sin in the life of the person afflicted.* Those who believe in biblical morality do *not* teach that *all* physical disease means that the person is guilty of specific sin. In John 9:1-3 we read of a man born blind:

> As Jesus passed by, He saw a man who was blind from birth. And His disciples asked Him, saying, "Rabbi, who sinned, this man or his parents, that he was born blind?" Jesus answered, "Neither this man nor his parents sinned, but that the works of God should be revealed in him."

Clearly this man's blindness was not the result of his own personal sin or that of his parents. 1 John 5:17 tells us that "all unrighteousness is sin, and there is sin not leading to death." Not all sinful behavior results in disease and/or death. *Some* of it does, but not all.

There are innocent victims of sexually transmitted disease, including babies in the wombs of mothers who are infected, as well as those who receive blood transfusions from infected blood donors.

5. *The Bible teaches that sexual sin and its results can be forgiven.* The good news of the gospel is that our sin can be forgiven through the death of Jesus Christ on the cross over 1900 years ago. His resurrection is the crowning proof of His victory of sin, death, and hell.

1 Corinthians 6:9,10 makes a list of sinful behavior that results in elimination from the kingdom of God. However, in verse 11 we read these encouraging words:

> And such were some of you. But you were washed, but you were sanctified, but you were justified in the name of the Lord Jesus and by the Spirit of our God.

2 Corinthians 5:17 adds:

> Therefore, if anyone is in Christ, he is a new creation; old things have passed away; behold, all things have become new.

You can become a brand-new person through the power of Jesus Christ. It is a spiritual rebirth that the Bible calls being "born again." Through faith in Jesus Christ for what He did when He died on the cross and rose again, thereby paying in full the price of your sins, you will live forever with the Lord.

It doesn't matter how much you have sinned and whatever physical consequences (including AIDS) you have experienced in the past or now experience in your body; there is complete forgiveness through Jesus Christ our Lord. The Bible speaks of *complete* cleansing, with your sins being washed away forever, as far as the east is from the west (Psalm 103:12). That is truly good news!

AIDS is a terrible disease, causing a horrible set of physical consequences and a terrifying death. Sonny was suffering the final stages of AIDS. His homosexual lifestyle, with its parade of multiple sex partners and experiences, was now costing him his health, happiness, and life. He was lonely, rejected by all his so-called friends.

In spite of the terminal condition he faced, he received a glimmer of hope as a hospital chaplain told him of God's love and forgiveness. Sonny heard the wonderful story of how he could one day receive a new body that was free from all sickness and death. Sonny accepted the good news that Jesus Christ died for his sins and that through His own resurrection guaranteed that Sonny would one day be resurrected with his own brand-new body.

A few weeks later Sonny died. At his funeral, the hospital chaplain told the audience that Sonny was with the Lord in heaven because of his decision to accept God's love and forgiveness. AIDS is a terrible plague, but it does not eliminate God's love from saving a person from sin, death, and hell.

WHAT SHOULD BE OUR RESPONSE?

Dealing with the problem of AIDS and sexual disease in our society is not easy. Emotions run high and hostilities abound. The medical profession is not unified or fully persuaded, because of a lack of information and a lack of time in terms of evaluation and research. AIDS remains a fatal disease, and the phenomenal rise in sexually transmitted diseases brings a multitude of solutions and a sense of panic. Something must be done... but what?

Consider carefully the following responses.

1) Do not tolerate or condone sexual immorality in your own lifestyle or in that of other people. Learn to confront it with love, compassion, understanding, and boldness.

2) Do not have sexual intercourse with any person outside of your marital spouse. This is the only position that involves "safe sex."

3) Do not use condoms; instead, practice abstinence.

4) Encourage and support all medical efforts that seek to find a cure for AIDS and other sexually transmitted diseases.

5) Be compassionate toward all who are sick and suffering regardless of the reasons that brought about their condition.

6) Understand that some people afflicted with sexual diseases are not guilty of sexual immorality. A spouse may be innocent, though infected by a spouse who was unfaithful. Some people may be suffering because of receiving blood from an infected donor.

7) Do not avoid the need of confession and repentance on the part of those guilty of sexual immorality and now suffering the consequences of their sinful behavior.

8) Be committed to the fact that a person's eternal destiny is more important than his or her physical condition.

9) Provide support, comfort, and help to family members of AIDS patients.

10) Support and encourage AIDS patients who suffer because of their sexual misconduct but who have sincerely confessed their sin and repented of it. Some will need special love and attention in order to face the final stages of their disease and the fact of approaching death.

11) In the care of children, do whatever is necessary to protect their health and to eliminate the possibility of contact with communicable diseases.

12) Do not support any effort that condones homosexual behavior or any other sexual sin. While the primary cause of AIDS appears to be multiple sex partners, the facts reveal that the majority of patients are former or present homosexuals.

13) Oppose any efforts by public schools that condone or encourage sexual behavior outside of marriage. Demand that sexual abstinence be taught for young people before marriage.

14) Oppose all attempts by television, movies, videos, and magazines to promote sexual immorality (premarital sex, rape, homosexuality, adultery, incest, prostitution, etc.) as something to be desired and experienced.

15) Understand that society's greatest need is spiritual change within the hearts of its citizens. A commitment to moral values is best achieved by a wholehearted commitment to Jesus Christ as Lord and Savior. The problem is not simply in the environment; it is in our own hearts!

8

The Death Penalty

In survey after survey, the moral issue that concerns the most Americans is that of a rising crime rate. Crime appears to be out of control, beyond the ability of our law enforcement agencies to stop it or even limit it.

On March 12, 1989, a major article on crime appeared in *USA Today* by staff writers Andrea Stone and Judy Keen. We have come to expect such articles because of our growing awareness that we live in a violent world. The article said:

> Murder rates in the nation's big cities are skyrocketing, and officials are blaming drugs, gangs and guns for the crisis.
>
> "It's an issue of the total breakdown of civilized standards and values," says Brooklyn, N.Y., District Attorney Elizabeth Holtzman.
>
> A sampling, as of mid-March (1989): In Washington D.C. homicides were up 65 percent over 1988; Philadelphia, up 57 percent; Columbus, Ohio, 57 percent; Chicago, 34 percent.

Quotations and statistics were given in the article to show that human life is no longer considered sacred.

> In San Jose, California, police chief Joseph McNamara says he's shocked by the "almost casual taking of human life. People lose their sense of right and wrong, and they don't have much to live for." Uniformed officers wear bulletproof vests when they're on duty.

> In Los Angeles, attacks on police are rising.
> Homicide detective John Zorn says it's no longer
> "the zip guns of 20 years ago." Now gangs are
> "heavily armed and have assault rifles."

On April 26, 1989, a newspaper article appeared in the Phoenix *Mesa Tribune*. It was written by Gordon Slovut of the *Minneapolis–St. Paul Star Tribune* and was entitled "Experts Seek to Discover Why Some Children Kill." The article points out that psychiatrists in a conference were attempting to discover why some children kill. The figures they were studying were based on 1986, in which 1400 murders were committed by juveniles. Over 300 of the child killers had murdered one or both of their parents.

Much to their surprise, these psychiatrists found that teenagers who kill during family conflicts usually have high IQ's and are frequently described by church and school officials as good children.

It was also pointed out in the article that children who killed lived in families where adults loosely threatened to kill others and where firearms and other lethal weapons were available.

CRIME AS A WAY OF LIFE

Crime is a way of life to millions of Americans. It's the only thing they know, and they have learned how to do it and get away with it at an early age. Many of our major cities are not safe for either tourists or residents. In the April 10, 1989, edition of *U.S. News and World Report*, an article was written by several staff writers on what are called "Dead Zones." This term refers to whole sections of urban America that are being written off as "anarchic badlands." Police officers fear to go into these zones. The article says that "this is Beirut, U.S.A." Consider these words from an exceptionally thorough article on crime and violence in our cities:

> Twenty years after nightly news programs
> spilled the carnage of Vietnam into our living

rooms, television and daily newspapers are bringing us live, another escalating war that we are losing. But this time the firefights are taking place on our own territory, within the hearts of our major cities. Every day there are haunting pictures of the dead being carried off in body bags, of angry, grieving families, of commandos breaking down doors of dilapidated buildings, of armed gangs and wounded children, of burned-out cars and the flash of gunfire.

From Gangland Los Angeles to Murder Capital Washington D.C., city after city now tolerates its own Beirut, a no-man's land where drug dealers shoot it out to command street corners, where children grow up under a reign of "narcoterror" and civil authority has basically broken down.

Slums, run-down housing projects and other bad areas have long been neglected by police and other city services, have always harbored drug dealers and users and have always been dangerous places to live or visit. But crack, a powerful and cheap derivative of cocaine, was the powder that ignited many of these neglected areas into actual war zones. Pharmacologists have proved that crack induces considerably more paranoia and violence than most other street drugs. Some 54 percent to 90 percent of those arrested for serious crimes in 11 big cities tested positive for drugs, according to a Justice Department study.

The article gives detail after detail describing the terrible breakdown of law and morality. One statement summarizes the condition of these "dead zones":

The most disturbing confirmation that cities now face combat conditions in some areas rather than traditional crime is the widely held view among law-enforcement professionals that police can no longer handle the problem alone.

A U.S. Attorney for Washington D.C., Jay Stephens, was quoted as saying:

> What we're seeing now is not aberrant
> criminal behavior but widespread disregard for
> the law, and lawlessness.

Jesus Christ said long ago in Matthew 24:12 that "lawlessness will abound" and that "the love of many will grow cold." The apostle Paul wrote in 2 Timothy 3:1-4 about these times when he said:

> Know this, that in the last days perilous
> times will come: For men will be lovers of
> themselves, lovers of money, boasters, proud,
> blasphemers, disobedient to parents, unthank-
> ful, unholy, unloving, unforgiving, slanderers,
> without self-control, brutal, despisers of good,
> traitors, headstrong, haughty, lovers of pleasure
> rather than lovers of God.

VIOLENCE ON THE SCREEN

As if the reality of what is happening on our streets is not enough, the television-and-movie industry has decided to bombard us with violence of all kinds, further stimulating impressionable minds and encouraging a violent society. So-called "good movies," those which come with G and PG ratings, can no longer be trusted. Many PG movies contain volumes of profanity, sexual acts and allurements, and much violence. The violence is not like that shown in movies of years ago, where a cowboy unloads his gun and his enemies fall over dead. No, today is different: We now show the gruesome details—how the bullet enters, how the body is maimed by the violence, and the more blood the better.

In a *Christianity Today* article of June 16, 1989, Roy M. Anker writes about the violence of Hollywood's movie industry. He describes a typical movie aimed at the teenage audience:

> A deranged and hideous man searches the
> night for victims, usually teens, whom he then

proceeds to hunt down, one by one, to mutilate
and kill. Always the camera's eye is the at-
tacker's as he spies and closes on the unsus-
pecting and then terrified women (male victims
do not merit this close cinematic attention). The
audience repeatedly enters his pursuit, slowly
approaching couples or girls caught in vulnerable moments, such as bathing or lovemaking.
Blades of all sorts—knives, axes, and chain
saws—slash and dismember. The camera then
pauses to appreciate the carnage pinned to walls
or splayed all over. The monster turns away only
when butchery finally satiates his thirst for pain
and murder. And there is no ending this phan-
tasm from hell. When the beast is finally killed,
the movie leaves ample suggestion that it has
not really died but will resurrect for even gorier
escapades of carnage.

Mr. Anker speaks truth when he says concerning the
impact of the movie industry upon our youth:

Of all the arts available to teens, movies
are perhaps the most potent. Film utilizes and
in many ways heightens several separate artistic
elements—story, picture, and melody—and thus
carries a kind of cumulative, synergistic clout.
The total psychic consequence can surpass the
sum of the ingredients. Ear and eye are fully
engaged; story, movement, sound—all combine
to provide a total experience that is brighter,
larger, and louder than life itself.
And the movies are becoming more and
more accessible. Hollywood thrives and prospers
by figuring out what will appeal to kids and,
given the lucrative enticements, is more than
eager to churn out film upon film.

This article presents the heart of our problem when it
analyzes the content of movies designed for children and youth
by saying:

Carnage, hurt, and dying now form the chief interest in almost all pictures made for children between the ages of 10 and 20. To be sure, violence has always been a strong component in American film, especially in Westerns and gangster pictures. Cowboys and private eyes did what they had to with their weapons, but behind the violence lay concern and care for justice and for the defenseless. And in those old movies, the hero's violence was always self-defensive and socially necessary, a way of keeping away a malignant, devouring chaos. The hero's code provided for force, but the motive was always protective, and its actual use was reluctant and restrained, only enough to subdue foes. The more realistic the violence became, the more likely the film was to depict its social and emotional consequences.

By any estimate, a sea of change has taken place in the climate of entertainment—not only in kid movies but in music and pro sports. Violence is now portrayed as pleasurable. Rambo kills with relish, again and again, pleasurably defusing his pent-up anger. Whether as a modern cop, Dirty Harry, or in the old West, as in Pale Rider and countless others, Clint Eastwood kills eagerly, promising his victims that their death will "make my day."

As violence is portrayed more positively and provoked with less and less motivation, as in the slasher films, it is ever more graphically depicted, both visually and verbally.

Slasher films exhibit every conceivable sort of mutilation and direct most of it toward women. With knives as phallic surrogates, predatory sexual assault forms the chief narrative interest: Who will get killed next and how, and how will the "monster" finally be defeated (they never die)? Body counts for a

single film range from 4 to 20. The level of bru-
tality astounds at times and is generally made
to seem fun. Since the monsters are always
male, sexual arousal mixes with the pleasure
of assault.

The article makes a tremendous point at its conclusion.
Mr. Anker, who is a member of the English department at
Northwestern College in Orange City, Iowa, writes:

Cultures that pander and gorge on violence
do not last long (the world before the Flood,
Sodom, Rome). God only knows our fate if we
further smother the Spirit's capacity for delight
in kindness and love. How long can we watch
and relish the cruel leer on the tormentor's face
without ourselves turning mean, just plain
mean?

An excellent question—how long can we continue to
watch the violence and not be affected by it?

IS THE DEATH PENALTY THE ANSWER?

This issue has been argued and debated for years. Is the
death penalty, capital punishment for capital crimes, a deterrent to crime? It is certainly a deterrent in the case of the one
who is put to death, since he obviously cannot commit another
crime!

But does the death penalty and its enforcement in our
society cause others to restrain themselves from committing
murder and serious crimes of violence against society?

Because the heart of a person is wicked, selfish, independent, arrogant, and violent, there is a sense in which the death
penalty or any law enforcement is helpless to control the individual's wicked desire or intent.

However, the Bible teaches that the law is intended for
the lawless person (1 Timothy 1:8-10). Law is necessary to
regulate society and to protect its citizens. The enactment of its
penalties is essential for the good of society as a whole. Without

law and its enforcement, anarchy is soon the result. Such a situation now exists in many cities of our country.

If we ask, "Does a person deserve to be put to death?" the question assumes that the right of the murderer to live is in a sense greater than the injustice he brought to the victim who died at his hands. Do any criminal acts at all deserve to be punished? Does a person who steals have a moral obligation to pay it back or pay a penalty for his refusal? Should children be punished if they have brought harm to other children deliberately? Does anyone deserve to pay for crimes he has committed?

Perhaps the question we should ask is whether the taking of another person's life (premeditated murder), an act which violates all standards of the sanctity and value of human life, can be punished justly *without* requiring the death penalty!

The problem behind our moral catastrophe is that we do not establish our moral values upon the authority of God and His revelation. The Bible is rarely consulted, even though our nation has historically considered biblical morality as foundational to our freedom and way of life.

The Bible argues that there is nothing wrong with God's laws as He gave them over 3000 years ago to Moses. The apostle Paul wrote in Romans 7:14, "We know that the law is spiritual." In verse 12 he said, "The law is holy, and the commandment holy and just and good." The law is a perfect reflection of the moral character and justice of the God who made us.

The law cannot save us or change our hearts. The law is not intended for a righteous man but for the ungodly, the person who seeks to do wrong.

The law was a protection for God's people. The law teaches that we have responsibilities to each other and that we must respect each other and one another's property. The law of Moses brought stability and a proper sense of freedom to God's people. That which makes a people "civilized" is very much a result of its laws and its respect for people's dignity and worth. The law of God protected the sanctity of human life and property.

Within that law, penalties were described. If a person did wrong, he had to pay the penalty. One of the penalties for serious crime was death itself. But what was it like before the law of Moses was ever given to people?

BEFORE THE LAW OF MOSES

The Bible teaches that death was a reality that society had to face even though there was at that time no direct revelation from God about what was right and wrong. Consider the following:

1. *Death was a consequence of Adam's sin.* Death came into the world because of Adam's sin. Romans 5:12-14 makes this clear:

> Through one man sin entered the world,
> and death through sin, and thus death spread
> to all men, because all sinned. For until the
> law sin was in the world, but sin is not im-
> puted when there is no law. Nevertheless death
> reigned from Adam to Moses, even over those
> who had not sinned according to the likeness of
> the transgression of Adam, who is a type of Him
> who was to come.

Like it or not, people died from Adam to Moses! You may not agree with the Bible's teaching on the subject, but the fact is that people died. Death was a reality.

The biblical story of creation tells us that God gave a command to Adam about the garden in which He placed him. In Genesis 2:16,17 we read:

> The Lord God commanded the man, saying,
> "Of every tree of the garden you may freely eat;
> but of the tree of the knowledge of good and evil
> you shall not eat, for in the day that you eat of
> it you shall surely die."

Death was to be a consequence of disobedience. In Genesis 3:17-19 God described the consequences to Adam for his sin of disobedience:

> Cursed is the ground for your sake; in toil
> you shall eat of it all the days of your life. Both

thorns and thistles it shall bring forth for you,
and you shall eat the herb of the field. In the
sweat of your face you shall eat bread till you
return to the ground, for out of it you were
taken; for dust you are, and to dust you shall
return.

Genesis 2:7 says that God formed man's body from the
dust of the ground. God now informs Adam that the result of his
disobedience is that his physical body will become dust again.
Job 34:14,15 adds this:

If he should set His heart on it, if He should
gather to Himself His Spirit and His breath, all
flesh would perish together, and man would
return to dust.

2. *Death was a curse in the lives of those who killed
someone.* The first murder occurred in the first family. Adam
and Eve had two sons initially, named Cain and Abel. The story
in Genesis 4:8-11 reveals how sin affects us all:

Cain talked with Abel his brother; and it
came to pass, when they were in the field, that
Cain rose against Abel his brother and killed
him. Then the Lord said to Cain, "Where is Abel
your brother?" And he said, "I do not know. Am
I my brother's keeper?" And He said, "What
have you done? The voice of your brother's blood
cries out to Me from the ground. So now you are
cursed from the earth, which has opened its
mouth to receive your brother's blood from your
hand."

Cain became concerned for his own life, fearing that
when his act would become known to his other brothers and
sisters, they would kill him. That fact alone suggests that our
deepest sense of justice argues for the death penalty in the case
of premeditated murder. God's answer to Cain was (Genesis
4:15):

Therefore, whoever kills Cain, vengeance
shall be taken on him sevenfold.

3. *Death was a condemnation by God upon the preflood
society.* The civilization before the flood (as recorded in the Book
of Genesis) could have easily numbered in the millions, due to
extended longevity and large families. But the entire culture
became dominated by sexual sin and violence, so God destroyed
it. Genesis 6:13 says:

God said to Noah, "The end of all flesh has
come before Me, for the earth is filled with
violence through them; and behold, I will
destroy them with the earth."

In verse 17 the Lord God repeats:

Behold, I Myself am bringing the flood of
waters on the earth, to destroy from under
heaven all flesh in which is the breath of life;
and everything that is on the earth shall die.

The death penalty was a condemnation by God Himself
upon a society that was corrupt and filled with violence. Before
any oral or written law came from the hand of God, the death
penalty was proclaimed by God as a just punishment for the
wickedness of mankind.

4. *Death was a command of God to Noah and his sons
after the flood.* One of the most significant biblical passages on
the death penalty is found in Genesis 9:6,7. Following the
destruction of the earth's population, the only people remaining
were Noah, his sons, and their wives—eight people on the
entire planet!

God's instruction is clear: Human life is to be honored and
protected, and the death penalty is to be used to uphold that
fact:

Whoever sheds man's blood, by man his
blood shall be shed; for in the image of God He
made man. And as for you, be fruitful and
multiply; bring forth abundantly in the earth
and multiply in it.

God's holiness and justice require payment for sin. The violence of planet Earth brought God's judgment, a worldwide flood that destroyed the first human civilization. Now, as life begins again, God makes if very clear that human life is to be protected, and that if anyone decides he has the right to take another person's life, his own life should be taken from him as a just penalty for his premeditated murderous act.

IN THE LAW OF MOSES

The law of Moses was not something that Moses himself invented or designed. The Bible teaches that God spoke these commandments directly to him. He was not to fill in the lines or give his own interpretation; he was to teach them to the people of God without additional comment. He was to leave nothing out and be careful to observe everything that God instructed him to do and say.

The famous Ten Commandments provided a simple but concise statement of God's righteousness and justice for His people to live together in harmony, peace, and safety. These commandments deal with our relationship to God as well as our relationship to each other. These commandments are the heart of God's law, the foundation, and everything else that God taught Moses and His people is built upon them. God gives many illustrations and clear statements as to how these commandments were to be applied in order to maintain the order and justice of society. Exodus 20:1-17 gives us these commandments:

1) *No other gods before Me.*

2) *No carved images or idolatry allowed.*

3) *Do not take the Lord's name in vain.*

4) *Keep the Sabbath day holy—no work to be done.*

5) *Honor your father and mother.*

6) *Do not commit murder.*

7) *Do not commit adultery.*

8) *Do not steal.*

9) *Do not bear false witness.*

10) *Do not covet what belongs to your neighbor.*

The sixth commandment of God in the law of Moses is "YOU SHALL NOT MURDER," or as it is worded in the King James Version of the Bible, "THOU SHALT NOT KILL." From that clear directive comes a multitude of applications, revealing that the death penalty was a just penalty for serious crimes against society. Consider the following:

1. *Murder*—Exodus 21:12-15.

> He who strikes a man so that he dies shall
> surely be put to death. But if he did not lie in
> wait, but God delivered him into his hand, then
> I will appoint for you a place where he may flee.
> But if a man acts with premeditation against
> his neighbor, to kill him with guile, you shall
> take him from My altar, that he may die.

Our American judicial system understands the difference between types of murder and refers to acts done in self-defense as manslaughter but not premeditated murder. The death of an individual can occur by accident, self-defense, carelessness, or premeditation. The latter deserves the death penalty.

Leviticus 24:17 says clearly, "Whoever kills any man shall surely be put to death." Such a statement always implies premeditation, an evil motive.

2. *Kidnapping*—Exodus 21:16.

> He who kidnaps a man and sells him, or
> if he is found in his hand, shall surely be put
> to death.

It is a terrible violation of the sanctity and dignity of human life to kidnap a person. The pornographic industry today kidnaps young children and young women, often enticing them with money, fame, and success but leading them to a life which destroys them. Kidnapping, according to God's sense of justice, demands the death penalty.

3. *Verbal abuse of parents*—Exodus 21:17.

He who curses his father or his mother
shall surely be put to death.

Today's society tolerates the rebellion of children, and
even encourages it in its television programming and its movie
industry. Children are disobedient to parents and think this is
their right. They have been led to believe that it is their fundamental right to do whatever they want to do, and that they do
not need to be obedient or submissive to their parents. But God
thinks differently; He says in Colossians 3:20 that children are
to obey their parents in all things.

If children verbally cursed or attacked their parents, the
death penalty was applied under the law of Moses. In Leviticus
20:9 God said:

Everyone who curses his father or his
mother shall surely be put to death. He has
cursed his father or his mother. His blood shall
be upon him.

Respect for the family is strong within the righteous law
and justice of God. Society is built upon the order and structure
of marriage, family, law, and government, all of which have a
chain of command.

4. *Death of a baby in the womb*—Exodus 21:22-25.

If men fight, and hurt a woman with child,
so that she gives birth prematurely, yet no
lasting harm follows, he shall surely be punished
accordingly as the woman's husband imposes
on him; and he shall pay as the judges determine. But if any lasting harm follows, then you
shall give life for life, eye for eye, tooth for tooth,
hand for hand, foot for foot, burn for burn,
wound for wound, stripe for stripe.

The principle of "life for life" clearly establishes that the
baby in the mother's womb is a real person and is entitled to the

full protection of the law. That is why the whole issue of abortion is so serious. Abortion, as a premeditated act to destroy the life of a baby in the womb, is an act of murder. The killing of a baby demanded the death penalty, for a baby in the womb had the full rights of any adult.

5. *Failure to control a wild animal*—Exodus 21:29.

> If the ox tended to thrust with its horn in
> times past, and it has been made known to his
> owner, and he has not kept it confined, so that
> it has killed a man or a woman, the ox shall be
> stoned and its owner also shall be put to death.

Our newspapers frequently record the attacks of wild animals upon people. In the Old Testament, if an owner of such an animal did not keep it confined, and it attacked and killed a person, then the animal and its owner were to be killed. Again, the wisdom of such a penalty can clearly be seen. This was not a judgment against an animal that had broken loose from its confinement, nor was it a judgment applied to an animal who attacked for the first time, with no evidence of any previous violence. The passage is clear: The owner knew the tendency of the animal to be violent but did not confine it.

6. *Sorcery*—Exodus 22:18.

Sorcery involves the occult, satanic rituals, astrological involvements, witchcraft, etc. The Bible's verdict about sorcery:

> You shall not permit a sorceress to live.

Leviticus 19:26 says:

> You shall not eat anything with the blood,
> nor shall you practice divination or soothsaying.

7. *Sex with animals*—Exodus 22:19.

> Whoever lies with a beast shall surely be
> put to death.

Leviticus 20:15,16 adds:

> If a man mates with a beast, he shall surely
> be put to death, and you shall kill the beast. If
> a woman approaches any beast and mates with
> it, you shall kill the woman and the beast. They
> shall surely be put to death. Their blood is upon
> them.

Pornographic interests portray people having sex with animals. School sex-education classes have mentioned such practices as though they are enjoyable for humans. God's verdict? Destroy the animal and the person! The death penalty is a just punishment for such abominable activity.

8. *Idolatry*—Exodus 22:20.

> He who sacrifices to any god except to the
> Lord only, he shall be utterly destroyed.

The first commandment of the Ten Commandments tells us that no other gods are to be put before the Lord, and the second commandment warns against making carved images and worshiping them. Idolatry is always condemned in the Bible in no uncertain terms.

Consider this passage in Deuteronomy 17:1-5:

> You shall not sacrifice to the Lord your God
> a bull or sheep which has any blemish or defect,
> for that is an abomination to the Lord your God.
> If there is found among you, within any of your
> gates which the Lord your God gives you, a man
> or a woman who has been wicked in the sight
> of the Lord your God, in transgressing His
> covenant, who has gone and served other gods
> and worshiped them, either the sun or moon
> or any of the host of heaven, which I have not
> commanded, and it is told you, and you hear of
> it, then you shall inquire diligently. And if it
> is indeed true and certain that such an abomi-
> nation has been committed in Israel, then you
> shall bring out to your gates that man or woman

who has committed that wicked thing, and shall
stone to death that man or woman with stones.

This law against idolatry applied to the people of God, the
children of Israel. It gives us an understanding of God's holiness
and righteous character. Idolatry violates God's original purpose in creation, since all things (including humanity) are to
worship, praise, honor, and glorify Him.

9. *Afflicting widows and orphans*—Exodus 22:22-24.

You shall not afflict any widow or fatherless
child. If you afflict them in any way, and they
cry at all to Me, I will surely hear their cry; and
My wrath will become hot, and I will kill you
with the sword; your wives shall be widows, and
your children fatherless.

God's protection of human life, property, and worth is
refreshing to see in a world where human life is so cheap and
worthless to people. The mistreatment of widows and orphans
is well-known. Instead of providing help and care for them,
people seek ways to rob them and take from them whatever
dignity and self-respect they may have left.

I have personally heard tragic stories from elderly widows
who have been cheated and lied to, and whose funds were stolen
from them under the guise of making them financially more
prosperous and providing additional security.

10. *Adultery*—Leviticus 20:10.

The man who commits adultery with
another man's wife, he who commits adultery
with his neighbor's wife, the adulterer and the
adulteress, shall surely be put to death.

Adultery is an attack upon marriage and the family. It is
a self-gratifying, often violent attempt to satisfy one's own
sexual desires apart from the circle of accountability, trust, and
respect which only marital fidelity and commitment can provide. God's verdict for this sin: the death penalty.

Deuteronomy 22:22 adds:

> If a man is found lying with a woman
> married to a husband, then both of them shall
> die, both the man that lay with the woman, and
> the woman; so you shall put away the evil
> person from Israel.

11. *Incest*—Leviticus 20:11,12,14.

> The man who lies with his father's wife has
> uncovered his father's nakedness; both of them
> shall surely be put to death. Their blood shall be
> upon them. If a man lies with his daughter-in-
> law, both of them shall surely be put to death.
> They have committed perversion. Their blood
> shall be upon them.
> If a man marries a woman and her mother,
> it is wickedness. They shall be burned with fire,
> both he and they, that there may be no wicked-
> ness among you.

Incest is a national tragedy today. In addition to thousands of reported incidents, many occurrences remain unknown,
primarily due to fathers' threats and the fear of daughters in
reporting their fathers' wicked advances toward them. The
total disdain which incest has for the sanctity of a person's life
and sexual privacy brings no other just penalty than death
itself. Many girls live in fear and suffer terrible future consequences to their emotional and sometimes physical health
because of the incestuous relationship which their fathers
imposed upon them while they were growing up. Helpless,
vulnerable, and naive, many daughters have endured and even
expected such relationships from their fathers, not knowing
that these sexual advances were an abomination to God and
proof of the father's lack of love and concern for the well-being of
his child.

12. *Homosexuality*—Leviticus 20:13.

> If a man lies with a male as he lies with
> a woman, both of them have committed an

abomination. They shall surely be put to death.
Their blood shall be upon them.

Such passages bring tremendous hostility from gay rights
groups and activists, and no wonder—the penalty that is deserved from homosexual behavior is death, the same penalty
required when adultery or incest is committed.

Our laws were built upon the ethical and moral codes of
the Mosaic law, and any lawyer or judge who knows his or her
legal history knows that to be fact. But today we have removed
ourselves so far from biblical morality that we now tolerate,
condone, and even approve of lifestyles which God says in His
Word deserve the death penalty!

13. *Premarital sex and prostitution by a priest's daughter*—Leviticus 21:9.

The daughter of any priest, if she profanes
herself by playing the harlot, profanes her
father. She shall be burned with fire.

In general terms, prostitution or premarital sex was
always considered to be a disgraceful thing to any family, and
especially to the reputation and role of a father. For example, in
Deuteronomy 22:13-21 we have the example of a man who, after
marrying, accuses his wife of shameful or immoral conduct. He
argues that she was not a virgin. The evidence is then presented, and if it is true, the woman is to be stoned to death,
according to Deuteronomy 22:21:

Then they shall bring out the young woman
to the door of her father's house, and the men
of her city shall stone her to death with stones,
because she has done a disgraceful thing in
Israel, to play the harlot in her father's house;
so you shall put away the evil person from
among you.

Premarital sex or prostitution was considered to be worthy of the death penalty. It was especially detrimental to the
character and responsibility of the priest, who was God's representative to bring the needs of the people to God and to take
God's directives to His people.

There is a wholesale acceptance of premarital sex in today's society that is far removed from traditional and moral values that used to permeate our culture. We encourage our young people to experiment and discover for themselves the meaning and pleasure of sex long before they are ready to be committed in marriage.

Studies reveal that our current population under the age of 40 frowns upon extramarital affairs but looks with favor upon premarital sexual involvements. Sex between singles is acceptable, while sex with a married person is not. God has no such double standards; sexual intercourse belongs only in marriage.

14. *Rape*—Deuteronomy 22:23-29.

These verses contain three examples of sex outside of marriage. The first deals with a virgin who is engaged, and is attacked within the city but does not cry out for help. The second example happens in the country, away from crowds and potential help; the woman is engaged, and the man rapes her. The third example is of a man who rapes a girl who is not engaged. The consequences vary in each illustration and demonstrate the righteous and just ways of God.

Case 1

If a young woman who is a virgin is betrothed [engaged] to a husband, and a man finds her in the city and lies with her, then you shall bring them both out to the gate of that city, and you shall stone them to death with stones, the young woman because she did not cry out in the city, and the man because he humbled his neighbor's wife; so you shall put away the evil person from among you.

The penalty for both the man and the woman is death. The woman does not cry out for help, and this fact alone reveals that her commitment to her fiancé is not what it should be.

Case 2

But if a man finds a betrothed young woman in the countryside, and the man forces

her and lies with her, then only the man who
lay with her shall die. But you shall do nothing
to the young woman; there is in the young
woman no sin worthy of death, for just as when
a man rises against his neighbor and kills him,
even so is this matter; for he found her in the
countryside, and the betrothed young woman
cried out, but there was no one to save her.

How interesting to observe God's righteousness concerning this experience of rape! He considers the rape the same kind of attack as murder; both deserve the death penalty.

It is also clear that God does not hold a woman accountable for seducing or attracting a man to attack her sexually if in fact the woman cried out for help. It is obviously a forcible rape, one in which the woman was not a willing participant.

It is tragic to see how many women who are raped are made to feel guilty for being an attractive woman, as though their appearance is to blame for the man's sexual aggression! The Bible teaches that a person is accountable for whatever sin he or she chooses to commit. James 1:13-15 teaches that every person is led away of his own lust. We cannot blame other people or the environment; the problem lies within each of us who sins.

Case 3

If a man finds a young woman who is a
virgin, who is not betrothed, and he seizes her
and lies with her, and they are found out, then
the man who lay with her shall give to the
young woman's father fifty shekels of silver, and
she shall be his wife because he has humbled
her; he shall not be permitted to divorce her all
his days.

It is clear that the consequences are different when the young woman is not engaged, since God always protects the sanctity of marriage. This woman is available, not tied down by commitment to another man. The penalty for this young man's sexual aggression is for him to now assume his responsibility toward her as a husband. To show that his actions were not acceptable or normal in terms of courtship, he must pay a heavy fine to the woman's father, and he will never be allowed to divorce his wife even if he thinks he has righteous grounds for doing so.

15. *Blasphemy*—Leviticus 24:15,16.

> You shall speak to the children of Israel, saying: "Whoever curses his God shall bear his sin. And whoever blasphemes the name of the Lord shall surely be put to death, and all the congregation shall certainly stone him, the stranger as well as him who is born in the land. When he blasphemes the name of the Lord, he shall be put to death.

Blasphemy is not the mere use of profanity or cursing; blasphemy is a deliberate rejection of the existence and authority of God, a denial of His divine character and holiness, and a rebellion against His laws and commandments. It is the attitude of an atheist.

When Jesus Christ said that one sin would never be forgiven He called it "the blasphemy against the Spirit" (Matthew 12:31,32). In the context of that passage, a demon-possessed man who was blind and deaf was healed by Jesus Christ. The Pharisees accused Jesus of performing this miracle by the power of Satan, not God. Their rejection of His messiahship and His divine ability to cast out demons was a blatant rebellion and rejection for which there would be no forgiveness. Any person who continues to deny the deity and power of Jesus Christ, to reject the teaching that it is the power of the Holy Spirit through Him that resulted in His miracles, and who argues that Christ must be in league with the devil to do what He does has no hope of forgiveness. That person is rejecting the only One who can save!

When Jesus Christ was on trial in front of the Jewish Sanhedrin and was asked by the high priest if He was the Messiah, the Son of God, Jesus answered: "It is as you said." The high priest then tore his clothes and blurted out the charge of blasphemy. The council responded that Jesus was deserving of death (Matthew 26:63-68). The reason? Blasphemy required the death penalty under the law of Moses.

Whenever Jesus indicated His equality with the heavenly Father, the Jews were ready to stone Him for blasphemy (cf. John 5:18; 10:28-31).

The penalty of death was attached to at least 15 different crimes among the children of Israel. However, there was a balance in this judicial system: Each offense required witnesses. Consider Deuteronomy 17:6,7:

> Whoever is worthy of death shall be put
> to death on the testimony of two or three
> witnesses, but he shall not be put to death on
> the testimony of one witness. The hands of the
> witnesses shall be the first against him to put
> him to death, and afterward the hands of all the
> people. So you shall put away the evil person
> from among you.

Deuteronomy 19:15 adds this:

> One witness shall not rise against a man
> concerning any iniquity or any sin that he
> commits; by the mouth of two or three witnesses
> the matter shall be established.

Israel had judges who would rule on all cases, and trials were conducted on the basis of proper evidence. Our entire judicial system, as tedious and ineffective as it seems at times, is based on the moral values and specific directives of biblical morality.

THE TEACHING OF JESUS CHRIST

Jesus Christ did not come to destroy the law; He came to fulfill it (Matthew 5:17). In His famous Sermon on the Mount He described the kind of righteousness that is needed to get into the kingdom of heaven. It was not the external performance of the scribes and Pharisees, but a righteousness that exceeded their concepts and dealt with the heart more than outward appearance.

In dealing with the law's teaching and His own, Jesus made some incredible statements about the moral intent of the

Mosaic law, especially as it relates to the death penalty. In
Matthew 5:21-25 we read:

> You have heard that it was said to those
> of old, "You shall not murder," and whoever
> murders will be in danger of the judgment. But
> I say to you that whoever is angry with his
> brother without a cause shall be in danger of
> the judgment. And whoever says to his brother,
> "Raca!" shall be in danger of the council. But
> whoever says, "You fool!" shall be in danger of
> hell fire. Therefore if you bring your gift to the
> altar, and there remember that your brother has
> something against you, leave your gift there
> before the altar, and go your way. First be
> reconciled to your brother, and then come and
> offer your gift. Agree with your adversary
> quickly, while you are on the way with him, lest
> your adversary deliver you to the judge, the
> judge hand you over to the officer, and you are
> thrown into prison.

The judgment that one faced for murder was the death
penalty. Jesus did not deny that fact or try to change the law's
demands. What He did was point out the root problem—anger.
You might think that anger does not deserve the severity of the
law's penalty for murder, but your murderous heart does not
escape the notice of God, and the final judgment by Him will
reveal it. The real danger is not the judgment of the "council"
but the terrifying reality of "hell fire."

Balanced with this teaching, consider the incident in
John 8:2-11, where a woman was caught in the act of adultery, a
sin which the Mosaic law said should be punished by death, and
in particular by stoning. Notice that Jesus never denied that
the woman was guilty or that she deserved to be punished.
What He said after writing something in the dirt with His
finger was, "He who is without sin among you, let him throw a
stone at her first." After they all departed, sensing that they
were not free of guilt (since it is entirely possible that they were
guilty of having sex with her in the past!), Jesus said to the

woman: "Woman, where are those accusers of yours? Has no one condemned you?" She answered, "No one, Lord." He then responded, "Neither do I condemn you; go and sin no more." Jesus did not condone her adultery, but rather said, "Sin no more." Here is a sense of justice mingled with mercy. The forgiveness of our Lord Jesus Christ is the heart of the good news of the gospel!

THE TEACHING OF THE APOSTLE PAUL

In Romans 1:32 the apostle Paul makes it clear that those who practice the sinful lifestyles that are condemned in God's law are "worthy of death." In Romans 13:1-4 he presents his case for government and its right to execute the penalties of the law.

> Let every soul be subject to the governing
> authorities. For there is no authority except
> from God, and the authorities that exist are
> appointed by God. Therefore whoever resists the
> authority resists the ordinance of God, and those
> who resist will bring judgment on themselves.
> For rulers are not a terror to good works, but to
> evil. Do you want to be unafraid of the au-
> thority? Do what is good, and you will have
> praise from the same. For he is God's minister
> to you for good. But if you do evil, be afraid; for
> he does not bear the sword in vain; for he is
> God's minister, an avenger to execute wrath on
> him who practices evil.

Government and its right to exercise authority is an institution established by God. Its commands, laws, ordinances, and policies are intended to curb the wicked. Its execution of penalties for breaking the law are commended by God, and we are warned not to resist their authority or their laws.

Verse 4 clearly says that the ruler "does not bear the sword in vain." The death penalty is intended by that remark, and it is clear that both before the law of Moses (Genesis 9:5,6) as well as in New Testament times (Romans 13:4) the death penalty was a moral response to certain capital crimes.

While some of the laws requiring the death penalty under the law of Moses might receive different treatment for secular nations of the world than for the children of Israel, the clear condemnation of premeditated murder in Genesis 9:6, written long before the law of Moses was ever given, argues for the validity of the death penalty in cases of premeditated murder that are committed today. The death penalty serves as a powerful reminder to all in our society that human life is sacred and cannot be violated without suffering the most severe penalty of all—death.

Romans 6:14 states that we as believers are not under the Mosaic law but under grace. The law does not save us, nor can it help us grow in Christ (Romans 3:28; 8:1-4; Galatians 3:1-3). The law was made for the ungodly, not the righteous (1 Timothy 1:9,10). But because we are not under the Mosaic law does not mean that the law serves no purpose for secular society. The basic principles of the law must be enforced in order for a just and stable society to exist, for criminals to be punished, and for the lives and properties of the innocent to be protected.

WHAT SHOULD BE OUR RESPONSE?

Violent crime is destroying our cities and threatening our civilization; it is a moral disaster! Law enforcement is well aware of the critical situation that exists. Criminals are more violent than ever before and are better equipped to attack, destroy, steal, threaten, and control. Our courts continue to release the criminal and protect his so-called "rights" while the victims remain in fear and frustration of the failure of our legal system and law enforcement personnel to control the spread of violence and crime in our society.

A step in the right direction is to reestablish moral values. A step in the right direction is to require the death penalty for premeditated murder. A step in the right direction is to enforce the laws we already have without compromise or fear of reprisal. A step in the right direction is to spend more money and time protecting the innocent and convicting the guilty. A step in the right direction is to demand stricter laws and stiffer penalties for those crimes that are clearly defined and described in the Bible.

What specifically can we do as individuals?

1) Respect the authorities that exist and honor their position and responsibilities.

2) Be willing to testify and speak up whenever you are an eyewitness of a criminal act.

3) Vote for judges and politicians who stand for law and order and believe in the death penalty as a proper punishment for premeditated murder.

4) Encourage law enforcement personnel and express thanks to them for risking their lives to protect our citizens.

5) Urge our public schools and institutions to display and promote the Ten Commandments as a moral guideline to our children, youth, and adults of what true morality and values are to be.

6) Understand that God's laws which require the death penalty for certain sinful actions are not foolish or unreasonable, but rather express the righteous, holy, and just character of God Himself.

7) Realize that the law cannot save or redeem anyone, but can only punish evildoers and protect the life and property of our citizens. It simply establishes what is right and wrong within society.

8) Believe that Jesus Christ paid the penalty of the law when He died on the cross, taking our place. Our hope of salvation, forgiveness, and a new life is not found in the law but in faith in the death and resurrection of Jesus Christ our Lord and Savior.

♦ 9 ♦

Alcoholism and Drug Abuse

Several years ago an article appeared in *Christianity Today* (August 5, 1983) in which Barbara Thompson, a freelance writer from New York, interviewed Dr. Anderson Spickard, Jr., Director of General Internal Medicine and also a professor of medicine at Vanderbilt University Medical Center. Dr. Spickard is a fellow of the American College of Physicians and a frequent speaker at medical schools on the subject of alcoholism.

The article begins with these challenging words:

> Heavy drinking has become almost as American as Super Bowl Sunday. The latest Gallup Poll on American drinking habits only confirms the suspicion that something is radically amiss: 81 percent of adults said they considered alcoholism to be a major national problem, and one out of three families reported that alcohol had caused trouble in their families.

Alcoholism, according to this article, is the third-largest health problem in the United States today, and is said to damage directly the lives of one out of every four or five Americans.

COMPOUNDING THE CRISIS

In terms of moral values, alcoholism has contributed to our present moral crisis. Dr. Spickard comments in this article:

Alcohol is a mood-altering drug that directly affects the part of our brain that controls inhibitions. We all have built-in prohibitions against certain kinds of behavior. When these restraints are lowered through the use of alcohol, we find it much easier to violate our own moral standards.

In the *American Family Journal* of August 1989, Dr. Spickard is quoted from his book *Dying for a Drink*:

Every 22 minutes another life is lost to a drunk driver. The cost to our society is estimated at fifty billion per year in the United States. Beyond these staggering statistics lie the ruined and priceless lives of millions of men, women and children.

In a recent Gallup Poll it was reported that one out of every three persons said that alcohol had caused trouble in his or her family. Heavy drinking is involved in 60 percent of all violent crimes, 30 percent of all suicides, and 80 percent of all fire and drowning accidents.

The suicide rate of alcoholics is *30 times* that of the general population!

Thousands of people are killed and millions injured each year in automobile accidents that are caused by drinking drivers. There are over 15 million known alcoholics in this country, and the number is increasing by several thousand each day. Surveys of divorce cases in our courts reveal that 50 to 60 percent of divorced persons had drinking problems as contributing causes to their marital problems.

While visiting the city of Canton, Ohio, my wife and I were confronted with a public school teacher of fourth-grade children who gave us these alarming statistics: One out of four children lives with an alcoholic, and one out of five already drinks alcoholic beverages, encouraged or allowed by the parents. By the sixth grade, one out of seven children in this public school has become addicted to either alcoholism or drug abuse!

During the prohibition era (1919-1933), crime decreased 54 percent and the death rate due to alcoholism decreased 43 percent. All but one of the 98 Keeley Alcoholics Clinics were closed for lack of patients, and all 60 of the Neil Cure Clinics closed for lack of patients afflicted with alcoholism! After the repeal of prohibition laws, drunkenness increased more than 350 percent, and over 50 percent of all fatal traffic accidents are alcohol-related. The story of the acceleration of crime affected by alcohol and drug abuse is tragically known by all of us.

DEATH ON THE HIGHWAY

An article appeared in the April 7, 1989, *USA Today* concerning the growing problem of alcoholism and its obvious connection to traffic fatalities and accidents. The article states that one out of every ten drivers on the road is drunk! Drinking drivers kill 24,000 people each year, and have been doing that for the past five years. They kill more young people than any other cause.

The article makes this clear statement about alcohol:

Alcohol is a depressant, like anesthesia. It makes it harder to make the decisions that driving demands. It slows reactions. It causes drowsiness, loss of alertness and concentration. It reduces and blurs vision.

Rachel Kelly writes in this *USA Today* article:

Alcohol is a drug, a sedative, a depressant. It's a mood-altering drug that slows down people's reflexes. Alcohol is a narcotic, a poison. Anyone who's consumed enough to be impaired is one who has overdosed on that drug.

She continues:

It's not the falling-down drunk who's killing people on the highways. It's the social drinker, the person who's been out to lunch or who's

returning from a ball game, has had a couple
of beers and gets in the car to drive.

It's the social drinker—the person who can
afford both to drink and to drive. It's not the
poverty-stricken person in the ghetto who's
causing this carnage. It's the social drinker, the
person who has money. It's the cocktail crowd.
It's the kid coming from a prom or a graduation
party.

She draws some hard conclusions:

But the real answer lies in educating our
kids not to drink—not to even start, total
abstinence.

Everybody is crying about the carnage on
the highways, but thousands of parents stand
by and let kids drink themselves to death. We
permit our young people to be brainwashed by
alcohol advertising, with its constant insinuation
that drinking, having fun and being athletic are
synonymous.

We've got to get back to our old-fashioned
morals—and parents have got to stop blaming
everybody else, especially teachers. It's parents'
position to teach children right and wrong—
including what's wrong about alcohol.

THE ALCOHOL PROMOTERS

Our problem is compounded by the music and media
industries. Their constant promotion of the value of alcohol and
drugs is adding to our moral catastrophe. On the album entitled
"Licensed to Kill" by the Beastie Boys (CBS Records, 1986), one
of the numbers, entitled "Hold It Now, Hit It," contains the
following words:

Well, I'm cruisin', I'm bruisin', I'm never
losin'. I'm in my car, I'm going far, and dust is

what I'm usin'. Head poppin', body rockin', doing
the do. Beer drinkin', breath stinkin', sniffin'
glue. I'll take no slack 'cause I got the knack.
I'm never dustin' out 'cause I trust that crack.

Worldwide, the liquor industry spends two billion dollars
annually to advertise alcoholic beverages. In the United States,
the sports and entertainment figures continue to tell television
viewers that drinking is the key to success, happiness, and the
good life. A recent study of the top television shows revealed
that an average of more than eight alcoholic drinks are taken
per television hour. No wonder our society has accepted and
tolerated indulgence in alcoholic beverages—we have been continually programmed to think and act that way!

In an article that appeared in the May 1989 issue of
Moody Monthly magazine, Robert Fischer writes:

> The general public has long accepted the
> proposition that small amounts of alcohol are
> not harmful to the user. Recent research, how-
> ever, indicates that this is not the case at all.
>
> For example, studies have shown that a
> blood-alcohol level of only 0.035 percent (most
> states define intoxication at 0.10 percent), which
> can be reached with only one drink, results in
> a decline in visual acuity and in the execution
> of simple and complex muscular tasks. Small
> amounts of alcohol affect hand-eye coordination
> more than mental and verbal activity. this
> means that a person may be unaware of im-
> paired performance, a situation that often
> results in tragedy on the road.
>
> Recent statistical studies have established
> a direct relationship between moderate use of
> alcohol and breast cancer. In one study, con-
> sumption of only two-thirds of a can of beer per
> week increased the risk by 40 percent, three
> drinks per week by 50 percent, and more than
> three drinks per week by 60 percent.

Commenting on the shift in moral values as it relates to

the use of alcoholic beverages, a book by James D. Hunter entitled *Evangelicalism: The Coming Generation* describes a survey of students in nine evangelical colleges:

> In 1951, 98 percent believed that drinking alcohol was wrong. In 1961, the figure for students then in college had dropped to 78 percent, and in 1982, it was 17 percent.

Significant changes have occurred in the past 40 years in this country with regard to the consumption of alcoholic beverages!

WHAT ABOUT DRUG ABUSE?

The drug-abuse problem has become a national tragedy that has far-reaching consequences upon the young people of our country. The violence and crime that the drug business brings to our culture is frightening, and its influence over political officials and law-enforcement personnel is alarming.

In the May/June 1989 issue of the *Psychiatric, Mental Health and Behavioral Medicine News Update*, a survey was reported by the *American Journal of Psychiatry*. A sampling of a nationwide group of 589 senior medical students found that 36 percent reported using cocaine at some time during their lives, and 17 percent during the past year, and 6 percent in the past month!

On May 7, 1989, the *Los Angeles Times* magazine put on its front cover a picture of guns and cocaine and entitled this issue "Losing the Cocaine War." The magazine describes in detail the connection between Colombia, the center of drug traffic for much of the world, and the rise of drug sales in Los Angeles. *USA Today* has stated that Los Angeles is the new drug capital of the United States, surpassing Miami, Florida. In 1988 more drug seizures were made in Los Angeles than in any other U.S. city. The cash surplus in the Federal Reserve Bank's Los Angeles branch jumped 23 times since 1985 to an astounding 3.8 billion dollars! U.S. Attorney Robert Bonner states that "staggering amounts of drug money are being funneled into Los Angeles for laundering." One group "laundered" 17 million dollars a week!

Street gangs, with 80,000 members, distribute cocaine and crack to 44 cities out of the Los Angeles area alone.

California seizures of cocaine have risen dramatically. In 1986, 1845 pounds of cocaine were confiscated; in 1988, 19,799 pounds of this deadly drug were captured. That is an increase of 973 percent in two years!

Washington D.C., our nation's capital, is another city infested with serious drug problems. In 1988 there were 371 murders, seven times the national average. The city has logged 46,000 drug arrests in the past two years.

William Bennett, the man in charge of doing something about our national drug problem, stated in a *USA Today* article last year (as well as in other newspapers) that the drug crisis is a national problem. The smuggling of drugs into the United States comes from the Bahamas, Haiti, Bolivia, Paraguay, Mexico, Honduras, and of course Colombia, a country controlled by the drug lords.

At a conference in Washington D.C. for mayors of our major cities who are confronted with drug problems that seem out of control, the answers were few and far between. Peter Reuter, an Australian researcher for the RAND Corporation, whose work is highly regarded by specialists on all sides of the narcotics field, told the mayors:

> At the moment, the conventional wisdom
> is that nothing works. It's a view that comes
> out of despair.

His report shows that the much-publicized patrolling of borders and policing of streets during the past eight years have failed to damage the drug trade in any significant way. Thomas C. Kelly, the deputy administrator of the federal government's Drug Enforcement Administration, told the mayors of American cities that "law enforcement is not the answer to our problem."

Frequently articles appear even in the *Wall Street Journal* concerning our national drug problem. Staff reporter Ronald G. Shafer wrote: "In America's nightmare of drugs, the most tragic victims are our children."

Lee Dogoloff, executive director of the American Council for Drug Education says, "Drug and alcohol use is the thing most likely to wrest children from their parents before they reach adulthood."

In a *USA Today* article by Dan Sperling in 1989, it was reported that overall drug use in the United States had dropped recently, but that cocaine addiction is increasing. Apparently the campaign to "say no to drugs" is paying off somewhat in terms of the *casual* use of drugs, but chronic and addictive cocaine use is still rising.

WHAT IS CRACK?

Crack is a popular drug whose impact is epidemic in America. Authorities and experts are overwhelmed with its awesome power to deceive our young people and destroy their lives. It is an inexpensive but highly potent and highly addictive form of cocaine. Pushers sell pellet-size "rocks" in tiny plastic vials for as little as ten dollars. Smoked rather than snorted, a single hit of crack provides an intense, wrenching rush in a matter of seconds. It goes straight to your head with great speed and sometimes feels like the top of your head is going to blow off!

Crack can be sold in tiny chips that give the user a 5- to 20-minute high. (When smoked, cocaine molecules reach the brain in less than ten seconds.) The high is usually followed by crushing depression, and the cycle of ups and downs reinforces the craving. Crack addicts may need another hit within minutes, and this addictive drug can become extremely habit-forming and expensive because of the need for so many hits. Dr. Arnold Washton, director of research for the National Cocaine Hotline, says: "In May 1985 I had never heard of crack. Today we get 700 to 900 calls a day from people having problems with the drug. The growth in the last several months is alarming."

Cocaine is a stimulant, and crack addicts are likely to be paranoid and highly active. The connection of crack with teenage crime is well-documented.

ALCOHOL AND DRUG ABUSE

While the message is frequently given that a person should not mix alcohol and drugs, the truth is that the two are very often used together. The number of people who use both is too great for us to ignore.

Dr. Andrew C. Ivy, former head of the Clinical Science Department of the University of Illinois, has made this statement about alcohol:

> Beverage alcohol is an intoxicating, hypnotic analgesic, an anesthetic narcotic, poisonous and potentially habit-forming, craving-producing or addiction-producing drug or chemical.

Apparently, from a number of sources that we have consulted, it is the ethyl alcohol in beer, whiskey, and other liquors that causes intoxication and addiction. Dr. Robert Flemming of the World Health Organization came to some interesting conclusions in a 56-page report:

> Most alcoholics are not psychiatric cases, but normal people.

> First, nobody is immune to alcoholism, and second, total abstinence is the only solution.

> Alcohol is a poison to the nervous system. The solubility of alcohol in water and fat enables it to invade the nerve cell. A person may become a chronic alcoholic without ever having shown symptoms of drunkenness.

In the book *Under the Influence*, by Dr. James R. Milam and Katherine Ketcham (Bantam Books, 1981, page 32), we read the following:

> The alcoholic starts drinking the same ways and for the same reasons the nonalcoholic starts drinking. He drinks to gain the effects of alcohol—to feel euphoric, stimulated, relaxed, or intoxicated. Sometimes he drinks to ease his frustrations; other times he drinks to put himself in a good mood. If he is tense, he may drink more than usual in an effort to unwind and get his mind off his troubles; if shy, he may drink to gain confidence; if extroverted, he may drink because he likes the company of other drinkers.

The alcoholic, like the nonalcoholic, is influenced in the way he drinks, where he drinks, how much, and how often he drinks by numerous psychological, social, or cultural factors. He may start drinking to impress his girlfriend, to prove he is not afraid of his parents' disapproval, or because he is taunted into it by his friends. He may drink regularly because alcohol makes him laugh and forget his troubles or because he feels self-assured after a few drinks. If his wife has a cocktail every night, he may drink to keep her company. If his coworkers are heavy drinkers, he may learn to drink heavily.

Alcohol often encourages young people to try drugs, because the "good feelings" that they are seeking in life are promised to them by the drug-pushers or their friends who have already experienced the "benefits" of taking drugs. The same feelings that are brought on by alcoholic beverages are also produced by various drugs. Frequently young people are told that the drugs are harmless. They are given the impression that it is an older generation and a less knowledgeable society that tries to stop people from taking drugs.

Peer-group friends are the major pressure upon young people in taking alcoholic beverages and using drugs. The "try it, you'll like it" philosophy is used along with promises that there are no serious side effects.

Many young people get involved in alcohol and drugs through events and occasions that are described as "party time." The phrase "let's party" can mean different things to different people, but its primary implication deals with alcohol, drugs, and sex. It promises everything—the fun and good times, the release of frustrations and inhibitions which parental authority has imposed, and of course the immediate acceptance and friendship of other young people who believe that the only way to be "cool" or "in" is to party.

The real tragedy behind all this alcohol and drug abuse is that parents are saying one thing to their kids and practicing another themselves. In the book *Children of Alcoholism: A*

Survivor's Manual, by Judith S. Seixas and Geraldine Youcha (Harper and Row, 1985), we read in the Introduction:

> There are at least 22 million adults in this country who have lived with an alcoholic parent. Most have survived the ordeal and are now out on their own. Nearly all of them, however, live with scars, psychic or physical, as a consequence of parental alcoholism. The quality of their lives ranges from devastation and misery to relative fulfillment and happiness.
>
> Why does alcoholism continue to be such a monumental problem in our culture? There are many reasons. Most of us are swamped daily, through the media, with powerful messages. They tell us that drinking will make us rich, beautiful, sexy, free, or successful or will carry us (don't ask how) to a beach in a warm, exotic land. These continuous entreaties to drink keep us from developing rational attitudes based on our own experience. We then combine the facts we have learned with the myths we want to believe.

My wife and I visited a local high school principal's office one day several years ago. We had an appointment to see him. Before he could stop his secretary, we were brought into his office at 11:00 A.M., where we found two students totally drunk. The principal was embarrassed and asked us to wait outside for a few minutes.

When he was finally able to see us, he felt obligated to tell us about the students. We asked about their background. As might be expected, their parents were alcoholics and their example had deeply affected these children. One of the students, a tenth-grade boy, had begun drinking alcoholic beverages when he was eight years old!

WHAT IS ALCOHOLISM?

In trying to answer the question "What is alcoholism?" the above-mentioned book on page 5 quotes Dr. Morris Chafetz, the first director of the National Institute of Alcohol Abuse and Alcoholism:

> Alcoholism is drinking too much, too often.
> It is permitting alcohol to play an inordinately
> powerful role in a person's life.

In the book *Recovering: How to Get and Stay Sober*, by L. Ann Mueller and Katherine Ketcham (Bantam Books, 1987), we read on page 9 a definition of alcoholism:

> A chronic, primary, hereditary, eventually
> fatal disease that progresses from an early
> physiological susceptibility into an addiction
> characterized by tolerance changes, physiological
> dependence, and loss of control over drinking.

On page 21 we read:

> Alcoholism is a complicated, catastrophic
> disease that, given enough time, will destroy
> your health and your happiness.

In the book *Addictive Drinking*, by Clark Vaughan (Penguin Books, 1982), the author makes a distinction between "heavy drinking" and "addictive drinking." On pages 3 and 4 we read:

> There are two kinds of people who habitu-
> ally or frequently drink very heavily and are
> often drunk, the heavy drinker and the addictive
> drinker. When they first begin drinking, the two
> are indistinguishable. Both appear to enjoy
> drinking heavily and the associations and
> feelings that go with it, and neither is addicted.
> A heavy drinker is a person who likes to
> drink for the feelings and associations that go
> with heavy drinking. He may be drinking much
> more than his family wishes; but as far as he

is concerned, no matter what his family may
say, the pleasure he finds in heavy drinking out-
weighs whatever disadvantages he is aware of.
In other words, he chooses to drink heavily
because he enjoys it, and he is willing to
pay the price, whatever that may be, for the
pleasure.

An addictive drinker is a person who likes
to drink for the feelings and associations that
go with heavy drinking—but with an added and
significant difference. He has lost control over
where, when, and how much he drinks.

Drug addiction is very similar to alcoholism, because the
fact is that alcoholism is drug abuse! Beverage alcohol is a
deadly drug that brings pleasurable feelings in the beginning
but ultimately destroys and kills all that is good, healthy, and
valuable in life.

How Does It Happen?

After examining several books that deal with medical
and social causes (books that often disagree with each other
over the causes and steps that lead to alcoholism and drug
abuse), it seems best to simplify matters into the following five
categories or steps that lead to alcoholism and drug abuse.

1. *Social drinking or the casual use of drugs.* There are
many people in our society who advocate the harmless nature of
such practice. They continue to insist (on the basis of only a few
examples) that the casual use of alcohol and/or drugs is no
problem. The facts prove otherwise.

Social drinking or the casual use of drugs is started because
you were offered it or it was made available to you and your
curiosity or your peer pressure motivated you to do it.

2. *Dependent drinking or drug usage.* People who take a
drink on a regular basis and use drugs regularly are now in the
"dependent" category. They normally use alcohol or drugs
when under severe stress. When the problems of life get too
much for them to handle, the message is "Have a drink." The
sedative qualities of alcohol and certain drugs relieve a person

temporarily, and produce feelings of relaxation and calm that are hard to ignore. The person realizes that, although artificial and dangerous, the immediate solution to many struggles in life is to take drugs or alcohol.

3. *Problem drinking and drug usage.* This stage is easily observable when a person drinks quickly, often gulping it down. This person will sneak drinks and drugs because of a strong desire to appear in control and not dependent upon alcohol or drugs. He will often lie about how many drinks he has had.

A problem drinker often controls the *time* when he or she *starts* to drink, but usually cannot stop when he or she wants to do so.

4. *Chronic drinking and habitual drug usage.* A person with a chronic problem has no control at all. This person does not know the difference between being drunk and being sober. He or she drinks all the time. The drug user who lives for a shot, pill, sniff, or whatever on a daily basis has a serious and chronic problem.

5. *Destructive drinking and drug abuse.* This person is easily recognized because physical deterioration is observable. Malnutrition is common, along with cirrhosis of the liver as well as nervous and gastric disorders. The most obvious fact about the destructive stage is the lack of personal hygiene. The eyes are bleary and the face is perpetually bloated and flushed. Our metropolitan streets are filled with such people, but the sad truth is that because of wealth, many of these people are protected from the view of society around them by the homes they live in and the money that allows them to continue their destructive habit.

The alcoholic cannot quit whenever he chooses; he is in the grip of a problem that is destroying him physically, mentally, and spiritually.

The tragedy is that the alcoholic does not see himself as he really is. He can sit in front of you dead drunk, with a swollen red nose and a liver falling down to his pelvic brim, and still deny that he is an alcoholic!

President George Bush was quoted in many articles and newspapers prior to his election with these words:

Alcohol must be recognized for what it is,
a drug, and drunk driving must be recognized
for what it is, a crime, and both should be dealt
with as such. Drugs are a cancer on our society,
and alcohol is the most common form of it. This
cancer has spread throughout our country, eating
away at the basic fabric of society, and more and
more often it is affecting our children.

WHAT DOES THE BIBLE SAY ABOUT ALCOHOL?

No subject can bring such controversy as deciding what
the Bible says about alcohol and the use of drugs. It is important to be careful with the Bible's evidence and not use it to
support one's personal preferences or habits. Consider carefully
the following:

1. *Drunkenness is always treated as a sin in the Bible, not
a disease.* Of course alcoholism *becomes* a terrible disease which
affects the mental, emotional, and physical processes of people.
However, it is extremely important to recognize that the Bible
deals with the problem of alcoholism from God's point of view,
and that victory is not found in simple medical solutions which
treat the physical consequences of drinking but do not treat the
root causes.

Deuteronomy 21:18-21 describes a young person who will
not obey his father and mother.

If a man has a stubborn and rebellious son
who will not obey the voice of his father or the
voice of his mother, and who, when they have
chastened him, will not heed them, then his
father and his mother shall take hold of him
and bring him out to the elders of his city, to
the gate of his city. And they shall say to the
elders of his city, "This son of ours is stubborn
and rebellious; he will not obey our voice; he
is a glutton and a drunkard." Then all the men
of his city shall stone him to death with stones;
so you shall put away the evil person from
among you, and all Israel shall hear and fear.

While the primary issue is the rebellion of the young person, it is interesting to note that the accusation included gluttony and drunkenness.

Romans 13:13,14 gives this admonition to believers:

> Let us walk properly, as in the day, not in
> revelry and drunkenness, not in licentiousness
> and lewdness, not in strife and envy. But put
> on the Lord Jesus Christ, and make no provision
> for the flesh, to fulfill its lusts.

Drunkenness is not only condemned, but it is described as fulfilling one's uncontrolled desires ("lusts").

1 Corinthians 6:9,10 gives a list of sins that, if continually practiced by a person without any desire for change or repentance, will result in eternal condemnation:

> Do you not know that the unrighteous will
> not inherit the kingdom of God? Do not be
> deceived. Neither fornicators, nor idolaters, nor
> adulterers, nor homosexuals, nor sodomites,
> nor thieves, nor covetous, nor drunkards, nor
> revilers, nor extortioners will inherit the king-
> dom of God.

The next verse gives great hope when it says, "And such *were* some of you."

Galatians 5:19-21 gives a list of sins for which a person "will not inherit the kingdom of God," and drunkenness is one of them.

In Ephesians 5:18 we have this command to Christians:

> Do not be drunk with wine, in which is
> dissipation; but be filled with the Spirit.

This is a plain, obvious command: "Do not be drunk with wine." Drunkenness is always considered sin in the Bible, According to the Bible, the only solution for sin is Jesus Christ, our Lord and Savior, who died on the cross over 1900 years ago to pay for our sins!

One of the great joys of sharing the good news of Jesus Christ with people is to see the change that comes to their lives. Bob was an alcoholic, divorced for five years, away from his family, lonely, and needing help. One of the men at church introduced Bob to Jesus Christ, and Bob made a commitment of his life, confessing his sin and his need of a Savior, and putting his trust in what the Bible teaches about Jesus Christ.

Bob started to attend a special meeting each week of people who have battled with alcoholism. It was there that he learned how to overcome his habit. Bob has not taken a drink now for many years. He was remarried to his former wife, and they and their children have a restored family life and are now active in their church.

The sin of alcoholism can be forgiven by Jesus Christ— that's the good news of the gospel!

2. *Nonmedicinal use of drugs is treated as sin in the Bible.* The Galatians 5:19-21 passage mentions "sorcery" in verse 20. That is based on the Greek word from which we get our English word "pharmaceutical," referring to drugs. Drugs were used in abundance in the ancient world of New Testament times, especially in relation to pagan religious rites and festivals.

Revelation 21:8 speaks of those who will be in hell, and says of them:

> The cowardly, unbelieving, abominable, murderers, sexually immoral, sorcerers [drug-users], idolaters, and all liars shall have their part in the lake which burns with fire and brimstone, which is the second death.

A similar point is made in Revelation 22:15, where the Bible describes those who are not in the heavenly city:

> Outside are dogs and sorcerers and sexually immoral and murderers and idolaters, and whoever loves and practices a lie.

Sorcery, or the use of drugs, is listed along with drunkenness as a sin in the Bible. To treat it in any other way is to ignore the plain evidence of the Bible. You may not agree with the

Bible's teaching, but before you reject it, at least face what it actually says!

3. *Wine was forbidden at certain times for certain people.* The word "wine" in the Bible needs to be carefully researched and evaluated. In the Hebrew language of the Old Testament, some 12 words are used in 251 places, and that does not count the usage of the word "to drink." In the Greek language of the New Testament, three words are used:

GLUEKOS — once in Acts 2:13.

LENOS — five times, referring to the winepress.

OINOS — 36 times, including three compound words:

OINOPOTES — "winebibber" in Matthew 11:19 and Luke 7:34.

OINOPHLUGIA — "drinking parties" in 1 Peter 4:3.

PAROINOS — "not given to wine" in 1 Timothy 3:3 and Titus 1:7.

In an excellent little book entitled *Bible Wines: Laws of Fermentation,* by William Patton (Sane Press, Oklahoma City, Oklahoma), there is a good deal of information, properly quoted and documented, concerning the ancient laws of fermentation. It is clear from historical information that people in Bible times understood and used processes by which wine was kept in unfermented stages.

It is also clear from the historical and scientific evidence that two kinds of wine were used in the ancient world. One was sweet, pleasant, refreshing, and unfermented. The other was intoxicating. Each was called "wine."

The Greek word *oinos* refers to wine in all of its stages, from being the grape on the vine to the total process of fermentation. This is the problem we have in examining the biblical evidence for the use of alcoholic beverages.

Fermentation begins immediately (the same day or next day) with a slight foam. Jewish tradition teaches that this initial stage makes the wine available for the wine tithe. After a week, violent processes subside and the wine is transferred to other jars or stronger wineskins. This is referred to as "new wine."

Up to 40 days the wine could be used for the "drink offering" mentioned in the Mosaic law. From this point on, the wine is deteriorating rapidly (fermentation is a decaying process) and is unacceptable for religious purposes. The rabbis of ancient times mixed the wine of Passover in the ratio of three parts water to one part wine in order to prevent any problem with fermentation or possible intoxication.

The longest time that wine was kept was three years. The term "old wine" seems to refer to that which is at least one year old.

Here is a list of the prohibitions in the Bible:

a) Priests while ministering—Leviticus 10:9.

b) Nazarites during the time of their vows—Numbers 6:3,20.

c) Prophets and priests while teaching or prophesying—Isaiah 28:7.

d) Kings or princes—Proverbs 31:4,5.

e) Elders and deacons—1 Timothy 3:3,8; Titus 1:7.

f) If it causes someone to stumble—Romans 14:21.

It is important to understand that the Bible condemns drunkenness and drug abuse, and also restricts various individuals and groups of people (on certain occasions and during the exercise of special responsibilities) from having any wine at all, regardless of the stage of fermentation.

4. *Wine in certain forms is always condemned.* Proverbs 20:1 says, "Wine is a mocker, intoxicating drink arouses brawling, and whoever is led astray by it is not wise." It should be

obvious by these words that we ought to practice abstinence from alcoholic beverages containing strong fermentation processes.

Proverbs 23:29-35 describes the condition of a person who takes "mixed wine":

> Who has woe? Who has sorrow? Who has contentions? Who has complaints? Who has wounds without cause? Who has redness of eyes? Those who linger long at the wine, those who go in search of mixed wine. Do not look on the wine when it is red, when it sparkles in the cup, when it swirls around smoothly; at the last it bites like a serpent, and stings like a viper. Your eyes will see strange things, and your heart will utter perverse things. Yes, you will be like one who lies down in the midst of the sea, or like one who lies at the top of the mast, saying: "They have struck me, but I was not hurt; they have beaten me, but I did not feel it. When shall I awake, that I may seek another drink?"

What a sad and tragic portrayal of a person who is drunk! Notice carefully that the wine was "mixed." Various grains and fruits were used to make the wine more intoxicating.

The words "strong drink" refer to highly intoxicating beverages, and the Bible recommends their use under only one condition—when a person is dying. Consider what Proverbs 31:4-7 says:

> It is not for kings, O Lemuel, it is not for kings to drink wine, nor for princes intoxicating drink; lest they drink and forget the law, and pervert the justice of all the afflicted. Give strong drink to him who is perishing, and wine to those who are bitter of heart. Let him drink and forget his property, and remember his misery no more.

The Bible recognizes that "strong drink" or "intoxicating drink" is a sedative and could be used to eliminate pain, especially in the case of someone who is dying.

5. *Wine at certain stages of fermentation was acceptable.* Although total abstinence from alcoholic beverages is the best solution to our alcoholic and drug-abuse problems in this country, it is important to note the occasions when wine was used and not condemned.

a) *For stomach problems*—1 Timothy 5:23.
Paul gave Timothy the following advice:

> No longer drink only water, but use a little wine for your stomach's sake and your frequent infirmities.

Timothy's physical problems were being intensified by the water he was drinking (which is often not safe in many parts of the world even today). Paul recommended wine with no evidence as to its condition. Since the nutritional value of wine (especially in the ancient processes) decreases with fermentation, it makes sense to believe that Paul was referring to the sweet, refreshing taste of grape juice, or wine that is unfermented.

b) *At the wedding of Cana of Galilee*—John 2:9-11.
Jesus and His disciples attended this wedding, and Jesus did not rebuke or confront the attendees for their wine-drinking. The problem involved a shortage of wine. Consider what was said by the master of the feast:

> When the master of the feast had tasted
> the water that was made wine, and did not know
> where it came from (but the servants who had
> drawn the water knew), the master of the feast
> called the bridegroom. And he said to him,
> "Every man at the beginning sets out the good
> wine, and when the guests have well drunk,
> then that which is inferior; but you have kept
> the good wine until now." This beginning of
> signs Jesus did in Cana of Galilee, and mani-
> fested His glory; and His disciples believed in
> Him.

To argue that the "good wine" which the miracle of Jesus produced was hard liquor is utterly ridiculous! It is far more likely to believe that it was closer to the sweet grape juice that was so highly prized and which took special processes of prevention to preserve. This "good" or "best" wine was usually served at the beginning, while older and more fermented wine would be brought out at the end, when people would be less likely to notice the difference. It is fascinating to notice that the governing official at this wedding immediately recognized the good quality of the wine which Jesus made from the water in the waterpots.

    c) *For celebrating*—Psalm 104:14,15; Ecclesiastes 9:7; 19:19.

In the beautiful passage in Psalm 104, the Psalmist exhorts us to consider the Lord's creation:

> He causes the grass to grow for the cattle,
> and vegetation for the service of man, that he
> may bring forth food from the earth, and wine
> that makes glad the heart of man, oil to make
> his face shine, and bread which strengthens
> man's heart.

This passage does not condone the drinking of alcoholic beverages! It simply teaches that everything God created was provided for man's strength and enjoyment. When man mixes other ingredients into the wine in order to produce an intoxicating drink, God condemns it (Proverbs 20:1; 23:29-35).

Ecclesiastes 9:7 says, "Drink your wine with a merry heart" and 10:19 adds "Wine makes merry." Once again, it is not commending the use of intoxicating beverages that dull the senses and sedate a person, and often cause him to do things he would not normally do. It is simply and refreshingly presenting the blessings of life which should be enjoyed and appreciated as they come from the hand of the Lord.

    d) *For Passover (Communion)*—Matthew 26:29.

The cup which was used at the Last Supper, when Jesus and His disciples shared in the Passover the night before He went to the cross to die for our sins, was not intoxicating drink. Jesus said in Matthew 26:29:

> I say to you, I will not drink of this fruit
> of the vine from now on until that day when I
> drink it new with you in My Father's kingdom.

As mentioned previously, the rabbis of ancient times mixed three parts water with one part wine (regardless of its stage of fermentation) to insure that it was not intoxicating.

e) *For worship*—Deuteronomy 14:22,23.
These verses refer to the tithe which the children of Israel were to bring in worship to the Lord:

> You shall truly tithe all the increase of your
> grain that the field produces year by year. And
> you shall eat before the Lord your God, in the
> place where He chooses to make His name
> abide, the tithe of your grain and your new wine
> and your oil, of the firstlings of your herds and
> your flocks, that you may learn to fear the Lord
> your God always.

This "new wine tithe" referred to wine that was 40 days old or less (cf. "drink-offering" in Numbers 28:7).

6. *The only position that avoids the appearance of evil is total abstinence.* In 1 Thessalonians 5:22 we read the following command:

> Abstain from every form of evil.

The word "form" or "appearance" does not refer to how something may appear to someone else, although that is a part of the warning here. The word speaks of the form which the actual evil or sin takes—not what we think it might be, but what form, structure, process, or tactics the sin or evil takes. It is a warning to be careful about getting close to evil and thinking you can handle it.

One of these evils is drunkenness, and consuming alcoholic beverages that are "mixed" and "strong" (since these are intended to make a person intoxicated). The "form" that it takes (from which we are to stay away) could be any alcoholic beverage. Social drinkers may argue vehemently that they are not drunkards and therefore do not violate the standards of the Bible, but are we not dangerously close to violating this principle of abstaining from *every* form of evil when we consume alcoholic beverages?

WHAT CAN BE DONE TO HELP?

There are many fine organizations in this country that are working hard to help alcoholics and drug-abusers and their families. One such organization, RAPHA (located in Houston, Texas), has provided 12 steps of help from a Christian and biblical perspective.

Step 1: I admit I have fouled up my life with chemicals over which I am powerless.

Romans 3:23; Galatians 5:16-21.

Step 2: I believe that someone with the wisdom and knowledge of God, through Jesus Christ, is necessary to guide me to sanity.

Acts 3:1-26; James 5:16.

Step 3: I believe that I am loved by God.

John 3:16; Romans 5:6.

Step 4: I know, with my mind's understanding, that Jesus Christ is able to fill the void in my life.

Psalm 111:10; John 14:6.

Step 5: I agree with God that I am not worthy to come to Him, but that Jesus Christ can make me worthy.

Romans 3:20-26; 5:8.

Step 6: I am entirely ready to have God, through Jesus Christ, remove all my rebellion against Him.

Acts 3:19; Colossians 1:19-22.

Step 7: I humbly ask God through Jesus Christ to take over as Master of my life.

Romans 10:8-11; Ephesians 2:8-10.

Step 8: I believe that my mind must be renewed to my significance in Christ.

Romans 8:28-39; Ephesians 1:3-23.

Step 9: I am making a searching and fearless moral inventory of myself—agreeing with God concerning the exact nature of my sins, and accepting His forgiveness.

Romans 12:1,2; 1 John 1:9.

Step 10: I am making a list of persons I have harmed and those who have harmed me, and am willing to forgive and to seek forgiveness.

Matthew 6:14,15; Ephesians 4:31,32.

Step 11: I am seeking through prayer, Bible study, and meditation to improve my conscious contact with God, praying only for knowledge of His will for me and the power to carry that out.

Psalm 119:11; Matthew 26:41; John 14:23-26.

Step 12: I am willing to help others!

Matthew 28:16-20; Acts 1:8.

WHAT SHOULD BE OUR RESPONSE?

No moral problem confronts the American family with greater tragedy and crisis than that of alcoholism and drug abuse. The problem is not going away; it is facing us every day with epidemic proportions! Millions of Americans are regular consumers of alcohol and millions are daily using drugs. These chemicals are causing terrible physical damage and increasing the violence and crime within our society and our families. It is time for strong action!

1) Say no to alcohol and drugs!

2) Get rid of wet bars and alcoholic beverages. Take nonmedicinal drugs out of your home and personal possessions.

3) Refuse to take a "social drink" unless it is a nonalcoholic beverage, and above all, stop the

alcoholic drinks during business contacts and meals.

4) Demand that our public schools take a strong stand against the use of alcoholic beverages and drugs. Insist that strong measures of discipline and punishment be applied to abusers and especially drug-pushers.

5) Do all you can to remove alcohol advertising from newspapers, television, and radio.

6) Vote for political candidates who are strong in their convictions and legislative goals against drugs and alcohol.

7) Promote and encourage stronger laws against drug dealers and pushers.

8) Insist on stronger laws against drunk drivers.

9) Show compassion to those addicted who want help and to their suffering families.

10) Develop programs with a biblical and Christian commitment to help alcoholics and those addicted to drugs.

11) Understand that alcoholics and drug-abusers can be delivered from these addictive habits.

12) Do not remove the responsibility and sin of those who become alcoholics and drug addicts from their understanding. Do not blame the environment or their past or their present problems, even though these may have contributed to their desire to escape through alcohol or drugs.

13) Urge any alcoholic or drug-user friend of yours to recognize his or her need of God's help in order to overcome the habit and to get delivered.

14) Do not make jokes about alcoholics and drug-users. Abuse is a serious and tragic problem in

our society that deserves more than humorous and condescending remarks.

15) Do not get discouraged. Alcoholics and drug-users have patterns that must be overcome. They will often abstain for a short period of time, only to fall into greater addiction. Don't give up on any person! They need your support, intervention, and confrontation.

16) Insist that leaders in your community and church totally abstain from alcoholic beverages and drug use. The Bible's standards for leadership are desperately needed in our country, communities, churches, and homes!

Las Vegas and Lotteries

Gambling is an epidemic in America that is destroying lives and homes. It is big business in this culture we call America, and it is no longer conducted only by the underworld of organized crime; the government is now capitalizing on the desire of many Americans to get rich quick and become millionaires overnight.

Art Schlichter, former Ohio State football star whose life was ruined by gambling, was quoted in *USA Today*:

> It grabs you. Your own mind is lying to you,
> telling you that your next bet is going to be
> better, that it's going to be the big winner. But
> it's not, it never is.

Millions of Americans do not agree. They have observed that there are many so-called "winners" in the statewide lotteries that are promoted throughout the country. This gambling fever is justified because its profits supposedly go to help public education and organizations worthy of our support.

In the summer of 1989, baseball superstar Pete Rose was suspended from baseball because of alleged gambling. From being a hero and idol of thousands of our nation's youth who follow baseball, Rose must now suffer the pain of disgrace and dishonor because of his desire to gamble. Although continuing to deny the many allegations against him, he accepted readily his suspension and caused most Americans to believe that he is indeed guilty.

What makes the above story so tragic is that what Pete Rose did to bring shame upon his career and future in baseball, millions of Americans are doing every week in a slightly different form.

Epidemic Proportions

Richard Richardson of the Maryland Compulsive Gambling Council says, "Without a doubt, compulsive gambling has reached epidemic proportions."

The cover of the April 24, 1989, edition of *Business Week* magazine was entitled "GAMBLING FEVER... IS IT GOOD FOR US?" A cover story of several pages was written to describe America's fascination with gambling.

It isn't the casinos of Las Vegas and Atlantic City that control the gambling industry of today; it is the state lotteries. Once considered vices promoted and controlled by the Mafia, lotteries are now run by state governments, which are drooling over the potential profits.

The cover story of the *Business Week* issue referred to above carried these facts:

> Every evening thousands of bingo players around the country lay out their cards, focus their eyes on video monitors, and start playing Mega-Bingo. Launched last February, it's the world's biggest and richest bingo game, with a $500,000 jackpot. Numbers drawn in a Tulsa bingo hall are telecast live via satellite to 15 other halls in eight states.
>
> In South Dakota, the legislature recently authorized the installation of new video gambling devices—electronic near-equivalents of slot machines—in bars and taverns. Within a year, 2500 of the machines should be in operation.
>
> In Maryland, Pimlico Race Course has just opened its huge "Sports Palace." Horseplayers can put bets on the Pimlico card and on races "simulcast" live from a dozen other tracks on huge TV screens. They can also watch an array of other sports events while keeping an eye on

a mural-size display of hundreds of scores and betting lines. Betting on sports such as football and baseball is illegal anywhere but in Nevada and Montana [other states, such as Oregon, have now made it legal as well]. But Pimlico's owners are getting set for its legalization nationally, which some observers believe will happen within a few years. The Pimlico Sports Palace could then become the country's largest sports-betting casino.

In Iowa, the state lottery recently began producing live TV game shows with teams of lottery players as contestants. Ratings have been higher than those for "Wheel of Fortune," in part because the shows also announce prizes for players at home. Lottery officials are considering arranging for home viewers to play along by calling in answers with touchtone telephones.

The article goes on to say:

At a pace that seems almost epidemic, gambling fever is sweeping the U.S., and raising disturbing questions about its possibly deleterious impact on society. Today gambling outlets are almost as ubiquitous and well-patronized as convenience stores. Gambling is part of the weekly, and even daily, routine of tens of millions of Americans, and of many millions more in Europe, the Far East, Latin America, Australia, and Canada. As University of Nevada gambling expert William N. Thompson puts it: "The world seems now to be engulfed in a veritable explosion of gambling activity." Last year, says industry consultant Eugene Martin Christiansen, Americans legally and illegally wagered more than $240 billion, a figure that is growing at about 10% annually.

The astounding thing is that the most lucrative future betting establishment, according to gambling experts, will be the private homes of millions of Americans.

Up until recent years, gambling was considered to be a

vice by the majority of Americans. It was always thought to be connected with prostitution, crime, and corruption. Eugene Christiansen said, "Gambling has gone through cycles of being prohibited and legalized. But now, for the first time, it is being legitimized. It's coming into the American mainstream."

Michael Rumbolz, former head of the Nevada Gaming Control Board (and who now runs Donald Trump's Nevada operations), said:

> You have a whole new generation of people
> who feel they can gamble without thinking that
> it reflects poorly on their character.

The numbers rackets of a few years ago and the presence of mob-affiliated bookies are now replaced with state governments, private charities, and religious organizations who have discovered the financial benefits of gambling for their needs and projects.

Iowa Lottery Commissioner Edward Stanek says, "Playing the lottery is a form of recreation that's no more harmful for most people than going to the movies or bowling." Officials who are reaping off the profits of gambling today are saying that the practice is a healthy escape from the frustrations of modern society.

On a cruise to Mexico aboard a ship called the *Tropicana,* my wife and I observed gambling up close. We saw people glued to slot machines and various gaming tables for hours. It seemed as though they were oblivious to the world around them. They seemed under some sort of spell, and the compulsion to gamble was totally dominating their lives.

WHAT'S HAPPENING IN LAS VEGAS?

On a short vacation trip to Las Vegas a few years ago, my wife and I stayed in one of the major hotels for an amazingly low price and ate delicious meals that were cheaper than anything we had experienced in our many years in Southern California. When we inquired why prices were so low, we were immediately told that the profits which these hotels and restaurants were making were coming from the gambling activities of their customers. Since we do not gamble, they obviously didn't make much money on the two of us! But that didn't seem to bother them, since they had plenty of customers. As we walked through the lobbies of various hotels on the Las Vegas strip, we were amazed at the attitudes and intensity which people displayed while gambling. In many ways it was frightening and depressing at the same time. To see so many people obsessed with a desire to get rich quick by gambling and betting their hard-earned money was very disturbing.

Some people go to Las Vegas for "fun," and insist that their gambling activities are harmless and not serious attempts to make money. What we saw was quite to the contrary. For every "fun-loving" weekender who predetermined the amount of money to be wasted at this strange "sport" of gambling, there were scores of other people whose faces revealed the pain, loneliness, and tragedy of gambling fever. It is truly a sickness which brings tragic consequences to many lives and homes.

In the midst of an explosion of gambling through a multitude of new methods sponsored by a new set of institutions and organizations, it is fascinating to see the growth of Las Vegas—it looks like a gold-rush town. Tourism is booming, and brand-new hotels and casinos are springing up in the desert surrounding the city.

Las Vegas spends millions marketing itself as a resort and convention center, but the fact is that 80 percent of profits come from slot machines. New technology is the reason: Electronic slots have replaced the one-armed mechanical slots of the past. The current craze is video poker, which adds a touch of skill to what is basically a game of chance.

Las Vegas is more popular today than ever before in American history. It is a common sight to see families involved, parents giving children money to use in slot machines and various video games of chance. The state lotteries are encouraging people to go to Las Vegas, a trip they might never have taken in the society of a few years ago. Today gambling is "in," and very few Americans seem to be aware of the moral revolution that has taken place in the past decade.

THE GAMBLING REVOLUTION

Our American culture has shifted its opinion about gambling in a very short period of time. It is indeed a revolution, a radical departure from the past that was done so quickly and so approvingly that it startles the imagination of social scientists and observers. What is causing this radical change? Why has America (and many other countries in the world) become so obsessed with gambling and lotteries?

The answer is found in the very nature of the "American dream." The materialism of our culture is deeply rooted in our value system. The word "success" means many things to many people, but in this country it mainly involves *money*. To get more money in order to buy the things they want is what the majority of Americans are seeking. Gambling seems to be a way to get what you want quickly, though the facts show that thousands of lives and homes are being ruined by gambling. It is especially sad to see people on welfare purchasing multiple lottery tickets.

In the minutes of a California State Lottery Commission meeting held in June 1989, the "staff objectives" are clearly stated: to achieve annual increases in revenue by creative means of gambling. In those minutes was a description of "LOTTO," which the report said experienced a "banner year" in 1988-89 with a sales increase of 50 percent over the previous year. Sales totaled almost two billion dollars!

The Lottery Commission has also introduced 750 Player Activated Terminals (PALS) in supermarkets to help increase sales. Many new games and technologies were suggested and proposed.

Goals for the next five years included the following:

1) Over the long term, provide constant dollars per student. Meet or exceed growth in: ADA and COLA.

2) Maintain positive public image.

3) Secure broad player participation before increasing player spending.

The Commission laid out key strategies in order to accomplish these goals:

1) Maintain current games.

2) Introduce new games.

3) Widen distribution network.

4) Improve communications.

Contracts were then approved and awarded to various advertising, public relations, and maintenance firms, some resulting in millions of dollars paid to companies who are reaping off the gambling fever.

Nine states permit card clubs, and it is big business. The Bicycle Club near Los Angeles is one of 350 clubs in California. It has 155 tables and attracts 2000 players every day! This club grosses 83 million dollars a year from seat-rental fees charged to players who bet against each other!

In Montana, 8400 video-gambling machines operate in bars and retail stores. Betting has doubled each year since legalization in 1985.

The sad news is that the most pervasive form of gambling is charitable games, primarily bingo, run by churches and various charity organizations. Charity bingo operates in 46 states and is run by professionals who help charities gross millions of dollars a year. Many of these charities run what are called "Las Vegas Nights" featuring casino-style games.

GAMBLING FEVER

Gambling fever has spread to horse racing, now enjoying its most profitable times. A few years ago experts were predicting its demise, but no longer. Attendance is soaring at the racetracks, and new tracks are being opened. At last tabulation, 43 states now allow betting on the horses. Greyhound racing is now run at more than 50 tracks in 15 states and is expanding every week.

In the *Business Week* article of April 24, 1989, the following evaluation was made:

Government-sanctioned lotteries during the 18th and 19th centuries eventually either collapsed or were banned because of scandals.

The current lottery era, beginning with New Hampshire in 1963, was nearly aborted for lack of interest. But increasingly sophisticated automation permitted lotteries to raise the frequency of drawings from monthly to weekly and daily, to introduce instant tickets, to switch from passive to active games where players could pick their own numbers, and, most recently, to roll out giant-jackpot lotto games. Each enhancement, especially lotto, precipitated a sharp sales jump.

The article makes these observations:

> Evidence suggests that, once people start playing the lottery, they often progress to other forms of gambling, including illegal gambling. Law-enforcement officials say state sponsorship of legal gambling has spurred illegal betting by helping to wipe out gambling's stigma.
>
> Critics also castigate lotteries' sales pitches, which stress the fantasy of huge jackpots but say little about the often astronomical odds against winning and the low payout. Typically only 50% of a lottery's sales is returned as prizes to players. Racetracks and casinos often pay out 80% or more. Says Penn State sociologist Vicki Abt: "The lottery is the worst game in town."

Duke University professor Philip J. Cook makes these remarks about the gambling phenomenon:

> It is troubling that the fantasy is sustained to such a large extent by ignorance and delusion. That a state should even be in the fantasy business is curious. Here you have the same outfit that is trying to educate our children selling images and hyperbole rather than factual information, and telling the public: "Play your hunch, you could win a bunch."

One of the most tragic consequences of state lotteries and the gambling fever is the impact upon the poor and working-class players. Poor people spend, according to recent research, a much bigger portion of their incomes on lotteries than high-income players. Many lottery players lose most of their pay-checks through gambling's enticements.

Compulsive gambling, in which a person cannot control his betting, has reached epidemic proportions. From 10 to 15 percent of Americans who gamble fall into the compulsive gambling category, and many experts believe the number is much higher.

Perhaps one of the most alarming facts about the current obsession for gambling is the surge in gambling by teenagers. Public schools have even sponsored events which promote gambling.

According to one study done in 1987 by Henry R. Lesieur of St. John's University, 86 percent of New Jersey high school students had gambled in the past year, and 32 percent had gambled at least once a week. Atlantic City casinos turned away 200,000 minors in 1987 and escorted 35,000 of them from their floors because they had slipped in unnoticed.

One story of gambling fever illustrates the problem that is growing in this country. In 1989 the Pennsylvania lottery reached a record jackpot of more than 100 million dollars. The huge jackpot set off a lottery mania. Players took planes, trains, and cars from around the country to join in the buying frenzy. In an average week, the state usually sells about four or five million tickets, but on one day alone, 24 million tickets were sold! The odds of any one ticket bearing seven winning numbers was one in 9.6 million. But that did not stop millions of Americans from trying to win. This lottery panic was reported in almost every major newspaper of the country. The tremendous emphasis on the excitement and allurement of this one lottery reveals how serious the problem has become in our country. We have lost our sense of values, and our desire for immediate success and wealth has blinded our minds and eyes to the realities and dangers of gambling.

DOES THE BIBLE APPROVE OF GAMBLING?

Believe it or not, some people have tried to support the gambling craze by pointing to the Bible's references to "casting the lot." In John 19:23,24 we have the fact of Roman soldiers casting the lot for the tunic of Jesus Christ while He was dying on the cross:

> Then the soldiers, when they had crucified
> Jesus, took His garments and made four parts,
> to each soldier a part, and also the tunic. Now
> the tunic was without seam, woven from the top
> in one piece. They said therefore among them-
> selves, "Let us not tear it, but cast lots for it,
> whose it shall be," that the Scripture might be
> fulfilled which says: "They divided My garments
> among them, and for My clothing they cast lots."
> Therefore the soldiers did these things.

The prophecy is in Psalm 22, which is called a messianic psalm. In verse 18 we read:

> They divide my garments among them, and
> for my clothing they cast lots.

Casting the lot (used several times in the Bible) was not gambling but an ancient form of decision-making, somewhat like voting. An example is found in Acts 1:21-26, where the disciples of Jesus were attempting to find a replacement for Judas, who had betrayed Jesus and committed suicide.

> Of these men who have accompanied us all
> the time that the Lord Jesus went in and out
> among us, beginning from the baptism of John
> to that day when He was taken up from us, one
> of these must become a witness with us of His
> resurrection. And they proposed two: Joseph
> called Barsabas, who was surnamed Justus, and
> Matthias. And they prayed and said, "You, O
> Lord, who know the hearts of all, show which
> of these two You have chosen to take part in this
> ministry and apostleship from which Judas by
> transgression fell, that he might go to his own

place." And they cast their lots, and the lot fell
on Matthias. And he was numbered with the
eleven apostles.

Casting the lot was used to determine which of the two
qualified men would be chosen. Both met the qualifications and
were acceptable. This was a method of decision-making; it did
not involve money and it was not gambling.

Proverbs 16:33 says:

The lot is cast into the lap, but its every
decision is from the Lord.

Human methods for determining matters must always be
understood in the light of the sovereignty of God.

Though the modern word "lottery" comes from the ancient word "lot," the modern practice of gambling is not the
ancient practice of decision-making.

WHAT IS WRONG WITH GAMBLING?

The way Americans are dealing with gambling today is a
far cry from the traditional and moral values of our past history.
Let's take a look at what the Bible teaches about gambling to
see what is right or wrong about it.

1. *It contributes to a person's lack of contentment.* In 1
Timothy 6:6-8 the apostle Paul gives this advice to his son in the
faith, Timothy:

Godliness with contentment is great gain.
For we brought nothing into this world, and it
is certain we can carry nothing out. And having
food and clothing, with these we shall be content.

Proverbs 15:16 adds:

Better is a little with the fear of the Lord
than great treasure with trouble.

Contentment is not the goal of gambling—it produces the exact opposite! Gambling creates dissatisfaction with your present state and lures you into believing that you deserve more than what you presently have, and that you don't need to wait to earn it—you can have it right now. On this basis alone, gambling is not good for us.

2. *It causes a person to fall into temptation and carnal desire.* 1 Timothy 6:9 brings this warning:

> Those who desire to be rich fall into temptation and a snare, and into many foolish and harmful lusts which drown men in destruction and perdition.

There is no doubt in any person's mind who has studied and engaged in gambling that it is built on the desire to be rich, which often controls the hearts of American people and is appealed to by our advertising and marketing agencies.

Proverbs 11:28 says:

> He who trusts in his riches will fall, but the righteous will flourish like foliage.

Proverbs 15:27 adds:

> He who is greedy for gain troubles his own house.

Proverbs 23:4,5 warns:

> Do not overwork to be rich; because of your own understanding, cease! Will you set your eyes on that which is not? For riches certainly make themselves wings; they fly away like an eagle toward heaven.

Remind yourself that these words were written by one of the wealthiest men in ancient times, King Solomon. His wisdom is well-known, but we don't seem to pay much attention to his advice and warnings about wealth. Our greed and desire to be rich drive us further and further into materialistic debt and tragedy.

The Bible says that the very desire to be rich is the problem. The rich have their own set of difficulties, but all of us who *desire* to be rich will face tremendous trouble because of it. The Bible calls this desire a "snare" or a trap. We get trapped by our desire and controlled by it, and as a result we fall into other kinds of temptation that have ruined people's lives.

3. *It conditions a person to accept and tolerate sinful attitudes and actions.* The apostle Paul continues his analysis of the problem in 1 Timothy 6:10:

> The love of money is a root of all kinds of evil.

We must point out that the Bible does not say that money itself is evil, but rather the *love* of money. However, 1 Timothy 6:17-19 gives this advice to the rich about their wealth:

> Command those who are rich in this present age not to be haughty, nor to trust in uncertain riches but in the living God, who gives us richly all things to enjoy. Let them do good, that they be rich in good works, ready to give, willing to share, storing up for themselves a good foundation for the time to come, that they may lay hold on eternal life.

Pride and a false sense of security are created by great wealth. The rich are warned about trusting in wealth. They should rather be "rich in good works," remembering that the greater issue is "eternal life."

When your goal is to get rich, you open yourself up to greater problems. Loving money leads to further sinful attitudes and actions.

In 1 John 2:15-17 we read these challenging words about the world's value system:

> Do not love the world or the things in the world. If anyone loves the world, the love of the Father is not in Him. For all that is in the

world—the lust of the flesh, the lust of the eyes,
and the pride of life—is not of the Father but
is of the world. And the world is passing away,
and the lust of it; but he who does the will of
God abides forever.

"The world" is the philosophy of a secular society, a viewpoint that is well-illustrated by the current craze to gamble. The lust for money, a part of "the things in the world," is not compatible with a commitment to God and His purposes in this world.

A few years ago a man shared with me his desire to get rich in a setting and conversation that seemed quite harmless. Little did I know what would happen in his life because of that desire! In a short time he was doing whatever he could to make money, and some of it by illegal means. The money he made brought demands that began to drown him. His marriage fell apart, and his children would have nothing to do with him. His craving for success and making lots of money gave him the ability to get into more trouble. Sex, alcohol, drugs, and crime became a way of life, and one day he was caught. He went to prison, his life in shambles. His love of money had led him into tragedy and disgrace. While he was "on his way up" his pride dominated him so that no friend, relative, or business associate could reach him. He thought he knew it all and was on top of everything. But in a few years he came crashing down. Payday someday!

4. *It changes a person's commitment to spiritual things.* Paul's advice to Timothy about the love of money in 1 Timothy 6:10 also included these words:

The love of money is a root of all kinds of
evil, for which some have strayed from the faith
in their greediness, and pierced themselves
through with many sorrows.

Some have "strayed from the faith in their greediness." The inability of the love of money to dwell in the same heart of the person who says he loves God is well-known. In Matthew

6:19-24 Jesus taught us the following about the dangers of wanting to be rich:

> Do not lay up for yourselves treasures on earth, where moth and rust destroy and where thieves break in and steal; but lay up for yourselves treasures in heaven, where neither moth nor rust destroys and where thieves do not break in and steal. For where your treasure is, there your heart will be also. The lamp of the body is the eye. If therefore your eye is good, your whole body will be full of light. But if your eye is bad, your whole body will be full of darkness. If therefore the light that is in you is darkness, how great is that darkness! No one can serve two masters; for either he will hate the one and love the other, or else he will be loyal to the one and despise the other. You cannot serve God and mammon.

"Mammon" is money. You cannot serve God and money! Lots of people try to, however, thinking that it is not a great problem. Yet their desire for money inevitably causes them to stray from their faith and confidence in the Lord. Love for God and love for money don't mix well!

Proverbs 10:22 says:

> The blessing of the Lord makes one rich, and He adds no sorrow with it.

Proverbs 15:6 continues:

> In the house of the righteous there is much treasure, but in the revenue of the wicked is trouble.

Proverbs 16:8 states:

> Better is a little with righteousness than vast revenues without justice.

Proverbs 21:25,26 reminds us:

> The desire of the slothful kills him, for his
> hands refuse to labor. He covets greedily all day
> long, but the righteous gives and does not spare.

5. *It controls your heart and your system of values.* Jesus said in Matthew 6:21:

> Where your treasure is, there your heart
> will be also.

If we desire the treasures that this world affords, and that is our goal in life, then that is where our heart will be. We all put our heart into whatever we value the most.

Jesus told a story about a rich young ruler who came to Him inquiring about eternal life. In Luke 18:18-30 Jesus told this rich ruler (who claimed to keep the commandments of God but wanted to know how he could inherit eternal life) that he should sell all that he had and give it to the poor. If he did this, Jesus said that he would have treasure in heaven. Jesus invited the rich young ruler to follow Him.

The Bible says in Luke 18:23:

> But when he heard this, he became very
> sorrowful, for he was very rich.

Upon seeing his sorrow, Jesus replied:

> How hard it is for those who have riches
> to enter the kingdom of God! For it is easier for
> a camel to go through a needle's eye than for
> a rich man to enter the kingdom of God.

The people who heard Him say this replied:

> Who then can be saved?

Jesus answered:

> The things which are impossible with men
> are possible with God.

In reply to Peter's remark that the disciples had left all to follow Jesus, Jesus said:

> Assuredly I say to you, there is no one who
> has left house or parents or brothers or wife or
> children, for the sake of the kingdom of God,
> who shall not receive many times more in this
> present time, and in the age to come everlasting
> life.

The truth is that our desire to be rich or even our riches themselves can keep us from following Jesus Christ. Our value system is controlled by our desire for wealth and the sense of security we feel when we have wealth.

When a person decides to follow Jesus Christ, it often requires a decision to leave all that he holds dear. But no sacrifice that we make in order to follow Christ will go unrewarded. The reward will come not only in this life but in the age to come.

6. *It characterizes those who are guilty of covetousness.* The Old Testament law is clear. Commandment number ten of the Ten Commandments (Exodus 20:17) says:

> You shall not covet your neighbor's house;
> you shall not covet your neighbor's wife nor his
> manservant, nor his maidservant, nor his ox,
> nor his donkey, nor anything that is your
> neighbor's.

Many people argue that gambling is not a violation of the law concerning covetousness. They say that this commandment only warns against the attitude of getting something that already belongs to your neighbor. Under this restrictive view, the word "covet" is similar to theft, taking something that does not belong to you. However, it is commandment number *eight* that says, "You shall not steal." This commandment is something more.

Ephesians 5:3-5 lists a number of sins, and remarks about them:

> But fornication and all uncleanness or
> covetousness, let it not even be named among

you, as is fitting for saints; neither filthiness,
nor foolish talking, nor coarse jesting, which
are not fitting, but rather giving of thanks. For
this you know, that no fornicator, unclean
person, nor covetous man, who is an idolater,
has any inheritance in the kingdom of Christ
and God.

Covetousness is condemned in no uncertain terms! It is
associated with fornication (sexual immorality) and all uncleanness. Covetousness is called idolatry because it is the
worship of things that you desire to have. It is greed, the desire
to be rich, the love of money.

"To covet" is much like the words "to lust." It is carnal
desire, wanting things you don't need to have and believing that
their possession will bring you happiness.

In Luke 12:14 Jesus said:

Take heed and beware of covetousness, for
one's life does not consist in the abundance of
the things he possesses.

He then gave them a parable about a certain rich man
who was very prosperous. When his crops became so productive
that he had more than he needed, he asked, "What shall I do,
since I have no room to store my crops?" He decided to tear down
his present barns and build bigger ones. He argued the following (Luke 12:19):

I will say to my soul, "Soul, you have many
goods laid up for many years; take your ease;
eat, drink, and be merry."

God's reply was (verse 20):

You fool! This night your soul will be
required of you; then whose will those things
be which you have provided?

Jesus summarized with these words in Luke 12:21:

> So is he who lays up treasure for himself,
> and is not rich toward God.

Covetousness is greed, the desire to find happiness in things and the belief that accumulation of wealth brings security.

Gambling is wrong; the Bible is clear on that point. Americans have forsaken biblical morality that made our country strong. We have decided that there are no serious consequences accompanying our new set of values, but a rude awakening is coming!

Early in his life Don became involved in criminal activity. The streets were "home" to him, and his family life was not worth mentioning. Using his fists, he got interested in boxing, and was undefeated in several professional bouts. Through his interest in boxing and his natural ability to handle himself he became attractive to organized crime. He was introduced to the gambling business in the days when it was all illegal. His specialty was slot machines, and he reaped greatly off the greed of people and his own desire to "make it big" and to "make a lot of money."

One day Don was visited at his home by two ladies from a local church. They knocked on his door by mistake, thinking he was a recent visitor to their church. Don made fun of them and tried to embarrass them and overwhelm them, but they were persistent and came back again and again. They also sent one of the pastors, who began to work on Don. This pastor would not give up. In spite of Don's background, his connections with organized crime, and the tragedies of his family and personal life, God's love and the message of the gospel motivated this pastor to keep after him and not give up in his efforts to win him to Jesus Christ.

Don finally saw that Christianity was real and that there was hope for him to be delivered from his sinful past and all his desire to make it big in the gambling rackets. He received Jesus Christ as his Lord and Savior, and today serves on the pastoral staff of a church in California. There is hope for all of us!

WHAT SHOULD BE OUR RESPONSE?

1. Don't gamble—ever!
2. Don't bet on anything even with your words.

3. Don't participate in any promotion or advertising gimmick that promises you something for nothing.

4. Don't argue that gambling is harmless for those who want to "have a little fun."

5. Express your displeasure at gambling devices and methods in grocery and retail stores.

6. Oppose parental associations and school administrations that promote gambling activities for our children and youth.

7. Teach your children why gambling is wrong and how it contributes to wrong attitudes and bad values in life.

8. Commit yourself to earning your living by hard work.

9. Don't put confidence in your money and possessions; instead, put your trust in the living God!

✦ 11 ✦

Religion and Politics: Do They Mix?

Perhaps the greatest moral issue of our time is the relationship of religion and politics. On the one hand are those who are unhesitatingly committed to the principle of a secular society: the complete and total separation of church and state, with neither one affecting the other (although proponents of this view usually desire state control of religious enterprises to "keep them in their place").

On the other hand are religious zealots who believe that the moral catastrophe facing our culture can only be resolved by a takeover: Religion must once again control all facets of society. Some Christian theologians argue that it is our God-given right and responsibility to "subdue the earth"—that God's principles must once again control our society, and that Christian people must establish the kingdom of God on earth. We are to have dominion over this world because this is a cultural mandate from the days of creation that has never been revoked.

In the book *Whatever Became of Sin?* (Hawthorn Books, 1973, and later Bantam Books, 1978), Karl Menninger refers to one of the signers of the Declaration of Independence, Dr. Benjamin Rush. Rush was the first American psychiatrist. He not only signed the Declaration of Independence but he also worked on the first drafts of our Constitution. He was one of the founders of the first public school systems and established the first free medical dispensary for the poor and one of the first colleges for women. He was involved in the first American prison reform movement and was the first American doctor to profess the specialty of psychiatry. He was also one of the founders of our American Psychiatric Association.

Benjamin Rush was deeply concerned about morality. In June 1788, in the midst of much work and travel intended to get the new Constitution ratified by the states, he wrote an open letter to clergymen of all faiths on the subject of American morality. He condemned many current sins, among them smoking, drinking, and horse-racing.

MORALLY NEUTRAL

Many people in our society today insist that our early forefathers wanted a society that was morally neutral. Is that true?

In *The Light and the Glory,* by Peter Marshall and David Manuel (Fleming H. Revell, 1977), an analysis is given of America since the assassination of President John Kennedy in 1963. On pages 14 and 15 the following is asserted:

> But perhaps the most mystifying indicator of all was the loss of moral soundness. To be sure, there had always been pockets of dissolution, but we had thought of them as isolated situations—surface cavities which needed to be drilled and filled. Now we were finding that what was actually needed was root-canal work, if it was not already too late.
>
> And yet, the sexual promiscuity, which we scrambled to accommodate through legalized abortion, permissive sex education, and ever more effective birth preventatives, was not in itself the most telling sign of the depth of the moral decay. Nor was it the disintegration of the family unit, the common thread which was all that was keeping the fabric of America from coming apart at the seams. And indeed, the American family seemed to be unraveling—a divorce rate that was approaching one marriage in two, when two generations ago divorce had been almost unheard of; the sudden prevalence of child abuse, which had been even rarer; the

wholesale abdication of parents from their traditional roles of leadership; and the determination
of each member of the family to achieve independence—as much and as soon as possible.

The most significant index of the extent
of our moral decay was our very indifference to
it. Pornography had insinuated itself into prac-
tically every level of our daily life, including our
language. Corrupt personal and business practices which once would have erupted into major
scandals, today seemed scarcely scandalous. But
where once we would have been up in arms,
speaking out, writing letters, and voting, now
we just shook our heads and counted it as
another sign of the times.

If any one event could be isolated as that
which marked the moment when our despair
had begun to harden into indifference, it was
when our President was caught lying to the
people, and then manipulating our trust in the
office in his attempt to cover up the lies.

This explains why, when the events of
Watergate tore down the idol of our "civil
religion," it was such a shattering experience
for so many. It also tells us why, after our initial
rage at the man (not so much for what he had
actually done, as for what he had destroyed), we
tended to put him completely out of our minds.
For as much as we would have liked to affix all
the blame to this one man, we sensed in our
hearts that his fall was merely a reflection of
what had happened to the American Dream.

THE SHATTERED DREAM

The American Dream has indeed been shattered. The
moral decline is catastrophic, and solutions do not come easily.
In the midst of this moral dilemnna we continue to fight over
the relationship of religion and politics. Do they mix?

Psalm 127:1 says:

Unless the Lord builds the house, they labor
in vain who build it; unless the Lord guards the
city, the watchman stays awake in vain.

Proverbs 14:34 states:

Righteousness exalts a nation, but sin is
a reproach to any people.

A similar passage in Proverbs 11:11 reads:

By the blessing of the upright the city is
exalted, but it is overthrown by the mouth of
the wicked.

Proverbs 29:2 warns:

When the righteous are in authority, the
people rejoice; but when a wicked man rules,
the people groan.

In the July/August 1989 *Saturday Evening Post,* an article appeared by Prime Minister Margaret Thatcher of Great Britain. It was entitled "We Can't Make It Without Religious Values." After stating her personal faith and convictions, she wrote:

None of this, of course, tells us exactly what
kind of political and social institutions that we
should have. On this point, Christians will very
often genuinely disagree, though it is a mark
of Christian manners that they will do so with
courtesy and mutual respect. What is certain,
however, is that any set of social and economic
arrangements which is not founded on the
acceptance of individual responsibility will do
nothing but harm. We are all responsible for our
own actions. We cannot blame society if we
disobey the law. We simply cannot delegate the
exercise of mercy and generosity to others.

Later in the article she wrote:

But intervention by the state must never
become so great that it effectively removes
personal responsibility.

She continued:

The Christian religion—which, of course, em-
bodies many of the great spiritual and moral truths
of Judaism—is a fundamental part of our national
heritage. I believe it is the wish of the overwhelming
majority of people that this heritage should be preserved and fostered. For centuries it has been our very
lifeblood. Indeed, we are a nation whose ideals are
founded on the Bible.

Also, it is quite impossible to understand our
history or literature without grasping this fact. That
is the strong practical case for ensuring that children
at school are given adequate instruction in the part
which the Judaic-Christian tradition has played in
molding our laws, manners, and institutions.

The truths of the Judaic-Christian tradition are
infinitely precious, not only, as I believe, because they
are true, but also because they provide the moral
impulse which alone can lead to that peace, in the
true meaning of the word, for which we all long.

To assert absolute moral values is not to claim
perfection for ourselves. No true Christian could do
that. What is more, one of the great principles of our
Judaic-Christian inheritance is tolerance.

People with other faiths and cultures have always
been welcomed in our land, assured of equality under
the law, of proper respect, and of open friendship.

There is absolutely nothing incompatible between
this and our desire to maintain the essence of our own
identity. There is no place for racial or religious
intolerance in our creed.

When Abraham Lincoln spoke in his famous
Gettysburg speech of 1863 of "government of the
people, by the people, and for the people," he gave the
world a neat definition of democracy which has since

been widely and enthusiastically adopted. But what
he enunciated as a form of government was not in
itself especially Christian, for nowhere in the Bible
is the word "democracy" mentioned. Ideally, when
Christians meet, as Christians, to take counsel together, their purpose is not—or should not be—to
ascertain what is the mind of the majority but what
is the mind of the Holy Spirit—something which may
be quite different.

Nevertheless, I am an enthusiast for democracy.
And I take that position not because I believe majority
opinion is inevitably right or true: indeed, no majority
can take away God-given human rights. But because
I believe it most effectively safeguards the value of the
individual, and more than any other system restrains
the abuse of power by the few. And that is a Christian
concept.

But there is little hope for democracy if the
hearts of men and women in democratic societies
cannot be touched by a call to something greater than
themselves. Political structures, state institutions,
collective ideals are not enough. Parliamentarians can
legislate for the rule of law. The Church can teach the
life of faith.

For, when all is said and done, a politician's role
is a humble one. I always think that the whole debate
about the Church and the State has never yielded
anything comparable in insight to that beautiful
hymn "I Vow to Thee My Country." It begins with a
triumphant assertion of what might be described as
secular patriotism, a noble thing indeed in a country
like ours: "I vow to thee my country all earthly things
above; entire, whole and perfect the service of my
love." It goes on to speak of "another country I heard
of long ago" whose King cannot be seen and whose
armies cannot be counted, but "soul by soul and
silently her shining bounds increase." Not group by
group or party by party or even church by church, but
soul by soul—and each one counts.

That is the country you chiefly serve. You may fight your causes under banners of many different churches. Your success matters greatly—as much to the temporal as to the spiritual welfare of the nation.

A remarkable statement by a remarkable lady—Prime Minister Margaret Thatcher of Great Britain.

CHRISTIAN—WITH FREEDOM

In an article by Don Feder (Heritage Features Syndicate) that appeared in the *American Family Journal* in August 1989, he makes a very interesting point:

I think one can safely say what a "Christian America" is not. It does not signify: the exclusion of non-Christians from public office or civic participation, the establishment of a state church, or promulgation of an official dogma.

When its devotees speak of America as a Christian nation they could mean one of the following: 1) America is Christian in the sense that an overwhelming majority of Americans are at least nominally Christian. 2) This nation was established by believing Christians, founded on Christian precepts: justice, charity, diligence, faith in divine providence. 3) America is a Christian nation today; the aforesaid values are reflected in our political/social institutions. 4) America should be—hopefully will become— a Christian commonwealth.

He goes on to argue that point number one is a truism. He then states that if point one is self-evident, then point three is an absurdity. He writes:

No one could reasonably argue that America currently is a Christian nation in terms of its essential ethos, as a glance at cable TV or

the front page of your daily paper will attest.
In fact, we are fast becoming an anti-Christian
nation, thanks to our friends in the ACLU,
People for the American Way and the Democratic Party.

Clearly this nation was established by
Christians. It was settled by men and women
of devout faith. The Puritans and Pilgrims had
the greatest impact on the development of our
political institutions. The Declaration of Independence contains no fewer than five separate
references to God, as: creator, supreme lawgiver,
source of rights and "protector and patron."

As a Jew, I'm entirely comfortable with the
concept of a Christian America. The morality
of Christianity, though not necessarily its theology, is my morality. After all, Christians got
their values from my Bible.

He concludes his article with these evaluations:

Our noble heritage notwithstanding, the
post-war era has witnessed the triumph of
secularism. Its more malignant manifestations
include the legalizing of abortion, outlawing of
school prayer, condoning perversion, moving
toward a gender-neutral society and public
school indoctrination, beginning—but regret-
tably not ending—with sex education.

Should America be a Christian nation? It
comes down to this: in any society, someone's
values must prevail. If America isn't animated
by the Judeo-Christian ethic it will be governed
by less enlightened doctrines. For the consequences of the latter, check out the latest statistics on drug use, rape and mental illness.

Don Feder is not a Christian; he is a Jew. Therefore his
remarks are all the more pertinent. Exactly whose morality do
we want controlling our national life, laws, families, communities, and institutions?

CHRISTIAN OR SECULAR?

In the excellent book *America, Christian or Secular?* edited by Jerry S. Herbert (Multnomah Press, 1984), Terry Eastland writes on page 50:

> It is only from history, not from cliches about history, that we can understand what we once were as a nation in regard to religion, and what we have since become. Let me therefore start with these propositions: that there was a principal religion in American life from 1620 until roughly 1920; that this religion was Protestant Christianity; and that Protestant Christianity has been our established religion in almost every sense of that phrase.

Eastland continued on page 52:

> State courts did their part to support the Protestant faith. In 1811 the New York state court upheld an indictment for blasphemous utterances against Christ, and in its ruling, given by Chief Justice Kent, the court said, "We are Christian people, and the morality of the country is deeply engrafted upon Christianity." Fifty years later this same court said that "Christianity may be conceded to be the established religion."
>
> The Pennsylvania state court also affirmed the conviction of a man on charges of blasphemy, here against the Holy Scriptures. The Court said: "Christianity, general Christianity, is and always has been a part of the common law of Pennsylvania...not Christianity founded on any particular tenets; nor Christianity with an established church and tithes and spiritual courts; but Christianity with liberty of conscience to all men."

After the end of World War I in 1918, there was a dramatic break with the morality and religious beliefs of the past. Following that tragic war, a period of laxity in morals and manners became quite obvious in American public life.

One of the most astounding changes in American life has been the disregard of moral and traditional values within the legal community. The old idea of law having its roots in the Judeo-Christian ethic is rarely discussed or debated today. The public philosophy of America has changed radically: Law is no longer religious but secular; no longer moral but political; no longer emphasizes the common good but rather the individual's rights.

In 1947 the United State Supreme Court (in the case Everson Versus Board of Education of Ewing Township) said that the First Amendment "requires the state to be neutral in its relations with groups of religious believers and non-believers." This inaugurated a doctrine of neutrality that now dominates American life and practice. It not only forbids the establishment of a religion, but has had the tendency to forbid the establishment of religious and moral convictions over that which is nonreligious or even irreligious.

In a multitude of similar examples in the last 40 years, the Supreme Court has made it clear that it considers the promotion of religious or moral values not to be in the public interest.

John R. Howe, Jr., in *The Changing Political Thought of John Adams* (Princeton University Press, 1966) quotes on page 185 a fascinating statement regarding morality that was made by John Adams in his first year as our first Vice-President:

> We have no government armed with power capable of contending with human passions unbridled by morality and religion. Our Constitution was made only for a moral and a religious people. It is wholly inadequate to the government of any other.

In an interesting book on freedom entitled *The Absence of Tyranny* (Multnomah Press, 1986), author Lloyd Billingsley concludes on page 192 with these words:

The greatest reason for hope is God. The God of the Bible is not the absentee landlord of deism or the vague Life Force capable of advancing our species from primeval slime to level "A" or beyond. He is not the Categorical Imperative of the classroom or some remote and forgotten First Cause. He is the Creator and Sustainer of everything. By him all things consist, and through him all things hold together. He is the Lord of history and even entered it in the Person of his Son, our Lord Jesus Christ. He is greater than all the nuclear bombs ever made. Before him they are less than nothing, a drop in a bucket. It is from ignorance and disregard of who and what God is that fear and despair proceed.

THE BIBLE ON RELIGION AND POLITICS

Romans 13:1-7 says:

Let every soul be subject to the governing authorities. For there is no authority except from God, and the authorities that exist are appointed by God. Therefore whoever resists the authority resists the ordinance of God, and those who resist will bring judgment on themselves. For rulers are not a terror to good works, but to evil. Do you want to be unafraid of the authority? Do what is good, and you will have praise from the same. For he is God's minister to you for good. But if you do evil, be afraid; for he does not bear the sword in vain; for he is God's minister, an avenger to execute wrath on him who practices evil. Therefore you must be subject, not only because of wrath but also for conscience' sake. For because of this you also pay taxes, for they are God's ministers attending continually to this very thing. Render therefore to all their due: taxes to whom taxes are due,

customs to whom customs, fear to whom fear,
honor to whom honor.

This passage was written by the apostle Paul during the
days of the Roman Empire, when Christians lived under totalitarian government and found it extremely difficult to survive.
Many Christians were persecuted, tortured, and killed for their
faith and commitment to Jesus Christ. Paul's teaching was hard
to accept but necessary for survival and for obedience to God.

Government is established by God, and God is obviously
not opposed to Christian faith and commitment. When we
separate God from government, we have separated the inven-
tion from the Inventor. The separation of church and state
guarantees that no religion will be established as an official or
state religion, but that in turn the government will not seek to
restrict the religious freedom of its citizens.

Paul made it clear in Romans 13:1 that "there is no
authority except from God, and the authorities that exist are
appointed by God." This statement does not justify all that
government does, nor does it defend the moral level of its
leaders. It simply establishes the fact that government is an
institution (regardless of the form it may take) which is designed
and approved by God. Mankind needs to be governed.

In Romans 13:2 we are told not to resist the government
or else we will suffer the consequences ("bring judgment on
themselves"). Jesus said in Matthew 5:39:

I tell you not to resist an evil person. But
whoever slaps you on your right cheek, turn the
other to him also.

That is hard teaching! It is the Christian's responsibility
in a secular society to live by what the Bible teaches, not by
what the majority believes or practices. The Christian walks to
a different drumbeat. In John 18:36 Jesus taught:

My kingdom is not of this world. If my
kingdom were of this world, my servants would
fight, so that I should not be delivered to the
Jews; but now my kingdom is not from here.

Jesus taught us in Matthew 6:33:

> Seek first the kingdom of God and His
> righteousness, and all these things shall be
> added to you.

The government of Rome was hardly moral in all its decisions and actions. Regardless, the Christians were to respect the principle of its authority and the right of that government to exercise its authority. Christians were exhorted not to resist the authority of government.

In addition to these admonitions, Christians are commanded to show honor and respect for the government, regardless of the moral character of its leaders. That is not always easy to do.

Romans 13:7 speaks of giving honor to the governing authorities. 1 Peter 2:17 says, "Honor all people. Love the brotherhood. Fear God. Honor the king." Titus 3:1,2 admonishes believers:

> Remind them to be subject to rulers and
> authorities, to obey, to be ready for every good
> work, to speak evil of no one, to be peaceable,
> gentle, showing all humility to all men.

THE ROLE OF GOVERNMENT

The Bible reveals at least three major roles which the government is to fulfill on earth.

1. *To protect human life.* Genesis 9:6, an instruction given to Noah and his sons after the deluge, gives this important role of government:

> Whoever sheds man's blood, by man his
> blood shall be shed; for in the image of God He
> made man.

No one but government has the right to take a person's life. A government may enforce capital punishment imperfectly, but according to the Bible it has the basic right to use this punishment. Romans 13:4 says:

He is God's minister to you for good. But
if you do evil, be afraid; for he does not bear the
sword in vain; for he is God's minister, an
avenger to execute wrath on him who practices
evil.

It is not the right of government to take innocent lives, but it is the role of government to punish evildoers. The death penalty is to be exercised when premeditated murder occurs.

2. *To protect personal and property rights.* In the Ten Commandments are prohibitions concerning stealing, adultery, bearing false witness, coveting, etc. In the details of the Mosaic law are strict requirements relating to property rights and inheritance rights.

Deuteronomy 19:14 says:

You shall not remove your neighbor's land-
mark, which the men of old have set, in your
inheritance which you will inherit in the land
that the Lord your God is giving you to possess.

The Bible teaches that God owns everything and that we are but stewards of it, managing it for His glory and His purposes. Yet God's ownership does not eliminate private ownership at the human level. In Acts 5:1-11 there is a story about a couple named Ananias and Sapphira who claimed that they had sold a possession for a certain price and had brought it as a gift to the apostles to help in distributing to the needy. But they lied about the amount. Peter said in Acts 5:4:

While it remained, was it not your own?
And after it was sold, was it not in your own
control?

Private ownership of property is clearly indicated. This couple had control over it and over the money they received from it. Their sin centered in the fact that they lied about what they did. Peter said, "You have not lied to men but to God."

3. *To handle disputes between people over their rights.*
The role of government is to establish the truth and make a
decision when its citizens have disputes. Deuteronomy 1:12-17
is a basic text on this role of government:

> How can I alone bear your problems and
> your burdens and your complaints? Choose wise,
> understanding, and knowledgeable men from
> among your tribes, and I will make them heads
> over you. And you answered me and said, "The
> thing which you have told us to do is good." So I
> took the heads of your tribes, wise and knowl-
> edgeable men, and made them heads over you,
> leaders of thousands, leaders of hundreds,
> leaders of fifties, leaders of tens, and officers
> for your tribes. Then I commanded your judges
> at that time, saying, "Hear the cases between
> your brethren, and judge righteously between a
> man and his brother or the stranger who is with
> him. You shall not show partiality in judgment;
> you shall hear the small as well as the great;
> you shall not be afraid in any man's presence,
> for the judgment is God's. The case that is too
> hard for you, bring it to me, and I will hear it."

In Deuteronomy 16:18-20 we read:

> You shall appoint judges and officers in all
> your gates, which the Lord your God gives you,
> according to your tribes, and they shall judge the
> people with just judgment. You shall not pervert
> justice; you shall not show partiality, nor take
> a bribe, for a bribe blinds the eyes of the wise
> and twists the words of the righteous. You shall
> follow what is altogether just, that you may live
> and inherit the land which the Lord your God
> is giving you.

In Deuteronomy 17:6 and 19:15-21 clear instruction is
given concerning trial procedures and the necessity of two or
more eyewitnesses in order to bring a conviction.

OUR RESPONSIBILITIES TO GOVERNMENT

Three chief responsibilities are laid upon Christians in terms of their attitudes and actions toward the government.

1) *Submission to the government*—Romans 13:1,5; Titus 3:1; 1 Peter 2:13-15 (it is the "will of God").

2) *Support of the government*—Matthew 22:15-22; Romans 13:7.

   We are to "render to Caesar the things that are Caesar's." We are to pay taxes. We may not like it, but we are to do it.

3) *Supplication and prayer for the government*—1 Timothy 2:1-4.

Our problems would be different if we spent more time in prayer for those in authority over us. Not only would our attitudes be different, but, according to the Bible, the peace and stability of society would be better.

The current moral crisis in our society and the helplessness of our government to do anything about it is rooted to some degree in the lack of prayer on the part of the believers who live in this society. How many of our public officials are on your regular prayer list? Do you pray at all for them?

OUR RELATIONSHIP TO GOD AND GOVERNMENT

The moral catastrophe confronts us every day, and sometimes we feel frustrated in what to do about it. Some Christians have opted for civil disobedience, believing it to be fully justified and approved by biblical example.

Our society has chosen to walk a path of professed moral neutrality, and has shoved religion outside of the mainstream of American life and practice. Yet a major part of our citizenry claims to be Christian, so what can we do about this catastrophe? Should we continue to allow secular humanism to prevail? As things stand right now, he who believes most gives way to him who believes least, and he who believes least often gives way to him who believes nothing. Is there anything we can do to change this pattern?

Many of us would like to work within the political and legislative framework of our society, but we are constantly told that religious opinions and traditional moral values are not to be presented, promoted, or imposed upon society. So exactly what is our responsibility to the government in the light of our moral catastrophe?

Consider the following four basic principles.

1. *Our position as believers in Jesus Christ.* The moment a person becomes a Christian, he or she is born into the kingdom of God. A different lifestyle and belief system governs his actions.

Jesus said in John 17:14-17:

> I have given them Your word; and the world
> has hated them because they are not of the
> world, just as I am not of the world. I do not
> pray that You should take them out of the world,
> but that You should keep them from the evil
> one. They are not of the world, just as I am not
> of the world. Sanctify them by Your truth. Your
> word is truth.

Jesus makes it clear that believers are "not of the world." The apostle Paul teaches in 1 Corinthians 5:9-13 that believers are not to keep company with other believers that are living in sinful habits and lifestyles. But he makes it clear that this only refers to *Christians,* not non-Christians. We are "in the world," but we are not "of the world." That biblical truth is not always easy to apply.

In John 18:36 Jesus teaches that His kingdom is not of this world; if it were, then His servants would fight. Paul reminds us in Philippians 3:20 that our "citizenship" is in heaven. In the spiritual sense we are not citizens of this country or planet but citizens of heaven. Everything changes when we become Christians; 2 Corinthians 5:17 says we are "new creations" in Christ. Paul tells us in Colossians 1:13 that we have been "delivered . . . from the power of darkness and translated . . . into the kingdom of the Son of His love." John tells us that we have passed "from death into life" (John 5:24).

The best thing we can do to bring about a moral change in our culture is to live what we say we believe. If all Christians would truly follow Jesus Christ, the resulting impact would be enormous.

2. *The preeminence of our commitment to God.* If government is wrong, it is wrong because it acts and decides in violation of the laws of God. The authority of government does not supersede the laws and authority of God Himself. That is precisely where our present moral dilemma lies. Christians and Jews believe that the laws and authority of God have been revealed within the pages of the Bible. The Bible is the revelation of God in written form, and it is the foundation of all that is morally right and good. It describes what is wrong and its declarations about morality and values are considered to be unalterable, final, authoritative, and reliable for human life and conduct.

However, many citizens in our society do not believe that the Bible should be taken and applied in this way. They feel that the Bible's viewpoints discriminate against the majority of the population and should not be enforced or imposed upon any of our citizens.

What should Christians do in such a pluralistic environment? What should be our response when our government legalizes what is morally wrong from God's point of view?

An interesting historical example of Christians in conflict with government is found in the Book of Acts. It involved the apostle Peter as well as the rest of the disciples of Jesus Christ. In Acts 4:18-21 we read:

> They called them and commanded them
> not to speak at all nor teach in the name of
> Jesus. But Peter and John answered and said
> to them, "Whether it is right in the sight of God
> to listen to you more than to God, you judge. For
> we cannot but speak the things which we have
> seen and heard." So when they had further threat-
> ened them, they let them go, finding no way
> of punishing them, because of the people, since
> they all glorified God for what had been done.

Peter makes it clear that believers must listen to God over the voice of men. In Acts 5:27-29 we read:

> When they had brought them, they set
> them before the council. And the high priest
> asked them, saying, "Did we not strictly com-
> mand you not to teach in this name? And look,
> you have filled Jerusalem with your doctrine,
> and intend to bring this Man's blood on us!"
> Then Peter and the other apostles answered and
> said: "We ought to obey God rather than men."

The principle is firmly established: Civil disobedience is a believer's necessary responsibility when the civil authorities demand that believers violate the commands of God. The result of their civil disobedience is recorded in Acts 5:40-42:

> They agreed with him, and when they had
> called for the apostles and beaten them, they
> commanded that they should not speak in the
> name of Jesus, and let them go. So they de-
> parted from the presence of the council, rejoicing
> that they were counted worthy to suffer shame
> for His name. And daily in the temple, and in
> every house, they did not cease teaching and
> preaching Jesus as the Christ.

The apostles were beaten for their civil disobedience and were instructed for the third time not to speak again about Jesus Christ. But once again they disobeyed the authorities and intensified their efforts in teaching and preaching the good news of the gospel. God commanded them to tell the whole world, so they had to disobey the command to stop which was given to them by the governing authorities.

Civil disobedience is an act on the part of a believer to disobey a law or command of human authority that requires that believer to disobey God. It does not give believers the right to impose their commitment upon nonbelievers. We may wish that all nonbelievers felt like we do about moral issues, and we should do all that is humanly possible through legal and legislative processes to stop the immoral acts of nonbelievers. But civil disobedience is a *believer's* response to what the governing authority is asking him to do or not to do; it does not apply to the actions and decisions of nonbelievers.

3. *The purpose of our Christian witness.* It is easy for us to lose sight of our real mission on this planet. Believers are commanded to make disciples of all nations, to preach the gospel to every creature, to be witnesses all over the world. Our goal is to take as many people to heaven with us as we possibly can.

Matthew 5:13-16 is a passage from the Sermon on the Mount. Jesus said:

> You are the salt of the earth; but if the salt loses its flavor, how shall it be seasoned? It is then good for nothing but to be thrown out and trampled under foot by men. You are the light of the world. A city that is set on a hill cannot be hidden. Nor do they light a lamp and put it under a basket, but on a lampstand, and it gives light to all who are in the house. Let your light so shine before men that they may see your good works and glorify your Father in heaven.

To "glorify your Father in heaven" is a statement refer-ring to nonbelievers becoming believers. Christians (disciples of Jesus Christ) are called "salt" and "light." The purpose of our influence is to cause unbelievers to glorify God or become believers. It is easy to lose sight of this fact and to believe that as "salt" we are to protect society from corruption and that as "light" we are to get rid of the darkness of this world. A cor-porate consciousness often develops from these passages as Christians see themselves as tools and instruments to bring social, moral, and political change in secular society. But that is not the main point of these verses. Christians are to so live that their influence will draw unbelievers to faith in Jesus Christ. The goal of the believer is not to change society per se but to change the hearts of those within society. Individual salvation is still the Christian's mandate. We are to win souls, not reform societies.

Christians who know God's salvation are taught in Titus 2:11-14 to stay away from "ungodliness and worldly lusts" and to live "soberly, righteously, and godly in this present age, looking for the blessed hope and glorious appearing of our great God and Savior Jesus Christ." The "blessed hope" is not the reformation of society but the return of our Savior, Jesus Christ our Lord! He will then change society as it has never been changed before in all of human history! 2 Peter 3:11-13 admonishes believers to live in "holy conduct and godliness" because all that we see here and now will be destroyed. What we are looking for instead is "new heavens and a new earth in which righteousness dwells."

4. *The priorities of our lives.* What we believe affects all of our priorities in life. Jesus said in Matthew 6:33:

Seek first the kingdom of God and His righteousness, and all these things shall be added to you.

Our priorities are not based on what our society thinks. As citizens of a heavenly kingdom, our priorities have changed. Our Savior and Lord told us in Matthew 28:19,20:

Go therefore and make disciples of all the nations, baptizing them in the name of the Father and of the Son and of the Holy Spirit, teaching them to observe all things that I have commanded you; and lo, I am with you always, even to the end of the age.

We are to "make disciples." The field is "all the nations," not just America. We are to baptize these disciples and teach them what Jesus commanded. That is our highest priority. Everything else becomes secondary.

WHAT SHOULD BE OUR RESPONSE?

The separation of church and state does not mean the separation of God, religious beliefs, and moral values from government and society. Our Constitution guarantees its citizens freedom of religion, without requiring any religious belief system to be imposed upon them. That wonderful document that has guided us through our history does not prohibit the free exercise of religion, nor does it establish a federal or state religion.

The early Christians lived under the heel of a totalitarian government, the Roman Empire. Christian principles apply to *all* believers, regardless of the secular society or form of government under which they must live. Our response should include:

1. Complete respect and honor for all governmental officials.

2. Exercising our right to vote.

3. Seeking changes through legal and political means.

4. Refusal to disobey God even if the government commands us to do so.

5. Commitment to the goal of making disciples of all nations.

6. Prayer for governmental leaders.

7. Obeying the laws of the land that do not require us to violate the laws of God.

8. Paying our taxes and never cheating the government.

9. Living a godly lifestyle in the midst of a secular environment that has lost its moral values.

Is It Too Late for America?

Psalm 33:12 says, "Blessed is the nation whose God is the Lord." Proverbs 14:34 adds, "Righteousness exalts a nation, but sin is a reproach to any people." Those two verses summarize the moral catastrophe of our country: We have forgotten the Lord God, and our sin and immorality are causing our decline and corruption.

The question is, *Is it too late for America?*

Some prophets of doom would say that it is, and the facts would certainly seem to back them up. In some respects we have gone too far. Our ability to change our attitudes, opinions, beliefs, and lifestyles seems almost gone. Abortion, pornography, adultery, homosexuality, sexual disease, murder, violence, alcoholism, drug abuse, divorce, and gambling are all strong indictments against a nation that says on its coins "In God we trust," and whose pledge of allegiance includes the words "one nation under God."

It is quite possible that we have passed the day of God's restraining patience, and that His plan for America is to judge her and humble her. According to the Bible, God's judgment upon a nation is usually brought by another nation who conquers her. Sometimes a nation decays from within long before the outward battle brings defeat by another nation.

Christians who study Bible prophecy have long wondered about the role of the United States in future events. While it is possible that some indirect references in biblical prophecies might apply to us, the general consensus is that we are not prominent in the events of the last days of planet Earth.

Many believers point to America's generosity and charitable giving as reasons for God's protection and tolerance. It is true that missionary enterprises around the world are often sustained and supported by American dollars. Our country has been a base for worldwide distribution of the Bible and the support of missionaries for many years. But does this guarantee that God will not judge us for our moral decline?

WHAT WE CAN LEARN FROM ISRAEL

In Israel's history of long ago lie admonitions for us today. After the united kingdom of Saul, David, and Solmon was divided into ten northern tribes (led by Jeroboam I, son of Nebat) and a southern kingdom of Judah and Benjamin (led by Rehoboam), the history of Israel becomes a fascinating study of how God treats nations who sin against Him. The northern kingdom was destroyed by God in 722 B.C. by the nation of Assyria and its citizens were led into captivity. The southern kingdom was finally destroyed by Babylon under King Nebuchadnezzar, the city and temple being destroyed in 586 B.C. While all the kings of Israel did evil in the sight of the Lord, the kings of Judah were mixed, with some good and some bad. One of the evil kings was named Manasseh. He came to power at the age of 12 and ruled for 55 years. He did terrible evil in the sight of the Lord, as did his son, Amon, who reigned for only two years. Following Amon, a wonderful boy came to the throne by the name of Josiah. He began his reign at eight years of age and ruled for 31 years. He did what was right in the sight of the Lord, but in spite of his loyalty to God, God's judgment could not be changed. 2 Kings 23:24-27 makes this remarkable analysis:

> Josiah put away those who consulted mediums and spiritists, the household gods and idols, all the abominations that were seen in the land of Judah and in Jerusalem, that he might perform the words of the law which were written in the book that Hilkiah the priest found in the house of the Lord. Now before him there was no king like him, who turned to the Lord with all his heart, with all his soul, and with all his might, according to all the law of Moses; nor after him did any arise like him. Nevertheless

the Lord did not turn from the fierceness of His great wrath, with which His anger was aroused against Judah, because of all the provocations with which Manasseh had provoked him. And the Lord said, "I will also remove Judah from my sight, as I have removed Israel, and will cast off this city Jerusalem which I have chosen, and the house of which I said, My name shall be there."

Though Josiah brought reforms in his society, the Lord's judgment would not be changed: Judah would suffer the same fate as the northern tribes of Israel had experienced some 135 years earlier.

The tragic story of why God brought judgment is recorded in 2 Kings 21:1-16. In order for you to appreciate fully the issues and circumstances involved, the entire passage is quoted here. Consider it carefully.

Manasseh was twelve years old when he became king, and he reigned fifty-five years in Jerusalem. His mother's name was Hephzibah. And he did evil in the sight of the Lord, according to the abominations of the nations whom the Lord had cast out before the children of Israel. For he rebuilt the high places which Hezekiah his father had destroyed; he raised up altars for Baal, and made a wooden image, as Ahab king of Israel had done; and he worshiped all the host of heaven and served them. He also built altars in the house of the Lord, of which the Lord had said, "In Jerusalem I will put My name." And he built altars for all the host of heaven in the two courts of the house of the Lord. Also he made his son pass through the fire, practiced soothsaying, used witchcraft, and consulted spiritists and mediums. He did much evil in the sight of the Lord, to provoke Him to anger. He even set a carved image of Asherah that he had made, in the house of which the Lord had said to David and to Solomon his son, "In this house and in Jerusalem, which I have chosen out of all the tribes of Israel, I will put My name forever; and I will not make the feet of Israel wander anymore from the land which I gave their fathers—only if they are careful to do according to all the law that My servant Moses commanded them." But they paid no attention, and Manasseh seduced them to do more evil than the nations whom the Lord had destroyed before the children of Israel. And the Lord spoke by His servants the prophets, saying, "Because Manasseh king of Judah has done these abominations (he has acted more wickedly than all the Amorites who were before Him, and has also made Judah sin with his idols), therefore thus says the Lord God of Israel: Behold I am bringing such calamity upon Jerusalem and Judah that whoever hears of it, both his ears will tingle. And I will stretch over Jerusalem the measuring line of Samaria and the plummet of the house of Ahab; I will wipe Jerusalem as one wipes a dish, wiping it and turning it upside down. So I will forsake the remnant of My inheritance and deliver them into the hand of their enemies; and they shall become victims of plunder to all their enemies, because they have done evil in My sight, and have provoked Me to anger since the day their fathers came out of Egypt, even to this day." Moreover Manasseh shed very much innocent blood, till he had filled Jerusalem from one end to another, besides his sin with which he made Judah sin, in doing evil in the sight of the Lord.

What a tremendous parallel to our present society and the moral catastrophe we now face in our country!

WHY GOD WILL JUDGE US

If we are to accurately compare the situation in our country with the events and circumstances in the ancient nation of Israel, we need to enumerate the reasons why God's judgment would come, and why the attempt at reform and the godly lifestyle of good King Josiah would not change God's judgment.

1. *Forsaking the Lord God*—2 Kings 21:21,22. This passage says of Amon, the son of Manasseh, that "he walked in all

the ways" of his father, serving and worshipping idols. But the key words are these: "He forsook the Lord God of his fathers, and did not walk in the way of the Lord."

In 2 Kings 22:16,17 God said that He would bring judgment "because they have forsaken Me." In 2 Chronicles 7:22 we learn that God's judgment would come "because they forsook the Lord God of their fathers... and embraced other gods, and worshiped them and served them."

We are a nation that has forsaken the Lord God. We have tried consistently to remove God out of our thinking and out of our politics. That pursuit is going to cost us dearly.

When Jeremiah reminded the people of Judah why God would bring the judgment of Babylon upon them, he continued to emphasize the fact that they had forsaken the Lord God. (Read Jeremiah 1:14-16; 2:13,17,19; 5:18,19; 9:12-16; 15:4-6; 16:10-13.)

2. *Following the occult and all its satanic methods and practices*—2 Kings 21:6; cf. 23:24,25. The Bible teaches that King Manasseh practiced, used, and consulted occultists. He was into astrology, spiritists, and mediums, and all of this was provoking the Lord to anger.

Today the New Age movement has created a monster of occultic belief and practice. People seek out "channelers" (a new term for old pagan practice) to get in touch with "spirit beings." Such practices are an abomination to God.

3. *Filling the land with innocent blood*—2 Kings 21:16; 24:3,4. The Bible says that Manasseh "shed very much innocent blood, till he had filled Jerusalem from one end to another." 2 Kings 24:4 says of this fact that "the Lord would not pardon." One cannot help but think of the terrible holocaust we call abortion. The lives of millions of unborn children have been killed. Abortion on demand has resulted in "very much innocent blood," not just in one city (as in Jerusalem), but throughout our nation. It will be a miracle if God does not judge us for this terrible crime.

Jeremiah 2:34 states, "On your skirts is found the blood of the lives of the poor innocents."

4. *Fulfilling sexual desires outside of marriage*—2 Kings 21:9; 23:7. The Bible says that Manasseh "seduced them to do more evil than the nations whom the Lord had destroyed." In the revival under King Josiah which followed the terrible reign

of Manasseh and his son, Amon, the Bible says that Josiah "tore down the ritual booths of the perverted persons that were in the house of the Lord, where the women wove hangings for the wooden image." The term "perverted persons" is referring to sexual immorality, acts of prostitution and homosexuality. The carved image of Asherah (2 Kings 21:7) was put in the temple of David and Solomon. Rites of fertility and sex from pagan customs and cultures were now dominating the people of God.

Jeremiah 2:33; 3:2,6-10; and 23:10,14 all speak of the terrible sexual immorality that dominated the land of Israel during the days of Manasseh, thereby bringing the verdict of judgment from the Lord God.

5. *Failing to respond to God's warnings*—2 Chronicles 36:15,16; Jeremiah 25:4-11. 2 Chronicles is the last book in the chronological system of the Hebrew Bible. It records the destruction of Judah by Babylon. In the last chapter (36), we read in verses 15 and 16:

> The Lord God of their fathers sent warnings
> to them by His messengers, rising up early and
> sending them, because He had compassion on
> His people and on His dwelling place. But they
> mocked the messengers of God, despised His
> words, and scoffed at His prophets, until the
> wrath of the Lord arose against His people, till
> there was no remedy.

The verdict? NO REMEDY! When a nation decides to mock and scoff at the prophets of God, the Lord's anger will not subside; His judgment is certain!

According to Jeremiah 25:4-11, the prophets urged the people to repent of their evil ways and doings, but the people refused to listen, so God's judgment came.

THE REPENTANCE THAT WE NEED

If there is any hope for America, it will be found in the repentance of God's people. The great tragedy in our present moral catastrophe is that it has affected a large majority of believers. Televangelist scandals were just the tip of the iceberg. The widespread toleration of sexual immorality and the failure of believers to judge themselves has resulted in a colossal moral decline among believers. The problems that affect the non-believers in our society have now overwhelmed the Christian community. The old standards of morality are gone, and there is a new liberty and freedom that includes things which God specifically calls sin. We are not fooling God or hiding these things from Him!

When Solomon finished his dedication of the temple, the Lord appeared to him and admonished him about obedience and loyalty to Himself. God predicted that judgment would come if the people would not turn to the Lord with all their hearts. In 2 Chronicles 7:14 God laid out a tremendous principle for the people of Israel that applies to the moral catastrophe in America today:

> If My people who are called by My name
> will humble themselves, and pray and seek My
> face, and turn from their wicked ways, then I
> will hear from heaven, and will forgive their sin
> and heal their land.

Four things are involved in the repentance of believers.

1. *Submit to God:* "Humble themselves."
In James 4:7-10 believers are challenged to get right with God:

> Therefore submit to God. Resist the devil
> and he will flee from you. Draw near to God and
> He will draw near to you. Cleanse your hands,
> you sinners; and purify your hearts, you double-
> minded. Lament and mourn and weep! Let your
> laughter be turned to mourning and your joy
> to gloom. Humble yourselves in the sight of the
> Lord, and He will lift you up.

Our arrogance will not do. Our self-confidence is not the answer. We are in desperate need of true humility, a real sub-mission to God that puts us on our knees, crying out to God for His mercy and deliverance.

2. *Spend time in prayer:* "Pray."

We talk more to ourselves than to God. How foolish of us to think that human personalities could help us more than the living God! Prayer should not be our last resort; it should be our first responsibility! The colossal lack of prayer among believers is contributing to the moral crisis. God answers prayer and we need to call upon the name of the Lord, to seek the Lord while He may be found!

3. *Seek the Lord and His will:* "Seek My face."

Seeking the face of the Lord means that we are consulting Him and His will, not spirit beings or professional counselors who do not point us to God and His Word. Psalm 1:1-3 puts it this way:

> Blessed is the man who walks not in the
> counsel of the ungodly, nor stands in the path
> of sinners, nor sits in the seat of the scornful;
> but his delight is in the law of the Lord, and in
> His law he meditates day and night. He shall
> be like a tree planted by the rivers of water, that
> brings forth its fruit in its season, whose leaf
> also shall not wither; and whatever he does shall
> prosper.

4. *Separate from sinful practices:* "Turn from their wicked ways."

One of the most amazing things about the story of Manasseh and how his sin brought the judgment of God is that he personally heeded the Lord's warnings and repented of his sin. That gives encouragement to all of us. Even though national judgment would be brought by God, individual salvation was available to all who would seek His face and separate from their sinful ways, even the king himself!

Consider the story in 2 Chronicles 33:12,13:

> When he was in affliction, he implored the
> Lord his God, and humbled himself greatly
> before the God of his fathers, and prayed to Him;

and He received his entreaty, heard his supplication, and brought him back to Jerusalem into
his kingdom. Then Manasseh knew that the
Lord was God.

What amazing grace, love, and forgiveness our Lord
brings to the heart that is humbled and calls upon Him! Israel's
wicked king, Manasseh, repented of his sin at the end of his life,
and God forgave him and answered him. That is indeed good
news!

Is there any hope for America? Maybe as a nation there is
not, though we all hope that God's patience will give us another
chance. But even if this nation is to be judged by God for our
moral decline, there is always hope for the individual who will
turn to the Lord.

Where do you stand? Have you humbled yourself before
God, acknowledged your sin, and trusted God's grace and forgiveness to save you from sin, death, and hell? God's good news
is that Jesus Christ died over 1900 years ago to pay for our sins.
His bodily resurrection is a guarantee that we will one day be
resurrected and live with God forever in a beautiful new world,
a heavenly city and a new earth that is changed by the power of
God. The Bible urges each person to make that commitment of
life and future to Jesus Christ. Believe on Him, for there is no
other hope or salvation for any of us. Acts 4:12 states:

Nor is there salvation in any other, for there
is no other name under heaven given among
men by which we must be saved.

When a Philippian jailer asked Paul and Silas, "Sirs,
what must I do to be saved?" they replied (Acts 16:31):

Believe on the Lord Jesus Christ, and you
will be saved, you and your household.

1 John 1:9 says:

If we confess our sins, He is faithful and
just to forgive us our sins and to cleanse us from
all unrighteousness.

Romans 10:9,10 makes the issue quite clear:

If you confess with your mouth the Lord
Jesus and believe in your heart that God has
raised Him from the dead, you will be saved.
For with the heart one believes to righteousness,
and with the mouth confession is made to
salvation.

Romans 10:13 summarizes by saying:

For whoever calls upon the name of the
Lord shall be saved.

Have you done this? If not, do it today!

ABOUT THE
AUTHOR

David Hocking is pastor of Calvary Church of Santa Ana and the radio Bible teacher on the "Biola Hour." Dr. Hocking has written several books, including *Good Marriages Take Time* and *Romantic Lovers*, both coauthored by his wife, Carole. In addition to several publications and tapes, David has conducted seminars on the subjects of marriage and family.

The Hockings—married since 1962—have three children and draw upon their years of marriage and family life to provide practical and down-to-earth insights in their books.

Other books authored by David Hocking include *Pleasing God, The Dynamic Difference*, and *Be a Leader People Follow*. All of the Hockings' books are available through the "Biola Hour."

Six Decades
of Broadcast Ministry

As a listener-funded ministry of Biola University, the purpose of the "Biola Hour" is to equip Christians to impact the world for Jesus Christ. This radio ministry also has the unique opportunity to present the gospel to the unsaved—as well as provide a biblical foundation from which Christians can grow.

On March 22, 1922, the Bible Institute of Los Angeles (BIOLA) transmitted its first broadcast over radio station KJS, soon renamed KTBI to represent "The Bible Institute." This station was among the first to be licensed in the U.S. for strictly religious programming, and featured devotional and educational programs taught by Institute faculty and guest speakers.

After the stock market crash of 1929, Biola and its supporters faced a grave financial crisis. In 1931, the Institute's radio station was sold for $37,500, and renamed KFAC. Under the new ownership, Biola secured several hours of daily air time and was able to broadcast only a portion of its regular programs.

In 1932, Dr. Louis T. Talbot, then president of Biola and pastor of the Church of the Open Door, picked up the pieces of the radio ministry and broadcast the programs at his own expense. Biola reinstated the "Biola Hour" in 1937 as a part of its outreach.

The program gained momentum and its constituency grew—and by 1946 it was aired over most of the 183 stations of the coast-to-coast Mutual Network.

In 1952, Dr. Al Sanders began his guidance of the "Biola Hour" as producer, director, and announcer—and he has continued in this role for the past three decades. Today, the "Biola Hour" features the teaching of Dr. David L. Hocking and can be heard on stations across the United States and Canada.

Other Good
Harvest House Reading

THE DYNAMIC DIFFERENCE
The Holy Spirit in Your Life
by *David Hocking*

Christians often talk about the inner peace and joy we are supposed to experience through Jesus Christ. Too often, however, instead of experiencing the joy of the Lord, Christians are plagued by discouragement and doubt. Why? Bestselling author and Bible teacher David Hocking says the key lies in our understanding of who we are in Christ and what it means to be Spirit-filled. *The Dynamic Difference* will help you discover and experience what it means to have God's power in your life.

GOOD MARRIAGES TAKE TIME
by *David and Carole Hocking*

Filled with teachings rooted in God's Word, this sensitive book offers help in four areas of married life: communication, sex, friends, and finances. Contains questions throughout the book for both husbands and wives to answer.

ROMANTIC LOVERS
The Intimate Marriage
by *David and Carole Hocking*

Here is romantic love for married couples that exceeds our greatest dreams and expectations! Greater intimacy is possible as we follow God's beautiful picture of marriage as found in the Song of Solomon.

WHATEVER HAPPENED TO HEAVEN?
by *Dave Hunt*

During the 1970s, when *The Late Great Planet Earth* was outselling everything, the rapture was the hot topic. Pastors preached about Heaven, and Christians eagerly anticipated meeting their Lord. When expected events didn't occur, disillusionment set in. Today, scarcely a sermon is preached about "the world to come." Whatever happened to Heaven? Dave Hunt addresses that question, shows that Heaven really is our home, and brings understanding to how that hope was lost and how it can be regained.

PEACE, PROSPERITY AND
THE COMING HOLOCAUST
by *Dave Hunt*

With fresh insight and vision, Dave Hunt dissects the influences that are at work to lull us into a state of euphoria and numb us to the reality of coming destruction. A startling account of the rapidly growing New Age Movement and the part it plays in the imminent return of Jesus Christ.

AMERICA: THE SORCERER'S NEW APPRENTICE
by *Dave Hunt* and *T.A. McMahon*

Many respected experts predict that America is at the threshold of a glorious New Age. Other equally notable observers warn that Eastern mysticism, at the heart of the New Age movement, will eventually corrupt Western civilization. *Who is right?* Will we be able to distinguish between the true hope of the Gospel and the false hope of the New Age?

Dave Hunt and T.A. McMahon break down the most brilliant arguments of the most-respected New Age leaders and present overwhelming evidence for the superiority of the Christian faith.

THE BONDAGE BREAKER
by *Neil Anderson*

Jesus intends for us to win the spiritual battles that confront us daily and He has provided everything we need to gain the victory. Yet instead of experiencing victory, we often find ourselves trapped in defeat—overcome with frustration, bitterness, and discouragement. If you have ever found yourself enslaved by negative thought patterns, controlled by irrational feelings, or caught in habitual sinful behavior, Neil Anderson can help you understand the strategy of Satan and fight back.

CLASSIC CHRISTIANITY
Life's too short to miss the real thing!
by *Bob George*

In his down-to-earth style, George shares the road back to joy and contentment in the Christian life. Clearly outlining the common pitfalls and misconceptions that hinder and rob so many Christians today, Bob confronts the question of why so many Christians start out as enthusiastic believers and then decide that Christianity doesn't "work" for them. He then provides the truth that will help Christians get back on track and stay there.